T0022793

THE ROUGH GUIDE TO
NEW ENGLAND

First edition written by Dan Stables.

This book includes extractions from The Rough Guide to the USA written by Maria Edwards, Stephen Keeling, Todd Obolsky, Annelise Sorensen, Georgia Stephens and Greg Ward, updated and published in 2021 by Apa Publications Ltd. A big thank you to all of the contributing authors to The Rough Guide to the USA.

ROUGH GUIDES

Contents

Introduction to
New England

New England is where it all began for the modern United States, unlikely as it may seem from the sleepy, pristine villages and old-growth forests which characterize the area today. This is where the Pilgrim Fathers disembarked the Mayflower in 1620, and where the first seeds of American independence were sown in the last decades of the 18th century. Today it remains one of the most pleasant and prosperous corners of the country, easy to reach thanks to the great city of Boston and nearby megalopolis of New York, but with pockets of countryside so quiet it feels like a different country. Its natural beauty, indeed, is up there with anything in the USA, with spectacular mountain ranges in New Hampshire and Vermont and a famously fiery display of changing leaves in the autumn.

The sheer size of the country prevents any sort of overarching statement about the typical American experience, just as the diversity of its people undercuts any notion of the typical American. This holds true for New England, which is home across some 70,000 square miles to Irish Americans, Italian Americans, African Americans, Chinese Americans and Latinos, as well as those who have upped sticks from elsewhere in the country: Texan cowboys and Bronx hustlers, Seattle hipsters and Alabama pastors, Las Vegas showgirls and Hawaiian surfers. Though it often sounds clichéd to foreigners, the only thing that holds this bizarre federation together is the oft-maligned "**American Dream**". While the USA is one of the world's oldest still-functioning democracies and the roots of its European presence go back to the 1500s, the palpable sense of newness here creates an odd sort of optimism, wherein anything seems possible and fortune can strike at any moment. New England may be most famous for its natural landscapes and social history, but it has produced its share of American pop culture icons, too: Jack Kerouac, Henry David Thoreau, Edgar Allan Poe and Stephen King are among the New England luminaries in the world of letters, while Aerosmith, the Dropkick Murphys, John Mayer and The Cars are among the pop music denizens to have emerged from this part of the country.

Aspects of American culture can be difficult for many visitors to understand, despite the apparent familiarity: the national obsession with guns; the widely held belief that "government" is bad; the real, genuine pride in the American Revolution and the US Constitution, two hundred years on; the equally genuine belief that the USA is the "greatest country on earth"; the wild grandstanding of its politicians (especially at election time); and the bewildering contradiction of its great liberal and open-minded traditions with laissez-faire capitalism and extreme cultural and religious conservatism. That's America: diverse, challenging, beguiling, maddening at times, but always entertaining and always changing. And while there is no such thing as a typical American person or landscape, there can be few places where strangers can feel so confident of a warm reception. All these curiosities and contradictions are as true of New England as they are of the rest of the country, even while generally speaking, New England is politically liberal and represented by the Democrats, Vermont, for example, has some of the most lax gun control laws in the country.

Where to go

The most rewarding American expeditions are often those that take in more than one town, city, or state. You do not, however, have to cross the entire continent from shore

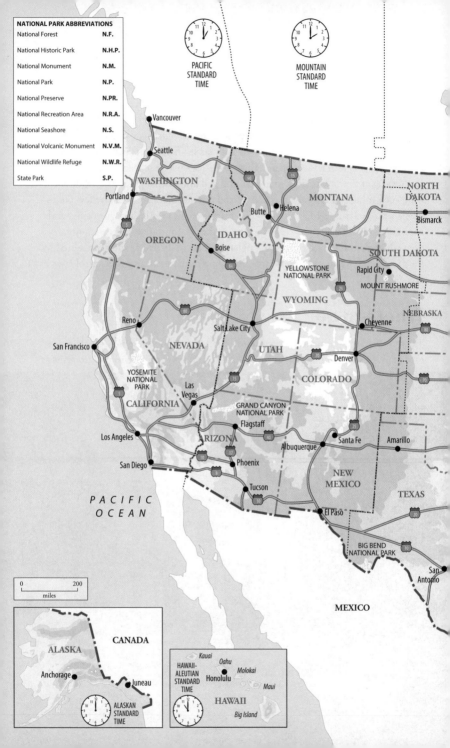

to shore in order to appreciate its amazing diversity; it would take a long time to see the whole country, and the more time you spend simply travelling, the less time you'll have to savour the small-town pleasures and backroad oddities that may well provide your strongest memories. Unless you're travelling to and within a centralized location such as Boston, you'll need a **car** – that mandatory component of life in New England, as elsewhere in the USA.

The obvious place to start for most people is **Boston** – the capital of Massachusetts, the cultural, political and financial hub of wider New England, and one of the most important cities in American history. The Freedom Trail, taking in some of the city's most important historical sights, is a must for history buffs; so too is a visit to Plymouth, Massachusetts, 'America's Hometown', where the Pilgrim Fathers first established a colony after stepping off the Mayflower in 1620.

Wider **New England** has a varied appeal; there's much more to the region once you venture beyond Boston's colonial history into its rural byways, which lead to centuries-old villages in Vermont, the White Mountains of New Hampshire, and the winding river valleys of Connecticut. History echoes through every forest and town in this storied interior, whether in the hallowed university halls of Cambridge or the haunted town of Salem, where dozens of people were killed as a result of mass hysteria in the tragic 17th-century witch trials. Such spectres lurk around every corner in New England, their potency enhanced by their juxtaposition with the white picket fences and neatly manicured lawns of the region's prosperous suburban settlements – such that, when you visit, it's easy to imagine why New England has proved such a fertile source of inspiration to the staggeringly successful horror writer Stephen King.

As captivating as the human history is the countryside which encloses it. To see New England in the fall, when the changing seasons turn its autumn leaves into a blazing inferno of red, ochre and gold, is a justifiably famous bucket-list activity – but this is a gorgeous place year-round. It's easy to share in the awe that must have been felt by early visitors to Maine's Mount Desert Island – now protected as the Acadia National Park – where craggy coastal bluffs are smothered in pine forest and Cadillac Mountain soars to the highest point in the eastern United States. Vermont is the sixth-smallest US state and the second-least populated behind the virtually empty Wyoming; its forest trails, winding from the Green Mountains to the Connecticut River, are ripe for road-tripping, cycling, and hiking.

Indeed, New England's variegated charms show no sign of abating as you approach the coast. Bayside Provincetown in Massachusetts is a vibrant town which has long served as a favoured vacation spot and lifestyle hub for the LGBTQ+ community, while the lobster-catching harbours and coastal mountains of Maine are characterised by a bold and rugged individualism, nowhere better expressed than in the thriving city of Portland.

Cape Cod and its surrounding islands, meanwhile, are waspy and wealthy, attracting well-heeled holidaymakers from New York and Boston to nestle in country inns and feast at farmhouse restaurants on cloistered outposts like Martha's Vineyard. Rhode Island, too, draws moneyed Americans and foreign visitors in equal measure, who moor their yachts in Newport to see and be seen in the town's oyster bars and the stately colonial architecture retains the classy patina of the Gilded Age.

Anyone of an intellectual inclination will be drawn to New England on a kind of academic pilgrimage, for this region is home to some of the most famous and prestigious universities not just in America, but in the whole world. The oldest and

NEW ENGLAND'S LITERARY LUMINARIES

The natural beauty, long and overwhelmingly evident history, world-class educational institutions and prosperous nature of New England have long made it one of America's most literary fertile regions. A whole host of iconic American writers have hailed from the Northeast, beginning right at the start of modern American history – the country's first printing press was set up, unsurprisingly, in Cambridge, Massachusetts.

Ralph Waldo Emerson was one New England native inspired to write by the region's abundant natural beauty. His conception of the 'transparent eyeball' was rooted in an approach to the natural world that did not reflect but absorbed, allowing for complete immersion. His exhortation to "Live in the sunshine, swim in the sea, drink the wild air" was an early credo for the American romantic movement, a flag proudly passed on to his protégé, Henry David Thoreau. Retreating to a woodland cabin near Concord, Massachusetts, Thoreau produced the 1854 work *Walden: an exercise in natural observation, self-reflection and self-reliance* – even if his mother still did his laundry.

As the decades wore on into the twentieth century, American changed, and New England's writers documented it feverishly. *On the Road*, Jack Kerouac's ripping yarn of footloose road-tripping across post-war America, was so influential on the counterculture of the 1950s and '60s that it has almost become hackneyed to invoke it, though it still continues to exert an iron grip on the imaginations of young and intrepid travellers. The same effect is wrought by the work of Paul Theroux, a fellow Massachusetts man who, with the publication of *The Great Railway Bazaar* in 1975, became one of the greatest modern names in travel writing, although he is primarily a novelist.

The title of New England's most successful author – financially, at least – must go to Stephen King. Born in Portland, Maine, and having remained in the Pine Tree State for most of his life, King has published a whopping 63 novels, which include American pop cultural icons such as *The Shining*, *Carrie*, and *It*. King's work is often set in Maine, and involves untold horrors lurking beneath the polished veneer of suburban New England gentility.

most recognisable is Harvard University, founded in 1636 in the Massachusetts city of Cambridge, itself named in honour of the famous British university. Harvard has produced hundreds of Nobel Prize laureates, eight presidents, and countless other leading lights in fields which transcend academia and extend to sporting excellence and the arts. Its museums of art and natural history are well worth a look, as is the adjoining Massachusetts Institute of Technology, whose contributions include the early development of the World Wide Web.

The Connecticut town of New Haven, meanwhile, is home to Yale University, Harvard's great rival ever since its founding in 1701. In terms of modern American political history, Yale has arguably been the more influential of the two prestigious colleges, with Gerald Ford, George H. W. Bush, George W. Bush, and Bill Clinton among its alumni. Other esteemed institutions of higher learning in New England include Brown University, in Providence, Rhode Island, and Dartmouth College, in Hanover, New Hampshire; in total, four out of the eight Ivy League universities are in New England.

When to go

A popular saying, attributed to Mark Twain, goes: "If you don't like the weather in New England, wait five minutes." Certainly, spend a few days in a harbourfront city like Boston, the starting point for most visitors' adventures in New England, and you'll likely see some evidence which supports the witticism. Boston endures long, cold and snowy winters, which eventually submit to sticky, humid summers; the in-between seasons of spring and autumn are more temperate, but unpredictable. Year-round, the city is battered by wind blowing in from the Atlantic, which adds a further headache for Boston's weather forecasters and makes dressing yourself reliably for the day something of a fool's errand – layers, including waterproof ones, are always to be advised.

That being said, the weather of New England varies a great deal, stretching as it does for hundreds of miles in each direction. The cities of Burlington, Vermont, Portland, Maine, and Manchester, New Hampshire receive around 45 inches of rain per year – that's more than in England's Manchester, Britain's quintessential 'Rainy City'. Trace a map south towards the coast of Rhode Island and the Connecticut border, however, and there is some respite, as the climate begins to shift from continental to temperate. The bite of the northern winters is not felt so harshly in areas around New Haven and Newport, although freezing temperatures remain the norm in the depths of winter, even while snow is less common. The coastal areas and islands tend to be cooler and windier in general as a result of being surrounded by the ocean and by sea breezes.

Cape Cod, while not exactly Californian, has a more temperate climate than much of New England, with both slightly warmer winters and slightly cooler

summers than cities like Boston. However, unfair as it may seem for a region which does not enjoy the perks of a tropical climate, cyclones and hurricanes are not unheard of, and sometimes have devastating effects in these parts. In 1954, the disarmingly named Hurricane Carol took the lives of 72 residents of Connecticut and Rhode Island, while more recent disasters include the 2013 North American blizzard, which claimed 18 lives in total.

Inland New England, while spared the brutal coastal winds, sees frigid winter temperatures, making this the best time for winter sport activities such as skiing in the resorts of Vermont. Come spring, wildflowers bloom in the mountains, and summers are short but warm as locals flock to the seaside resorts. Autumn is a popular and beautiful time to visit rural New England on account of the changing autumn foliage, which put on a dazzling display of fiery colours, particularly in woodland areas. The tourists who come to see this phenomenon are known, rather pleasingly, as 'leaf peepers', and they fill up the inns and B&Bs quickly at this time of year.

AVERAGE TEMPERATURE (°F) AND RAINFALL

To convert °F to °C, subtract 32 and multiply by 5/9

	Jan	Feb	Mar	Apr	May	Jun	Jul	Aug	Sep	Oct	Nov	Dec
BOSTON												
Max/min temp	37/23	39/24	46/31	56/40	67/50	76/60	82/66	80/65	73/58	62/48	52/38	42/29
Days of rain	12	11	12	12	12	11	9	9	9	11	10	12
BURLINGTON												
Max/min temp	29/13	32/14	41/24	55/36	69/48	78/57	82/62	80/60	72/53	59/42	46/32	35/21
Days of rain	15	12	13	13	13	13	13	11	11	13	13	15
BRIDGEPORT												
Max/min temp	38/24	40/25	47/32	58/41	68/51	77/61	83/68	82/67	75/59	64/48	53/38	44/30
Days of rain	11	10	11	11	12	11	9	9	8	9	10	11
CONCORD												
Max/min temp	32/13	35/15	44/24	58/33	70/44	78/54	83/60	82/57	74/49	61/38	48/29	37/20
Days of rain	11	10	12	11	12	13	11	10	9	11	11	12
PORTLAND												
Max/min temp	32/16	35/17	42/26	54/35	54/46	64/55	74/61	80/60	79/52	71/41	60/32	38/24
Days of rain	11	10	11	11	13	12	11	9	9	11	11	12
PROVIDENCE												
Max/min temp	38/22	41/24	48/30	59/40	69/49	78/59	84/65	83/64	75/57	64/45	53/36	44/28
Days of rain	11	10	12	12	12	11	9	9	9	10	10	12
MANCHESTER												
Max/min temp	34/17	37/19	45/27	59/38	70/48	78/58	84/64	82/62	75/54	62/42	50/33	39/24
Days of rain	10	10	11	11	12	13	11	10	9	11	10	11

Author picks

Some personal highlights as chosen by our hard-travelling authors:

Most scenic drives The Mohawk Trail runs for 63 miles from Athol to Williamstown through villages and forests. New Hampshire's Kancamagus Highway is an awesome drive through the White Mountains, while Vermont's Route 100 winds for 217 miles through snowy mountains, green forests, and historic towns. Park Loop Road, on Maine's Mount Desert Island, is a great introduction to Acadia National Park.

Best seafood New England's long and fertile coast make this one of the best places in the USA to feast on seafood. In Portland, there's world-beating lobster rolls at Eventide Oyster & Co. (see page 113) and unforgettable Maine mussels at Fore Street (see page 113), while Boston boasts the excellent Island Creek Oyster Bar (see page 65) and magnificent seafood pasta at Waypoint (see page 65).

Classic diners Few American icons are so beloved as the roadside diner, where burgers, apple pie and strong coffee are often served 24/7. In Boston there's Paramount (see page 64), open since 1937, while Providence's Haven Brothers (see page 85), a diner on wheels, has been a local favourite since way back in 1888. Blue Benn Diner (see page 95) is well worth stopping off US-7 while driving through Vermont, while Brattleboro's Chelsea Royal (see page 95) puts a Cajun spin on classic diner cuisine. The pancakes at Littleton Diner (see page 108) are just the thing after a day in the White Mountains.

Top wildlife spots National and state parks such as Acadia (see page 118) and Baxter (see page 121) especially good at preserving herds of elk and deer, moose and black bears, with the latter also home to muskrats, raccoons, coyotes and river otters. Shad Island, on the shores of Lake Champlain in Vermont (see page 100), is home to elegant great blue herons, while whale-watching tours depart from many coastal cities (see page 56) mid-April to October. Mount Desert Island (see page 117) is a haven for seals.

> Our author recommendations don't end here. We've flagged up our favourite places – a perfectly sited hotel, an atmospheric café, a special restaurant – throughout the Guide, highlighted with the ★ symbol.

KANCAMAGUS HIGHWAY, NEW HAMPSHIRE

HUMPBACK WHALE OFF CAPE COD

15

things not to miss

It's obviously not possible to see everything that New England has to offer in one trip. What follows is a selective and subjective taste of the country's highlights: unforgettable cities, spectacular drives, magnificent parks, spirited celebrations and stunning natural phenomena. All highlights are colour-coded by chapter and have a page reference to take you straight into the Guide, where you can find out more.

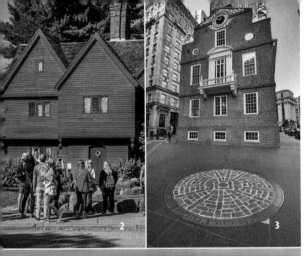

1 FALL FOLIAGE
See page 94
The Berkshires are among the many places in New England to witness a glorious inferno of red and orange leaves in the autumn.

2 SALEM, MA
See page 68
A gruesome history hangs over Salem thanks to the infamous 17th-century witch trials, documented in fascinating detail in this beautiful Massachusetts town.

3 THE FREEDOM TRAIL
See page 49
Trace the footsteps of the heroes of the early United States on this intriguing walking trail in the historic city of Boston.

4 THE WHITE MOUNTAINS
See page 105
It's no secret where this range of mighty mountains in New Hampshire and Maine got its name, and the snow which dusts its peaks makes for great winter skiing.

5 HARVARD, CAMBRIDGE, MA
See page 59
Stroll the hallowed corridors and visit the several fascinating museums of Harvard University, a world-renowned seat of learning.

6 FRESH LOBSTER IN MAINE
See page 115

The picture-perfect towns and harbours of Maine are a rich source of crab and lobster, best eaten freshly boiled at a local fish shack.

7 PROVINCETOWN, MA
See page 73

A thriving arts scene and bustling waterfront characterise "P-town", long a favoured vacation spot for the LGBTQ+ community.

8 A LIVE BASEBALL GAME IN BOSTON
See page 58

Boston's Fenway Park is the oldest ballpark in the country, and remains one of the best places to catch America's favourite game.

9 ACADIA NATIONAL PARK, ME
See page 118

This collection of islands off the coast of Maine includes lonely lighthouses on craggy bluffs, forests, ponds, and windswept moorlands.

10 CAPE COD, MA
See page 71

Spend a day or two on the spectacular beaches of Cape Cod and you'll soon see why it's so popular.

11 PLYMOUTH, MA
See page 69
"America's Hometown" is where it all began when the Pilgrims stepped off the Mayflower in 1620.

12 MARTHA'S VINEYARD, MA
See page 76
New England's largest offshore island is a place of chocolate-box villages and wild beauty – and, yes, a few vineyards.

13 NEWPORT, RI
See page 86
This exclusive port city in Rhode Island evokes the Gilded Age, while the yachts in the marina nod to its upmarket reputation.

14 MYSTIC, CT
See page 88
Famous pizza joints, superb art galleries and museums, and the enchanting Mystic Seaport are some highlights.

15 HARTFORD, CT
See page 90
Explore the life and legacy of America's great writer and wit, Mark Twain, in this extremely pleasant city.

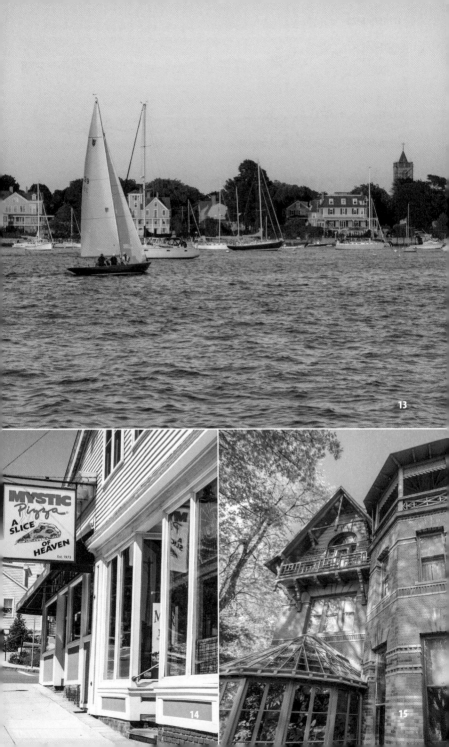

Itineraries

The following itineraries span the length and breadth of this incredibly diverse region, from the towns and villages which birthed the modern nation to the most glamorous cities and monied island resorts. Given the distances involved, you may not be able to cover everything, but New England is more manageable than some parts of America in this regard, and even picking a few highlights will give you a deeper insight into its natural and historic wonders.

NORTH–SOUTH COASTAL ROAD TRIP

This week-long road trip gives an excellent introduction to New England's gorgeous countryside, historic villages and coastal cities, and it's a great trip to make at any time of year. Set off following Route 1 down the east coast from Portland to New Haven and on into Massachusetts.

❶ Portland, ME Maine's biggest city is an atmospheric place of enviable waterfront warehouses and pleasing open green spaces, home to fantastic museums and some of the finest seafood you'll come across anywhere in the US. See page 110

❷ Kennebunkport, ME Numerous presidents have chosen to pass their summers in Kennebunkport, and for good reason. It's a small resort town that is home to glorious beaches, lovely architecture and superb restaurants. See page 109

❸ Ogunquit, ME Stop off in Maine to linger, surf or stroll on one of the East Coast's finest beaches, in the gay-friendly community of Ogunquit. See page 109

❹ Portsmouth, NH Beautiful 17th- and 18th-century architecture tells of Portsmouth's long and esteemed history as an early colonial settlement and later as an artists' refuge. See page 102

❺ Salem, MA Haunting and intriguing history awaits in the town of Salem, the site of New England's infamous 17th-century witch trials. See page 68

❻ Boston, MA The cultural and commercial capital of New England was once known as the Athens of America, and remains a thriving hub for the arts. See page 49

❼ Plymouth, MA The place where the Pilgrims disembarked the Mayflower to found modern America is well worth a visit for history buffs. See page 69

8 Providence, RI A thriving university scene, stately 18th-century architecture and a buzzing arts scene converge on the state capital of Rhode Island. See page 83

9 New Haven, CT The rarefied home of Yale, one of the world's finest universities, is also the place for iconic pizza joints and some brilliant museums. See page 92

RIDING THE RAILS IN THE NORTHEAST

While renting a car is the best way to get around in New England, it's by no means the only option. The USA's skeletal Amtrak rail network, along with connecting lines, is more extensive in the Northeast than in some other areas, and makes for a relaxing and scenic way to explore the region.

1 Freeport, ME Lovers of the great outdoors will find much to divert them in prosperous Freeport, home to toe legendary clothing company L.L. Bean and some lovely parkland. See page 113

2 Boston, MA America's early history is nowhere better explored than Boston, which is now a thriving modern metropolis. See page 49

3 New London, CT Explore the legacy of playwright and Nobel Prize winner Eugene O'Neill in the former whaling port of New London, now an up-and-coming coastal city. See page 89

4 Pioneer Valley Jump off the Amtrak at Springfield and explore the hiking and biking trails of the Pioneer Valley, also home to the lovely towns of Amherst and Northampton. See page 80

5 Killington, VT The fiery fall foliage gives way to frosty winters in Vermont – all the better for skiing at the celebrated resort of Killington. See page 96

6 Littleton, NH There's hiking and skiing galore at the New Hampshire town of Littleton, where feasting on pancakes and maple syrup at the Littleton Diner is another must. See page 108

7 Mount Desert Island, ME Finish your Northeast train tour by disembarking at Bangor, Maine, and exploring the gorgeous Acadia National Park, a protected coastal area which covers half the wilderness of Mount Desert Island. See page 117

NATIONAL AND STATE PARKS

New England is home to only one national park, Acadia National Park in Maine, but boasts a great number of state parks and protected coastline areas which combine to form a superb road trip itinerary.

1 Baxter State Park, ME Mount Katahdin is a holy grail for hikers as the endpoint of the Appalachian Trail, but hikers of all ability levels will love exploring Baxter's forests, mountains, and streams. See page 121

2 Acadia National Park, ME Covering a collection of islands off the coast of Maine, including the ruggedly beautiful Mount Desert Island and Isle au Haut, Acadia National Park is home to coniferous forests, granite coastal formations, and atmospheric old lighthouses. See page 118

3 Camden Hills State Park, ME Spectacular views of the Maine coastline, stretching all the way to Mount Desert Island on a clear day, can be had from the tower atop Mount Battie in Camden Hills. See page 116

4 Wolfe's Neck Woods State Park, ME On a wooded peninsula off the coast of Maine lies the strikingly named Wolfe's Neck Woods, where

NORTH SOUTH COASTAL ROAD TRIP

RIDING THE RAILS IN THE NORTHEAST

NATIONAL AND STATE PARKS

forests of pine and hemlock run down to salty marshlands. See page 113

6 Mount Washington State Park, NH The eastern USA's highest mountain is well worth a climb, or can also be reached by a cog train. The views over the foothills from the summit are unforgettable. See page 106

6 Franconia Notch State Park, NH Ascend into the White Mountains, where the spectacularly sited Franconia Notch mountain valley sees sheer granite cliffs and the gorgeous Echo Lake. See page 105

7 Smugglers' Notch State Park, VT The caves which burrow through this mountain pass were once used as hideaways for smugglers; today they're a scenic diversion from the ski resorts of Vermont. See page 99

8 Quechee State Park, VT The Quechee Gorge plummets in spectacular fashion down to the Ottauquechee River, spanned by a spectacular bridge and covered in thick forest. See page 98

9 Walden Pond State Reserve, MA Channel your inner Henry David Thoreau at the pond and woodlands where the transcendentalist writer penned his masterpiece, Walden. See page 68

THE NORTHEAST BY ROAD

The northeast of America and especially New England is rich in history, with stunning scenery and invariably empty stretches of road the further north you get. This two- to three-week tour is best experienced by car, but you could also do this one by bus.

1 Portland, ME Succulent seafood, historic waterfront architecture and voguish bars draw hipsters and outdoorsy types in equal measure to the endlessly charming city of Portland. See page 110

2 Hartford, CT Visit the Connecticut capital to pay homage to Mark Twain, Harriet Beecher Stowe and the astonishing art at the Wadsworth Atheneum. See page 90

3 Nantucket, MA Take the ferry to the "Little Gray Lady", a once great whaling community still redolent of the era of *Moby Dick*. See page 78

4 Cape Cod, MA Take a day or two to explore the historic towns, tranquil beaches and fish shacks of this hook-shaped peninsula, famously known as the setting for the iconic *Jaws* movies. See page 71

5 Plymouth, MA Where it all began for the modern USA was the town of Plymouth, where the disembarkation of the Pilgrims from the Mayflower is marked by Plymouth Rock. See page 69

6 Salem, MA This historic city has much to recommend it, not least some gorgeous old buildings and museums. And for many visitors who come here it harbours a gruesome intrigue as the site of the infamous 17th-century witch trials. See page 68

7 Boston, MA New England's lively capital oozes colonial history, but also boasts enticing restaurants, top art museums and some of the USA's best sports teams. See page 49

8 White Mountains, NH Across into New Hampshire the mountains become bigger and wilder, perfect for hiking and biking, and culminating in mighty Mount Washington. See page 105

9 Acadia National Park, ME Maine's coastline of wooded bays and small villages snakes northeast to this pristine section of rolling, mist-shrouded hills, fir forests and lobster pounds. See page 118

ISLANDS AND COAST

Some of New England's greatest charms equally lie offshore on its many islands, which are by turn unspoilt and gentrified, naturally beautiful and magnets for the beautiful people. The same is true of the historic and often exclusive coastal cities that punctuate the coastline and serve as embarkation points for the islands.

1 Cape Cod National Seashore, MA Well-heeled Cape Cod is one of the most exclusive postcodes in America, and boasts some glorious beaches along its hundreds of miles of coastline. See page 71

2 Provincetown, MA Long renowned as a haven of tolerance and inclusivity, "P-town" is also a hub for the arts and is home to some lovely, dune-fringed beaches. See page 73

3 Martha's Vineyard, MA Rugged moorland, picturesque gingerbread-house villages, and yet more gorgeous beaches characterise the popular holiday island of Martha's Vineyard. See page 76

4 Nantucket, MA Literature buffs will recognise Nantucket as a setting in the great American novel, *Moby Dick*; today, this former whaling port is home to elegant old houses and interesting museums telling of the island's legacy. See page 78

⑤ Providence, RI The state capital of Rhode Island echoes with centuries of history and reverberates with an artsy buzz thanks to its student population. See page 83

⑥ Newport, RI Long associated with the glamour of the Gilded Age, preserved today in its stately mansions, Newport's charms are far from faded – as the yachts moored in the harbour illustrate. See page 86

⑦ Monhegan Island, ME Eleven miles off the mainland, the unspoilt island of Monhegan has long attracted fisherfolk and artists alike to its hiking trails, old lighthouse, historic inns and lobster-rich waters. See page 116

⑧ Mount Desert Island, ME Perhaps New England at its most beautiful: get back to nature as you drive across the one road onto this rugged island of fjords, forests, flower meadows and craggy coastal bluffs. Come here outside of summer for pure escapism. See page 117

⑨ Bar Harbor, ME Once a summer retreat for the USA's richest families, Bar Harbor is now an appealing tourist town with some great seafood restaurants and places to stay. See page 117

FROM COAST TO MOUNTAINS

Take in the best that New England has to offer travelling from Maine through New Hampshire, on into Vermont and finishing up in Massachusetts. Encounter the vibrant cities of the coast and the snow-capped mountains and bucolic villages of the interior on this epic road trip.

① Portland, ME Hipsters and history buffs converge on the vibrant city of Portland, where lobster shacks serve some of the USA's finest seafood. See page 110

② Mount Washington State Park, NH Drink in the views atop the summit of mighty Mount Washington, the eastern USA's highest mountain, a couple of hours inland from Portland. See page 106

③ Littleton, NH The charming town of Littleton, home to some lovely historic inns and diners, makes the perfect base from which to hike, bike and ski in the White Mountains. See page 108

④ Montpelier, VT Explore the pint-sized charms of the nation's smallest state capital,

with some lovely cafes and restaurants to repair to after exploring the elegant State House. See page 98

⑤ Burlington, VT Continue west to the border with New York and the buzzy city of Burlington, a green, eminently liveable place rich in Revolutionary Way history and lovely lake views. See page 98

⑥ Green Mountains, VT The leafy spine of Vermont is formed by the Green Mountains, best explored on foot along walking routes such as the epic, 272-mile Long Trail. See page 94

⑦ Brattleboro, VT Quirky charm abounds at this mountain town, where yoga studios and vintage bookstores are peopled with a lively student population. See page 95

⑧ Killington, VT Ski or snowboard in the winter, hike and bike in the summer (or go tubing or explore rope courses if you're feeling adventurous) at this popular resort. See page 96

⑨ The Berkshires, MA Hills and forests enclose the well-to-do Berkshires, with some excellent farm-to-table restaurants dotted about the place and glorious autumn foliage adding to the general aura of wholesomeness. See page 80

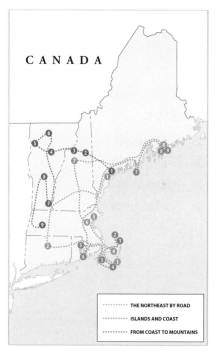

THE NORTHEAST BY ROAD

ISLANDS AND COAST

FROM COAST TO MOUNTAINS

THE WHITE MOUNTAINS, NEW HAMPSHIRE

Basics

Getting there

New England is relatively easy to reach from abroad, whether flying direct into Boston or travelling by train, bus or car via New York.

In general, ticket prices are highest from July to September, and around Easter, Thanksgiving and Christmas. Fares drop during the shoulder seasons – April to June, and October – and even more so in low season, from November to March (excluding Easter, Christmas and New Year). Prices depend more on when Americans want to head overseas than on the demand from foreign visitors. Flying at weekends usually costs significantly more so it's worth looking out for mid-week deals..

Flights from the UK and Ireland

It's possible to fly direct to Boston from London, a flight time of just under eight hours, and from Dublin, which takes a little over seven hours. Manchester and London both have several daily non-stop flights to New York, from where it's easy to transfer to a domestic flight to Boston, Stamford, Providence, and other New England hubs.

As for fares, Britain remains one of the best places in Europe to obtain flight bargains, though prices vary widely. In low or shoulder season, you should be able to find a return flight to East Coast destinations such as Boston and New York for as little as £400, or to California for around £500, while high-season rates can more than double. These days the fares available on the airlines' own websites are often just as good as those you'll find on more general travel websites.

With an open-jaw ticket, you can fly into one city and out of another, though if you're renting a car remember that there's usually a high drop-off fee for returning a rental car in a different state than where you picked it up. An air pass can be a good idea if you want to see a lot of the country. These are available only to non-US residents, and must be bought before reaching the USA.

Flights from Australia, New Zealand and South Africa

For passengers travelling from Australasia to the USA (when travel between the two regions has resumed, projected to be sometime in 2022), the most expensive time to fly has traditionally been during the northern summer (mid-May to end Aug) and over the Christmas period (Dec to mid-Jan), with shoulder seasons covering March to mid-May and September, and the rest of the year counting as low season. Fares no longer vary as much across the year as they used to, however.

Various add-on fares and air passes valid in the continental US are available with your main ticket, allowing you to fly to destinations across the States. These must be bought before you go.

AIRLINES

Aer Lingus Ⓦ aerlingus.com
Air Canada Ⓦ aircanada.com
Air France Ⓦ airfrance.com
Air New Zealand Ⓦ airnewzealand.com
Alaska Airlines Ⓦ alaskaair.com
American Airlines Ⓦ aa.com
British Airways Ⓦ ba.com
Delta Air Lines Ⓦ delta.com
JetBlue Ⓦ jetblue.com
Qantas Airways Ⓦ qantas.com.au
Southwest Ⓦ southwest.com
United Airlines Ⓦ united.com
Virgin Atlantic Ⓦ virgin-atlantic.com

AGENTS AND OPERATORS

Adventure World Australia Ⓦ adventureworld.com.au, New Zealand Ⓦ adventureworld.co.nz
American Holidays Ireland Ⓦ americanholidays.com
Wotif? Australia Ⓦ wotif.com

Getting around

Amtrak provides a skeletal but often scenic rail service, and there are usually good bus links between the major cities. Even in rural areas, with advance planning,

A BETTER KIND OF TRAVEL

At Rough Guides we are passionately committed to travel. We believe it helps us understand the world we live in and the people we share it with – and of course tourism is vital to many developing economies. But the scale of modern tourism has also damaged some places irreparably, and climate change is accelerated by most forms of transport, especially flying. We encourage all our authors to consider the carbon footprint of the journeys they make in the course of researching our guides.

PACKAGES AND TOURS

Although independent travel is usually cheaper, countless flight and accommodation packages allow you to bypass all the organizational hassles. A typical package from the UK might be a return flight plus mid-range hotel accommodation in Boston.

Fly-drive deals, which give cut-rate car rental when a traveller buys a transatlantic ticket from an airline or tour operator, are always cheaper than renting on the spot, and give great value if you intend to do a lot of driving. They're readily available through general online booking agents such as Expedia and Travelocity, as well as through specific airlines. Several of the operators listed here also book accommodation for self-drive tours.

you can usually reach the main points of interest without too much trouble by using local buses and charter services.

That said, travel between cities is almost always easier if you have a car. Many worthwhile and memorable New England destinations are far from the cities: even if a bus or train can take you to the general vicinity of one of the great national parks, for example, it would be of little use when it comes to enjoying the great outdoors.

By rail

Travelling on the national Amtrak network (Ⓦ amtrak.com) is rarely the fastest way to get around, though if you have the time it can be a pleasant and relaxing experience. As you will note from our map, the Amtrak system isn't comprehensive, although New England is better covered than some parts of the country.

For any one specific journey, the train is usually more expensive than taking a Greyhound bus, but is a more pleasant experience. Special deals, especially in the off-peak seasons (Sept–May, excluding Christmas), can bring the cost of a coast-to-coast return trip down. Money-saving passes are also available.

Even with a pass, you should always reserve as far in advance as possible; all passengers must have seats, and some trains, especially between major East Coast cities, are booked solid. Sleeping compartments include three full meals, in addition to your seat fare. However, even standard Amtrak quarters are surprisingly spacious compared to aeroplane seats, and

there are additional dining cars and lounge cars (with full bars and sometimes glass-domed 360° viewing compartments). Finally, if you want to make your journey in the Northeast in a hurry, hop aboard the speedy Acela service, which can shave anywhere from thirty minutes to an hour off your trip, though tends to cost more than a fare on a standard Amtrak train.

By bus

If you're travelling on your own and plan on making a lot of stops, buses are by far the cheapest way to get around. The main long-distance operator, Greyhound (Ⓦ greyhound.com), links all major cities and many towns. Out in the country, buses are fairly scarce, sometimes appearing only once a day, if at all. However, along the main highways, buses run around the clock to a full timetable, stopping only for meal breaks (almost always fast-food chains) and driver changeovers.

To avoid possible hassle, travellers should take care to sit as near to the driver as possible, and to arrive during daylight hours – many bus stations are in dodgy areas, at least in large cities. In many smaller places, the post office or a gas station doubles as the bus stop and ticket office. Reservations can be made in person at the station, online or on the toll-free number. Oddly they do not guarantee a seat, so it's wise to join the queue early – if a bus is full, you may have to wait for the next one, although Greyhound claims it will lay on an extra bus if more than ten people are left behind. For long hauls there

HISTORIC RAILROADS

While Amtrak has a monopoly on long-distance rail travel, a number of historic or scenic railways, some steam-powered or running along narrow-gauge mining tracks, bring back the glory days of train travel. Many are purely tourist attractions, doing a full circuit through beautiful countryside in two or three hours, though some can drop you off in otherwise hard-to-reach wilderness areas. Fares vary widely according to the length of your trip. We've covered the most appealing options in the relevant Guide chapters.

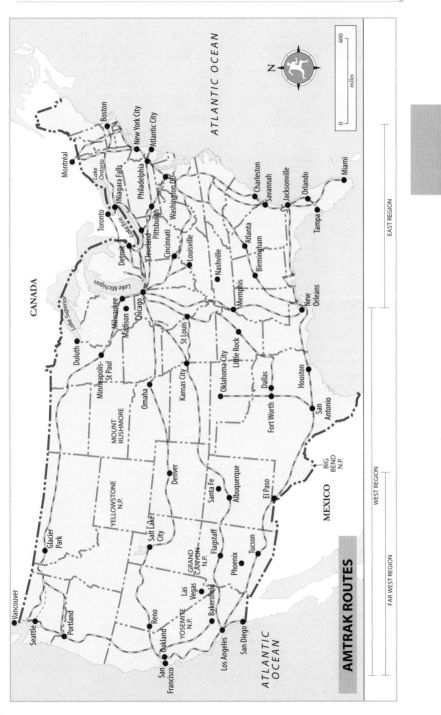

AMTRAK ROUTES

are plenty of savings available – check the website's discounts page.

Other operators include Trailways (Ⓦtrailways.com), whose regional divisions cover some parts of the country more comprehensively; Megabus (Ⓦus.megabus.com), whose low-cost service includes the Northeast; and fellow Northeast operator Peter Pan (800 343 9999, Ⓦpeterpanbus.com).

By plane

Despite the presence of good-value discount airlines – most notably Southwest and JetBlue – air travel is a much less appealing way of getting around the country than it used to be. With air fuel costs escalating even faster than gas costs, and airlines cutting routes, demanding customers pay for routine services and jacking up prices across the board, the days of using jet travel as a spur to vacation adventuring are long gone. By American standards, New England covers a relatively small area, so car, bus or train is the best way to get around.

By car

For many, the concept of cruising down the highway, preferably in a convertible with the radio blasting, is one of the main reasons to set out on a tour of the USA. The romantic images of countless road movies are not far from the truth, though you don't have to embark on a wild spree of drinking, drugs and sex to enjoy driving across America. Apart from anything else, a car makes it possible to choose your own itinerary and to explore the astonishing wide-open landscapes that may well provide your most enduring memories of the country.

Driving in the cities, on the other hand, is not exactly fun, and can be hair-raising. Yet in larger places a car is by far the most convenient way to make your way around, especially as public transport tends to be spotty outside the major cities.

Renting a car

To rent a car, you must have held your licence for at least one year. Drivers under 25 may encounter problems and have to pay higher than normal insurance premiums. Rental companies expect customers to have a credit card; if you don't, they may let you leave a cash deposit, but don't count on it. All the major rental companies have outlets at the main airports but it can often be cheaper to rent from a city branch. Reservations are handled centrally, so the best way to shop around is either online, or by calling their national toll-free numbers. Potential variations are endless; certain cities and states are consistently cheaper than others, while individual travellers may be eligible for corporate, frequent-flier or AAA discounts. You can get some good deals from strictly local operators, though it can be risky as well. Make reading up on such inexpensive vendors part of your pre-trip planning.

Even between the major operators, there can be a big difference in the quality of cars. Industry leaders like Alamo, Hertz and Avis tend to have newer, lower-mileage cars and more reliable breakdown services. Always be sure to get unlimited mileage and remember that leaving the car in a different city from the one where you rented it can incur a drop-off charge of hundreds of extra dollars.

PRE-TRIP PLANNING FOR OVERSEAS TRAVELLERS

AMTRAK PASSES

The USA Rail Pass (15-day/8 segments, 30-day/12 segments/, 45-day/18 segments all available) covers the entire Amtrak network for the designated period, though you are restricted to a set number of individual journeys. Passes can be bought from the Amtrak website (Ⓦamtrak.com).

AIR PASSES

The main American airlines offer air passes for visitors who plan to fly a lot within the USA. These must be bought in advance and are often sold with the proviso that you cross the Atlantic with the same airline or group of airlines (such as Star Alliance). Each deal will involve the purchase of a certain number of flights, air miles or coupons. Other plans entitle foreign travellers to discounts on regular US domestic fares, again with the proviso that you buy the ticket before you leave home. Check with the individual airlines to see what they offer and the overall range of prices. However you do it, flying within the USA is only a wise choice for travel in regions where fares are low anyway; distances within New England rarely merit taking a plane.

DRIVING FOR FOREIGNERS

Foreign nationals from English-speaking countries can drive in the USA using their full domestic driving licences (International Driving Permits are not always regarded as sufficient). Fly-drive deals are good value if you want to rent a car (see above), though you can save up to fifty percent simply by booking in advance with a major firm. If you choose not to pay until you arrive, be sure you take a written confirmation of the price with you. Remember that it's safer not to drive right after a long transatlantic flight – and that most standard rental cars have automatic transmissions.

Small print and insurance

When you rent a car, read the small print carefully for details on Collision Damage Waiver (CDW), sometimes called Liability Damage Waiver (LDW). This form of insurance specifically covers the car that you are driving yourself – you are in any case insured for damage to other vehicles. This charge can add substantially to the total cost, but without it you're liable for every scratch to the car – even those that aren't your fault. Increasing numbers of states are requiring that this insurance be included in the weekly rental rate and are regulating the amounts charged to cut down on rental-car company profiteering. Some credit card companies offer automatic CDW coverage to customers using their card; contact your issuing company for details. Alternatively, European residents can cover themselves against such costs with a reasonably priced annual policy from Insurance4CarHire (Ⓦ insurance4carhire.com).

The American Automobile Association, or AAA (800 222 4357, Ⓦ aaa.com), provides free maps and assistance to its members and to members of affiliated associations overseas, such as the British AA and RAC. If you break down in a rented car, call one of these services if you have towing coverage, or the emergency number pinned to the dashboard.

CAR RENTAL AGENCIES

Alamo USA 800 462 5266, Ⓦ alamo.com
Avis USA 800 230 4898, Ⓦ avis.com
Budget USA 800 527 0700, Ⓦ budget.com
Dollar USA 800 800 3665, Ⓦ dollar.com
Enterprise USA 800 261 7331, Ⓦ enterprise.com
Hertz USA 800 654 3131, Ⓦ hertz.com
Holiday Autos USA 866 392 9288, Ⓦ holidayautos.com
National USA 800 227 7368, Ⓦ nationalcar.com
Thrifty USA & Canada 800 847 4389, Ⓦ thrifty.com

Cycling

Cycling is another realistic mode of transport. An increasing number of big cities have cycle lanes and local buses equipped to carry bikes (strapped to the outside), while in country areas, roads have wide shoulders and fewer passing motorists. Unless you plan to cycle a lot and take your own bike, however, it's not especially cheap. Bikes can be rented for a fixed fee per day, or at discounted weekly rates, from outlets that are usually found close to beaches, university campuses and good cycling areas. Local visitor centres have details.

The national non-profit Adventure Cycling Association (Ⓦ adventurecycling.org) publishes maps of several lengthy routes, detailing campgrounds, motels, restaurants, bike shops and places of interest. Many individual states issue their own cycling guides; contact the state tourist offices (see page 43). Before setting out on a long-distance cycling trip, you'll need a good-quality, multispeed bike, panniers, tools and spares, maps, padded shorts and a helmet (legally required in many states and localities). Plan a route that avoids interstate highways (on which cycling is unpleasant and usually illegal) and sticks to well-maintained, paved rural roads. Of problems you'll encounter, the main one is traffic: RVs, huge eighteen-wheelers and logging trucks can create

HITCHHIKING

Hitchhiking in the United States is generally a bad idea, especially for women, making you a potential victim both inside (you never know who you're travelling with) and outside the car, as the odd fatality may occur from hitchers getting a little too close to the highway lanes. At a minimum, in the many states where the practice is illegal, you can expect a steep fine from the police and, on occasion, an overnight stay in the local jail. The practice is still fairly common, however, in more remote rural areas with little or no public transport.

intense backdraughts capable of pulling you out into the middle of the road.

Backroads Bicycle Tours (W backroads.com), and the HI-AYH hostelling group (see page 31 (W hiusa. org) arrange multi-day cycle tours, with camping or stays in country inns; where appropriate we've also mentioned local firms that offer this.

Greyhound, Amtrak and major airlines will carry passengers' bikes – dismantled and packed into a box – for a small fee.

Accommodation

The cost of accommodation is significant for any traveller exploring New England, especially in the cities, but wherever you travel, you're almost certain to find a good-quality, reasonably priced motel or hotel. If you're prepared to pay a little extra, wonderful historic hotels and lodges can offer truly memorable experiences.

The prices we give in the Guide represent the cheapest double room in high season. Typical rates in motels and hotels start at $75 per night in rural areas, more like $95 in major cities, though substantial discounts are available at slack times. Unsurprisingly, the sky's the limit for luxury hotels, where exclusive suites can easily run into four figures. Many hotels will set up a third single bed for around $25 extra, reducing costs for three people sharing. For lone travellers, on the other hand, a "single room" is usually a double at a slightly reduced rate at best. A dorm bed in a hostel usually costs $25–45 per night, but standards of cleanliness and security can be low, and for groups of two or more the saving compared to a motel is often minimal. In certain parts of New England, camping makes a cheap – and exhilarating – alternative. Alternative methods of finding a room online are through wairbnb.com and the free hosting site W couchsurfing.org.

Wherever you stay, you'll be expected to pay in advance, at least for the first night and perhaps for further nights, too. Most hotels ask for a credit card imprint when you arrive, but many still accept cash for the actual payment. Reservations – essential in busy areas in summer – are held only until 6pm, unless you've said you'll be arriving late. Note that some cities – probably the ones you most want to visit – tack on a hotel tax that can raise the total tax for accommodation to as much as fifteen percent.

Note that as well as the local numbers we give in the Guide, many hotels have freephone numbers (found on their websites), which you can use within the USA.

Hotels and motels

The term "hotels" refers to most accommodation in the Guide. Motels, or "motor hotels", tend to be found beside the main roads away from city centres, and are thus much more accessible to drivers. Budget hotels or motels can be pretty basic, but in general standards of comfort are uniform – each room comes with a double bed (often two), a TV, phone and usually a portable coffeemaker, plus an attached bathroom. Above $95 or so, the room and its fittings simply get bigger and include more amenities, and there may be a swimming pool and added amenities such as irons and ironing boards, or premium cable TV (HBO, Showtime, etc). Almost all hotels and motels now offer wi-fi, albeit sometimes in the lobby only.

The least expensive properties tend to be family-run, independent "mom 'n' pop" motels, but these are rarer nowadays, in the big urban areas at least. When you're driving along the main interstates there's a lot to be said for paying a few dollars more to stay in motels belonging to the national chains. These range from the ever-reliable and cheap Super 8 and Motel 6 (from $70) through to the mid-range Days Inn and La Quinta (from $70) up to the more commodious Holiday Inn Express and Marriott (from $90).

During off-peak periods, many motels and hotels struggle to fill their rooms, so it's worth bargaining to get a few dollars off the asking price, especially at independent establishments. Staying in the same place for more than one night may bring further reductions. Also, look for discount coupons, especially in the free magazines distributed by local visitor centres and welcome centres near the borders between states. These can offer amazing value – but read the small print first. Online rates are also usually cheaper, sometimes considerably so.

Few budget hotels or motels bother to compete with the ubiquitous diners by offering full breakfasts, although most will provide free self-service coffee, pastries and if you are lucky, fruit or cereal, collectively referred to as "continental breakfast".

B&Bs

Staying in a B&B is a popular, sometimes luxurious, alternative to conventional hotels, and there are some lovely historic properties in New England. Some B&Bs consist of no more than a couple of furnished rooms in someone's home, and even the larger establishments tend to have fewer than ten rooms, sometimes without TV or phone, but often laden with potpourri, chintzy cushions and an assertively precious Victorian atmosphere. If this cosy, twee setting appeals to you, there's a range of choices throughout the region, but keep a few things in mind.

ACCOMMODATION PRICE CODES

Throughout the guide, accommodation is categorized according to a price code, which roughly corresponds to the following price ranges. Price categories reflect the cost of a double room per night, without breakfast, in peak season.

$\overline{\underline{\$}}$ under $100
$\overline{\underline{\$\$}}$ $100–200
$\overline{\underline{\$\$\$}}$ $200–350
$\overline{\underline{\$\$\$\$}}$ over $350

For one, you may not be an anonymous guest, as you would in a chain hotel, but may be expected to chat with the host and other guests, especially during breakfast. Also, some B&Bs enforce curfews, and take a dim view of guests stumbling in after midnight after an evening's partying. The only way to know the policy for certain is to check each B&B's policy online – there's often a lengthy list of do's and don'ts.

The price you pay for a B&B – which varies from around $85 to $300 for a double room – always includes breakfast (sometimes a buffet on a sideboard, but more often a full-blown cooked meal). The crucial determining factor is whether each room has an en suite bathroom; most B&Bs provide private bath facilities, although that can damage the authenticity of a fine old house. At the top end of the spectrum, the distinction between a "boutique hotel" and a "bed-and-breakfast inn" may amount to no more than that the B&B is owned by a private individual rather than a chain. In many areas, B&Bs have united to form central booking agencies, making it much easier to find a room at short notice; we've given contact information for these where appropriate.

Historic hotels and lodges

Throughout New England, many towns still have historic hotels, many dating from the arrival of the railroads. So long as you accept that not all will have up-to-date facilities to match their period charm, these can make wonderfully ambient places to spend a night or two. Those that are exceptionally well preserved or restored may charge $200 or more per room, but a more typical rate for a not overly luxurious but atmospheric, antique-furnished room would be more like $120–150.

Hostels

Hostel-type accommodation is not as plentiful in the USA as it is in Europe, but provision for backpackers

and low-budget travellers does exist. Unless you're travelling alone, most hostels cost about the same as motels; stay in them only if you prefer their youthful ambience, energy and sociability. Many are not accessible on public transport, or convenient for sightseeing in the towns and cities, let alone in rural areas.

These days, most hostels are independent, with no affiliation to the HI-AYH (Hostelling-International-al-American Youth Hostels; http://hiusa.org) network. Many are no more than converted motels, where the "dorms" consist of a couple of sets of bunk beds in a musty room, which is also let out as a private unit on demand. Most expect guests to bring sheets or sleeping bags. Rates range from $25 to about $50 for a dorm bed, and from $50–90 for a double room, with prices in the major cities at the higher end. Those few hostels that do belong to HI-AYH tend to impose curfews and limit daytime access hours, and segregate dormitories by sex.

Food and drink

The USA is not all fast food. Every state offers its own specialities, and regional cuisines are distinctive and delicious. In addition, international food turns up regularly – not only in the big cities, but also in more unexpected places. Portuguese restaurants, dating from whaling days, line the New England coast, and the region's seafood is particularly fresh and delicious, with clam chowder and lobster rolls both unmissable dishes to try.

In Boston, you can pretty much eat whatever you want, whenever you want, thanks to the ubiquity of restaurants, 24-hour diners, and bars and street carts selling food well into the night. Also, along all the highways and on virtually every town's main street, restaurants, fast-food joints and cafés try to outdo one another with bargains and special offers. Whatever you eat and wherever you eat it, service is usually prompt, friendly and attentive – thanks in large part to the institution of tipping. Waiters depend on tips for the bulk of their earnings; fifteen to twenty percent is the standard rate, with anything less sure to be seen as an insult.

New England cuisine

Many regions of the USA have developed their own cuisines, combining available ingredients with dishes and techniques of local ethnic groups, and New England is no exception. Shellfish, highly spiced and eaten whole or made into soups and chowders, is the dish of choice on the East Coast; Maine lobsters and steamers (clams), eaten whole or mixed up in a chowder, are reason alone to visit New England. Inland, maple syrup and cranberries are among the bounty of New England's fertile forests, along with hearty treats like pumpkin pie.

Other cuisines

In big cities, Boston in particular, where centuries of settlement have created distinctive local neighbourhoods, each community offers its own take on the cuisine of its homeland. Boston is particularly known for its Italian restaurants, but also has French Canadian establishments in spades, along with the Chinese, Jewish and Mexican eateries common to all American cities.

Drink

You need to be 21 years old to buy and consume alcohol in the USA, and it's likely you'll be asked for ID if you look under 30, and possibly even if you don't. Foreign driving licences are usually accepted as proof of age, but beware of bored bouncers on a power trip.

"Blue laws" – archaic statutes that restrict when, where and under what conditions alcohol can be purchased – are held by many states, and prohibit the sale of alcohol on Sundays; on the extreme end of the scale, some counties and towns (known as "dry") don't allow any alcohol, ever. These are not common in New England, but they include the Massachusetts towns of Alford, Chilmark, Dunstable, Gosnold, Hawley, Montgomery, Mount Washington, and Westhampton, and Ellsworth, New Hampshire. Rest assured, though, that in Boston alcohol can be bought 24/7, except on Sundays, but can be serviced in bars between 8am until 4am the next day, seven days a week.

Note that if a bar is advertising a happy hour on "rail drinks" or "well drinks", these are cocktails made from the liquors and mixers the bar has to hand (as opposed to top-shelf, higher-quality brands).

Beer

The most popular American beers may be the fizzy, insipid lagers from national brands, but there is no lack

EATING PRICE CODES

Throughout the guide, restuarants and diners are categorized according to a price code, which roughly corresponds to the following price ranges. Price categories reflect the cost of a two-course meal for two, with a drink.
$\overline{\underline{\mathsf{S}}}$ under $25
$\overline{\underline{\mathsf{SS}}}$ $26–40
$\overline{\underline{\mathsf{SSS}}}$ $41–60
$\overline{\underline{\mathsf{SSSS}}}$ over $61

of alternatives. The craze for microbreweries started in northern California several decades ago, and has long since reached New England. Indeed, microbreweries have undergone an explosion in most parts of the country in recent years and brewpubs can now be found in virtually every sizeable US city and college town. Almost all serve a wide range of good-value, hearty food to help soak up the drink. For more on craft beers, see ⓦ craftbeer.com. The old guard still reign supreme, though: look for Boston-based Samuel Adams and its mix of mainstream and alternative brews.

Festivals

In addition to the main public holidays – on July 4, Independence Day, the entire country takes time out to picnic, drink, salute the flag, and watch or participate in fireworks displays, marches, beauty pageants, eating contests and more, to commemorate the signing of the Declaration of Independence in 1776 – there is a diverse multitude of engaging local events in New England: arts-and-crafts shows, county fairs, ethnic celebrations, music festivals, rodeos, sandcastle-building competitions, chilli cookoffs and countless others.

Thanksgiving Day, on the fourth Thursday in November, is more sedate. Relatives return to the nest to share a meal (traditionally, roast turkey and stuffing,

VEGETARIAN EATING

In Boston and large cities at least, being a vegetarian – or even a vegan – presents few problems. However, don't be too surprised in rural areas if you find yourself restricted to a diet of eggs, grilled-cheese sandwiches and limp salads. The abundance of high-quality seafood along the New England coast means that pescatarians are particularly well catered for.

cranberry sauce, and all manner of delicious pies) and give thanks for family and friends. Ostensibly, the holiday recalls the first harvest of the Pilgrims in Massachusetts, though Thanksgiving was a national holiday before anyone thought to make that connection.

Annual festivals and events

For further details of the festivals and events listed below, including more precise dates, see the relevant page of the Guide (where covered) or access their websites. The state tourist boards (see page 43) can provide more complete calendars for each area.

JANUARY

County Snow Fest Aroostook County, ME Ⓦ visitmaine.com.

FEBRUARY

Mount Washington Chocolate Festival Intervale, NH Ⓦ mwvskitouring.org/Chocolate-Festival.html.

MARCH

St. Patrick's Day Parade Boston, MA

APRIL

Boston Marathon Boston, MA Ⓦ baa.org

MAY

Cape Cod Maritime Days Cape Cod, MA Ⓦ capecodchamber.org

JUNE

Harvard-Yale Regatta New London, CT

JULY

Newport Folk Festival and Newport Jazz Festival Newport, RI Ⓦ newportfolkfest.org, Ⓦ newportjazzfest.org (latter sometimes Aug).

AUGUST

Maine Lobster Festival Rockland, ME Ⓦ mainelobsterfestival.com.

SEPTEMBER

Vermont State Fair Rutland, VT Ⓦ vermontstatefair.org

OCTOBER

Festival of the Dead Salem, MA Ⓦ festivalofthedead.com.

NOVEMBER

Thanksgiving Celebration Plymouth, MA Ⓦ seeplymouth.com.

DECEMBER

Boston Tea Party Reenactment Boston, MA Ⓦ oldsouthmeetinghouse.org

The outdoors

Coated by dense forests and home to some gorgeous coastline, New England is blessed with fabulous backcountry and wilderness areas. Even the heavily populated East Coast has its share of open space, notably along the Appalachian Trail, which winds from Mount Katahdin in Maine to the southern Appalachians in Georgia – some two thousand miles of untrammelled woodland. On the downside, be warned that in many coastal areas, the shoreline can be disappointingly hard to access, with a high proportion under private ownership.

National parks and monuments

The National Park Service administers both national parks and national monuments. Its rangers do a superb job of providing information and advice to visitors, maintaining trails and organizing such activities as free guided hikes and campfire talks.

In principle, a national park preserves an area of outstanding natural beauty, encompassing a wide range of terrain and prime examples of particular landforms and wildlife. Thus Acadia has lovely tide pools, granite cliffs and wild islands, while Cape Cod national seashore preserves coastal meadows and beaches. A national monument is usually much smaller, focusing perhaps on just one archaeological site or geological phenomenon, such as Katahdin Woods and Waters in Maine.

While national parks tend to be perfect places to hike – almost all have extensive trail networks – all are far too large to tour entirely on foot. Even in those rare cases where you can use public transport to reach a park, you'll almost certainly need some sort of vehicle to explore it once you're there.

Most parks and monuments charge admission fees, ranging from $5 to $30, which cover a vehicle and all its occupants for up to a week. For anyone on a touring vacation, it may well make more sense to buy the Inter-agency Annual Pass, also known as the "America the Beautiful Pass". Sold at all federal parks and monuments, or online at Ⓦ store.usgs.gov, this grants unrestricted access for a year to the bearer, and any accompanying passengers in the same vehicle, to all national parks and monuments, as well as sites managed by such agencies as the US Fish and Wildlife Service, the Forest Service and the BLM (Bureau of Land Management). It does not, however, cover or reduce additional fees like charges for camping in

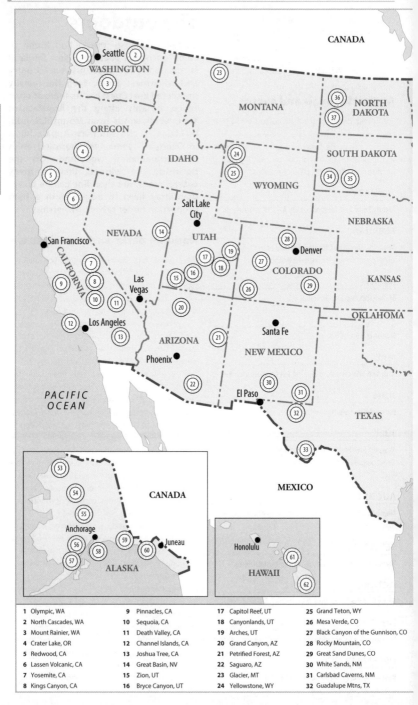

1 Olympic, WA	**9** Pinnacles, CA	**17** Capitol Reef, UT	**25** Grand Teton, WY
2 North Cascades, WA	**10** Sequoia, CA	**18** Canyonlands, UT	**26** Mesa Verde, CO
3 Mount Rainier, WA	**11** Death Valley, CA	**19** Arches, UT	**27** Black Canyon of the Gunnison, CO
4 Crater Lake, OR	**12** Channel Islands, CA	**20** Grand Canyon, AZ	**28** Rocky Mountain, CO
5 Redwood, CA	**13** Joshua Tree, CA	**21** Petrified Forest, AZ	**29** Great Sand Dunes, CO
6 Lassen Volcanic, CA	**14** Great Basin, NV	**22** Saguaro, AZ	**30** White Sands, NM
7 Yosemite, CA	**15** Zion, UT	**23** Glacier, MT	**31** Carlsbad Caverns, NM
8 Kings Canyon, CA	**16** Bryce Canyon, UT	**24** Yellowstone, WY	**32** Guadalupe Mtns, TX

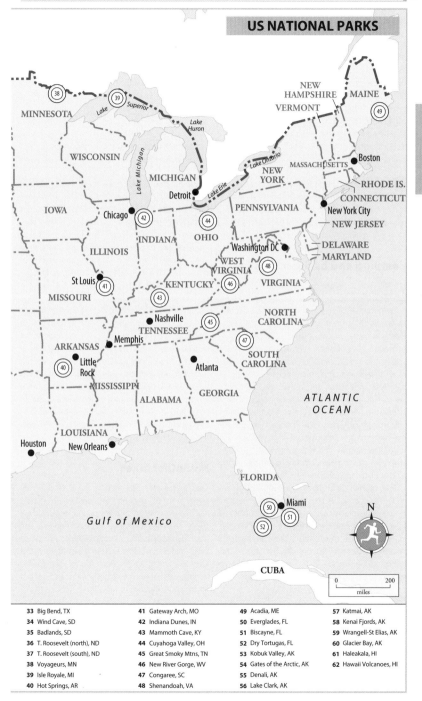

US NATIONAL PARKS

MINNESOTA

Lake Superior

WISCONSIN

Lake Michigan

Lake Huron

MICHIGAN

Detroit

Lake Erie

Lake Ontario

NEW HAMPSHIRE   MAINE

VERMONT

Boston

MASSACHUSETTS

NEW YORK

RHODE IS.

CONNECTICUT

New York City

NEW JERSEY

IOWA

Chicago

INDIANA

OHIO

PENNSYLVANIA

ILLINOIS

DELAWARE

MARYLAND

Washington DC

WEST VIRGINIA

ST Louis

MISSOURI

KENTUCKY

VIRGINIA

Nashville

TENNESSEE

NORTH CAROLINA

ARKANSAS

Memphis

Little Rock

SOUTH CAROLINA

Atlanta

MISSISSIPPI

GEORGIA

ATLANTIC OCEAN

ALABAMA

LOUISIANA

Houston

New Orleans

FLORIDA

Miami

Gulf of Mexico

N

CUBA

0   200

miles

33 Big Bend, TX	**41** Gateway Arch, MO	**49** Acadia, ME	**57** Katmai, AK
34 Wind Cave, SD	**42** Indiana Dunes, IN	**50** Everglades, FL	**58** Kenai Fjords, AK
35 Badlands, SD	**43** Mammoth Cave, KY	**51** Biscayne, FL	**59** Wrangell-St Elias, AK
36 T. Roosevelt (north), ND	**44** Cuyahoga Valley, OH	**52** Dry Tortugas, FL	**60** Glacier Bay, AK
37 T. Roosevelt (south), ND	**45** Great Smoky Mtns, TN	**53** Kobuk Valley, AK	**61** Haleakala, HI
38 Voyageurs, MN	**46** New River Gorge, WV	**54** Gates of the Arctic, AK	**62** Hawaii Volcanoes, HI
39 Isle Royale, MI	**47** Congaree, SC	**55** Denali, AK	
40 Hot Springs, AR	**48** Shenandoah, VA	**56** Lake Clark, AK	

official park campgrounds, or permits for backcountry hiking or rafting.

Two further passes, obtainable at any park or online, grant free access for life to all national parks and monuments, again to the holder and any accompanying passengers, and also provide a fifty-percent discount on camping fees. The Senior Pass is available to any US citizen or permanent resident aged 62 or older, while the Access Pass is issued free to blind or permanently disabled US citizens or permanent residents. While hotel-style lodges are found only in major parks, every park or monument tends to have at least one well-organized campground. Often, a cluster of motels can be found not far outside the park boundaries. With appropriate permits – subject to restrictions in popular parks – backpackers can also usually camp in the backcountry (a general term for areas inaccessible by road).

Camping and backpacking

The ideal way to see the great outdoors – especially if you're on a low budget – is to tour by car and camp in state and federal campgrounds. Typical public campgrounds range in price from free (usually when there's no water available, which may be seasonal) to around $50 per night. Fees at the generally less scenic commercial campgrounds – abundant near major towns, and often resembling open-air hotels, complete with shops and restaurants – are more like $25–50. If you're camping in high season, either reserve in advance or avoid the most popular areas.

Backcountry camping in the national parks is usually free, by permit only. Before you set off on anything more than a half-day hike, and whenever you're headed for anywhere at all isolated, be sure to inform a ranger of your plans, and ask about weather conditions and specific local tips. Carry sufficient food and drink to cover emergencies, as well as all the necessary equipment and maps. Check whether fires are permitted; even if they are, try to use a camp stove in preference to local materials. In wilderness areas, try to camp on previously used sites. Where there are no toilets, bury human waste at least six inches into the ground and 100ft from the nearest water supply and campground.

Health issues

Backpackers should never drink from rivers and streams; you never know what acts people – or animals – have performed further upstream. Giardia – a water-borne bacteria that causes an intestinal disease characterized by chronic diarrhoea, abdominal cramps, fatigue and weight loss – is a serious problem. Water that doesn't come from a tap

MAIN ATTRACTIONS IN NATIONAL PARKS

The Park Service website, ⓦ nps.gov, details the main attractions of the national parks, plus opening hours, the best times to visit, admission fees, hiking trails and visitor facilities.

should be boiled for at least five minutes or cleansed with an iodine-based purifier or a giardia-rated filter.

Hiking at lower elevations should present few problems, though near water mosquitoes can drive you crazy; Avon Skin-so-Soft or anything containing DEET are fairly reliable repellents. Ticks – tiny beetles that plunge their heads into your skin and swell up – are another hazard. They sometimes leave their heads inside, causing blood clots or infections, so get advice from a ranger if you've been bitten. One species of tick causes Lyme disease, a serious condition that can even affect the brain. Nightly inspections of your skin are strongly recommended.

Beware, too, of poison oak, which grows throughout the west, usually among oak trees. Its leaves come in groups of three (the middle one on a short stem) and are distinguished by prominent veins and shiny surfaces. If you come into contact with it, wash your skin (with soap and cold water) and clothes as soon as possible – and don't scratch. In serious cases, hospital emergency rooms can give antihistamine or adrenaline shots. A comparable curse is poison ivy, found throughout the country. For both plants, remember the sage advice, "Leaves of three, let it be".

Mountain hikes

Take special care hiking at higher elevations. Late snows are common, and in spring avalanches are a real danger, while meltwaters make otherwise simple stream crossings hazardous. Weather conditions can also change abruptly. Altitude sickness can affect even the fittest of athletes: take it easy for your first few days above 7000ft. Drink lots of water, avoid alcohol, eat plenty of carbohydrates and protect yourself from the sun.

Skiing

Downhill ski resorts can be found in New England, particularly in Vermont but also New Hampshire and Maine. Expect to pay $50–100 per day (depending on the quality and popularity of the resort) for lift tickets, plus another $35 or more per day to rent equipment.

A cheaper alternative is cross-country skiing, or ski touring. Backcountry ski lodges dot mountainous areas along both coasts and in the Rockies. They offer a range of rustic accommodation, equipment rental and lessons, from as little as $20 a day for skis, boots and poles, up to about $250 for an all-inclusive weekend tour.

Wildlife

Watch out for bears, deer, moose, and mountain lions in the backcountry, and consider the effect your presence can have on their environment.

Other than in a national park, you're highly unlikely to encounter a bear. Even there, it's rare to stumble across one in the wilderness. If you do, don't run, just back away slowly. Most fundamentally, it will be after your food, which should be stored in airtight containers when camping. Ideally, hang both food and garbage from a high but slender branch some distance from your camp. Never attempt to feed bears, and never get between a mother and her young. Young animals are cute; their irate mothers are not.

Snakes and creepy-crawlies

Though New England is not often associated with poisonous snakes, there are two species to be found: the timber rattlesnake and the eastern copperhead. To avoid trouble, observe obvious precautions. Don't attempt to handle wildlife; keep your eyes open as you walk, and watch where you put your hands (and feet) when scrambling over obstacles; shake out shoes, clothing and bedding before use; and back off if you do come up close to a creature, giving it ample room to escape.

If you are bitten or stung, current medical thinking rejects the concept of cutting yourself open and attempting to suck out the venom. Whether snake or spider is responsible, apply a cold compress to the wound, constrict the area with a tourniquet to prevent the spread of venom, drink lots of water and bring your temperature down by resting in a shady area. Stay as calm as possible and seek medical help immediately.

Sports

As well as being good fun, catching a baseball game at Boston's Fenway Park on a summer afternoon or joining the screaming throngs at a Patriots football game in Foxborough can give visitors an unforgettable insight into a town and its people. Professional teams almost always put on the most spectacular shows, but big games between college rivals, Minor League baseball games and even Friday night high-school football games provide an easy and enjoyable way to get on intimate terms with a place.

Specific details for the most important teams in all the sports are given in the various city accounts in this Guide. They can also be found through the Major League websites: Wmlb.com (baseball); Wnba.com (basketball); Wnfl.com (football); Wnhl.com (ice hockey); and Wmlssoccer.com (soccer).

Major spectator sports

Baseball, because the Major League teams play so many games (162 in the regular season, usually at least five a week from April to September, plus October playoffs), is probably the easiest sport to catch when travelling. It's also among the cheapest sports to watch (from around $15–25 a seat for the bleachers), and tickets are usually easy to come by.

Pro football, the American variety, is quite the opposite. Tickets are exorbitantly expensive and almost impossible to obtain (if the team is any good), and most games are played in huge, fortress-like stadiums far out in the suburbs; you'll do better in a bar to watch it on TV. College football is a whole lot better and more exciting, with chanting crowds, cheerleaders and cheaper tickets.

Basketball also brings out intense emotions. The protracted pro playoffs run well into June. The men's month-long college playoff tournament, called "March Madness", is acclaimed by many as the nation's most exciting sports extravaganza, taking place at venues spread across the country in many small to mid-sized towns.

Ice hockey, usually referred to simply as hockey, was long the preserve of Canada and cities in the far north of the USA, but now penetrates the rest of the country, with a concentration around the East Coast. Tickets, particularly for successful teams, are hard to get and not cheap.

Other sports

Soccer remains much more popular as a participant sport, especially for kids, than a spectator one, and those Americans who are interested in it usually follow foreign matches like England's Premier League, rather than their home-grown talent. The good news for international travellers is that any decent-sized city will have one or two pubs where you can catch games from England, various European countries or

Latin America; check out ⓦ livesoccertv.com for a list of such establishments and match schedules.

Golf, once the province of moneyed businessmen, has attracted a wider following in recent decades due to the rise of celebrity golfers such as Tiger Woods and the construction of numerous municipal and public courses. You'll have your best access at these, where a round of golf may cost from $15 for a beaten-down set of links to around $50 for a chintzier course. Private golf courses have varying standards for allowing non-members to play (check their websites) and steeper fees – over $100 a person for the more elite courses.

Travel essentials

Costs

When it comes to average costs for travelling expenses, much depends on where you've chosen to go. A road trip around New England will see the cost of gas add up – this varies from state to state, but at the time of writing the average price was around $3.60 per gallon. By contrast, getting around a large city such as Boston will be relatively cheap, but you'll pay much more for your hotel, meals, sightseeing and shopping. New Hampshire has no state sales tax, but others do, and goods may be liable to some other form of tax from county to county.

Unless you're camping or staying in a hostel, accommodation will be your greatest expense while in New England. A detailed breakdown is given in the Accommodation section, but you can reckon on at least $50–100 per day, based on sharing, more or less double that if travelling solo. Unlike accommodation, prices for good food don't automatically take a bite out of your wallet, and you can indulge anywhere

from the lowliest (but still scrumptious) burger shack to the choicest restaurant helmed by a celebrity chef. You can get by on as little as $25 a day, but realistically you should aim for more like $50.

Where it exists, and where it is useful (which tends to be only in the larger cities), public transport is usually affordable, with many cities offering good-value travel passes. Renting a car is a far more efficient way to explore the broader region, and, for a group of two or more, it could well work out cheaper. Drivers staying in larger hotels in the cities should factor in the increasing trend towards charging even for self-parking; this daily fee may well be just a few dollars less than that for valet parking.

For attractions in the Guide, prices are quoted for adults, with children's rates listed if they are significantly lower or when the attraction is aimed primarily at youngsters; at some spots, kids get in for half-price, or for free if they're under six.

Tipping

In the USA, waiters earn most of their income from tips, and not leaving a fair amount is seen as an insult. Waiting staff expect tips of at least fifteen percent, and up to twenty percent for very good service. When sitting at a bar, you should leave at least a dollar per round for the barkeeper; more if the round is more than two drinks. Hotel porters and bellhops should receive at least $2 per piece of luggage, more if it has been lugged up several flights of stairs. About fifteen percent should be added to taxi fares, rounded up to the nearest 50¢ or dollar.

Crime and personal safety

No one could pretend that America is crime-free, although away from the urban centres crime is often remarkably low. This is particularly true in New England. All the major tourist areas and the main nightlife zones in cities are invariably brightly lit and well policed. By

---

MARIJUANA AND OTHER DRUGS

Over recent years, the legalization of marijuana for recreational purposes has been introduced in a number of states. The first to pass the measure included Massachusetts, Maine, and Vermont. Pot, as it is commonly referred to in America, is now on sale at licensed shops in these states, though there are no Amsterdam-style coffeeshops anywhere as of yet. Rules as to whether only local residents can buy it and how much vary from state to state; smoking in public is usually still illegal.

Paradoxically, the substance is still illegal at the federal level but this has not been creating problems in the above states. More than twenty other states allow the usage of medical marijuana but only with a licence. Note that in states where pot is still illegal, you can be prosecuted even if you have bought it legally elsewhere, so it's wise not to take it across state lines in such cases. Also note that all other recreational drugs remain illegal at both state and federal level, so even simple possession can get you into serious trouble.

planning carefully and taking good care of your possessions, you should, generally speaking, have few problems.

Car crime

Crimes committed against tourists driving rented cars aren't as common as they once were, but it still pays to be cautious. In major urban areas, any car you rent should have nothing on it – such as a particular licence plate – that makes it easy to spot as a rental car. When driving, under no circumstances should you stop in any unlit or seemingly deserted urban area – and especially not if someone is waving you down and suggesting that there is something wrong with your car. Similarly, if you are accidentally rammed by the driver behind you, do not stop immediately, but proceed on to the nearest well-lit, busy area and call ☎ 911 for assistance. Hide any valuables out of sight, preferably locked in the trunk or in the glove compartment.

Electricity

Electricity runs on 110V AC. All plugs are two-pronged and rather insubstantial. Some travel plug adapters don't fit American sockets.

Entry requirements

At the time of writing, the citizens of several countries were not permitted to enter the US, due to measures to limit the spread of Covid-19. The situation may remain subject to specific restrictions for some time to come, and testing or proof of a negative Covid test may be required, even after the border has reopened. For the latest information, consult https:// travel.state. gov/content/travel/en/traveladvisories/ea/require-ments-for-air-travelers-to-the-us.html.

Temporary restrictions aside, citizens of 35 countries – including the UK, Ireland, Australia, New Zealand and most Western European countries – can enter under the Visa Waiver Program if visiting the United States for a period of less than ninety days. To obtain authorization, you must apply online for ESTA (Electronic System for Travel Authorization) approval before setting off. This is a straightforward process – simply go to the ESTA website (westa.cbp.dhs.gov), fill in your info and wait a very short while (sometimes just minutes, but it's best to leave at least 72hr before travelling to make sure) for them to provide you with an authorization number. You will not generally be asked to produce that number at your port of entry, but it is as well to keep a copy just in case, especially in times of high-security alerts – you will be denied entry if you don't have one.

Prospective visitors from parts of the world not mentioned above require a valid passport and a non-immigrant visitor's visa for a maximum ninety-day stay. How you'll obtain a visa depends on what country you're in and your status when you apply; check ⓦ travel.state.gov. Whatever your nationality, visas are not issued to convicted felons and anybody who owns up to being a communist, fascist, drug dealer or guilty of genocide (fair enough, perhaps). On arrival, the date stamped on your passport is the latest you're legally allowed to stay.

FOREIGN EMBASSIES IN THE USA

Australia 1601 Massachusetts Ave NW, Washington DC 20036, 202 797 3000, ⓦ usa.embassy.gov.au
Canada 501 Pennsylvania Ave NW, Washington DC 20001, 202 682 1740, ⓦ international.gc.ca
Ireland 2234 Massachusetts Ave NW, Washington DC 20008, 202 462 3939, ⓦ dfa.ie/irish-embassy/usa
New Zealand 37 Observatory Circle NW, Washington DC 20008, 202 328 4800, ⓦ mfat.govt.nz
South Africa 3051 Massachusetts Ave NW, Washington DC 20008, 202 232 4400, ⓦ saembassy.org
UK 3100 Massachusetts Ave NW, Washington DC 20008, 202 588 6500, ⓦ ukinusa.fco.gov.uk

Health

If you have a serious accident while in the USA, emergency medical services will get to you quickly and charge you later. For emergencies or ambulances, dial ☎ 911, the nationwide emergency number.

Should you need to see a doctor, consult the Yellow Pages telephone directory under "Clinics" or "Physicians and Surgeons". The basic consultation fee is $150–200, payable in advance. Tests, X-rays etc are much more. Medications aren't cheap either – keep all your receipts for later claims on your insurance policy.

Foreign visitors should bear in mind that many pills available over the counter at home – most codeine-based painkillers, for example – require a prescription. Local brand names can be confusing; ask for advice.

Inoculations aren't required for entry to the USA.

Covid-19

The global Covid-19 pandemic impacted the US from early 2020 and by January 2022, it had claimed the lives of 875,000 Americans, the highest number in the world by some margin, and a total that was still climbing at time of writing. More positively, the US's vaccination programme to protect citizens from future infections was well underway, with 200 million vaccine shots given before President Biden's 100th day in office, doubling his original pledge made. However, vaccine hesitancy remains more of a problem in the USA than in many other countries.

ROUGH GUIDES TRAVEL INSURANCE

Rough Guides has teamed up with WorldNomads.com to offer great travel insurance deals. Policies are available to residents of over 150 countries, with cover for a wide range of adventure sports, 24hr emergency assistance, high levels of medical and evacuation cover and a stream of travel safety information. Roughguides.com users can take advantage of their policies online 24/7, from anywhere in the world – even if you're already travelling. And since plans often change when you're on the road, you can extend your policy and even claim online. Roughguides.com users who buy travel insurance with WorldNomads.com can also leave a positive footprint and donate to a community development project. For more information go to ⓦ roughguides.com/travel-insurance.

Visitors should check what health precautions are necessary at both federal and state level, in particular with regards to mask-wearing and social distancing.

MEDICAL RESOURCES FOR TRAVELLERS

CDC ⓦ cdc.gov/travel. Official US government travel health site.
International Society for Travel Medicine ⓦ istm.org. Full listing of travel health clinics.

Insurance

In view of the high cost of medical care, all overseas travellers should be sure to buy some form of travel insurance. American and Canadian citizens should check whether they are already covered – some homeowners' or renters' policies are valid on holiday, and credit cards such as American Express often include some medical or other insurance, while most Canadians are covered for medical mishaps overseas by their provincial health plans. If you only need trip cancellation/interruption coverage (to supplement your existing plan), this is generally available at a cost of about six percent of the trip value.

Internet

Almost all hotels and many coffeeshops and restaurants offer free wi-fi for guests, though some upmarket hotels charge for access. As a result, cybercafés, where you can use a terminal in the establishment for around $5–10 an hour, are increasingly uncommon. Nearly all public libraries provide free internet access, but often there's a wait and machine time is limited.

LGBTQ travellers

The LGBTQ scene in New England is heavily concentrated in the major cities, but people in general are tolerant and liberal by American standards. Provincetown has been associated with the LGBTQ scene since the 1950s, and Boston has many gay-friendly bars and clubs. Visit ⓦ ptowntourism.com and ⓦ queerintheworld.com for more information.

Mail

Post offices are usually open Monday to Friday from 8.30am to 5.30pm, and Saturday from 9am to 12.30pm, and there are blue mailboxes on many street corners. At time of publication, first-class mail within the USA costs 58¢ for a letter weighing up to 28 grams (an ounce), $1.30 for the rest of the world. Airmail between the USA and Europe may take a week.

In the USA, the last line of the address includes the city or town and an abbreviation denoting the state ("MA" for Massachusetts; "ME" for Maine, for example). The last line also includes a five-digit number – the zip code – denoting the local post office. It is very important to include this, though the additional four digits that you will sometimes see appended are not essential. You can check zip codes on the US Postal Service website, at ⓦ usps.com.

Maps

The free road maps distributed by each state through its tourist offices and welcome centres are usually fine for general driving and route planning.

The American Automobile Association, or AAA ("Triple A"; 800 222 4357, ⓦ aaa.com) provides free maps and assistance to its members, as well as to British members of the AA and RAC. Call the main number to get the location of a branch near you; bring your membership card or at least a copy of your membership number.

The best supplier of detailed, large-format map books for travel through the American backcountry is Benchmark Maps (ⓦ benchmarkmaps.com).

Money

The US dollar comes in $1, $2, $5, $10, $20, $50 and $100 denominations. One dollar comprises one hundred

OPENING HOURS AND PUBLIC HOLIDAYS

The traditional summer holiday period runs between the weekends of Memorial Day, the last Monday in May, and Labor Day, the first Monday in September. Many parks, attractions and visitor centres operate longer hours or only open during this period and we denote such cases as "summer" throughout the Guide. Otherwise, specific months of opening are given.

Government offices (including post offices) and banks will be closed on the following national public holidays:

Jan 1 New Year's Day
Third Mon in Jan Martin Luther King, Jr's Birthday
Third Mon in Feb Presidents' Day
Last Mon in May Memorial Day
July 4 Independence Day
First Mon in Sept Labor Day
Second Mon in Oct Columbus Day
Nov 11 Veterans' Day
Fourth Thurs in Nov Thanksgiving Day
Dec 25 Christmas Day

cents, made up of combinations of one-cent pennies, five-cent nickels, ten-cent dimes and 25-cent quarters. You can check current exchange rates at ⓦx-rates.com; at the time of writing one pound sterling will buy around $1.34 and a euro around $1.20.

Bank hours generally run from 9am to 5pm Monday to Thursday, and until 6pm on Friday; the big bank names are Wells Fargo, US Bank and Bank of America. With an ATM card, you'll be able to withdraw cash just about anywhere, though you'll be charged $2–5 per transaction for using a different bank's network. Foreign cash-dispensing cards linked to international networks, such as Plus or Cirrus, are also widely accepted – ask your home bank or credit card company which branches you can use. To find the location of the nearest ATM, call AmEx (800 227 4669); Cirrus (800 424 7787); Accel/The Exchange (800 519 8883); or Plus (800 843 7587).

Credit and debit cards are the most widely accepted form of payment at major hotels, restaurants and retailers, even though a few smaller merchants still do not accept them. You'll be asked to show some plastic when renting a car, bike or other such item, or to start a "tab" at hotels for incidental charges; in any case, you can always pay the bill in cash when you return the item or check out of your room.

Phones

The USA currently has well over one hundred area codes – three-digit numbers that must precede the seven-figure number if you're calling from abroad (following the 001 international access code) or from a different area code, in which case you prefix the

ten digits with a 1. It can get confusing, especially as certain cities have several different area codes within their boundaries; for clarity, in this Guide, we've included the local area codes in all telephone numbers. Note that some cities require you to dial all ten digits, even when calling within the same code. Numbers that start with the digits 800 – or increasingly commonly 888, 877 and 866 – are toll-free, but these can only be called from within the USA itself; most hotels and many companies have a toll-free number that can easily be found on their websites.

If you are planning to take your mobile phone (more often called a cell phone in America) from outside the USA, you'll need to check with your service provider whether it will work in the country: you will need a tri-band or quad-band phone that is enabled for international calls. Using your phone from home will probably incur hefty roaming charges for making calls and charge you extra for incoming calls, as the people calling you

CALLING HOME FROM THE USA

For country codes not listed below, dial 0 for the operator, consult any phone directory or log onto ⓦcountrycallingcodes.com.
Australia 011 + 61 + area code minus its initial zero.
New Zealand 011 + 64 + area code minus its initial zero.
Republic of Ireland 011 + 353 + area code minus its initial zero.
South Africa 011 + 27 + area code.
UK 011 + 44 + area code minus its initial zero.

will be paying the usual rate. Depending on the length of your stay, it might make sense to rent a phone or buy a compatible prepaid SIM card from a US provider; check ⓦtriptel.com or ⓦtelestial.com. Alternatively, you could pick up an inexpensive pay-as-you-go phone from one of the major electrical shops.

Senior travellers

Anyone aged over 62 (with appropriate ID) can enjoy a vast range of discounts. Both Amtrak and Greyhound offer (smallish) percentage reductions on fares, and any US citizen or permanent resident aged 62 or over is entitled to free admission to all national parks, monuments and historic sites using a Senior Pass. This free admission applies to all accompanying travellers in the same vehicle and also gives a fifty-percent reduction on park user fees, such as camping charges.

Time

New England is in the Eastern time zone, five hours behind Greenwich Mean Time (GMT), so 3pm London time is 10am in Boston. The USA puts its clocks forward one hour to daylight saving time on the second Sunday in March and turns them back on the first Sunday in November.

Travelling with children

Children under 2 go free on domestic flights and for ten percent of the adult fare on international flights – though that doesn't mean they get a seat, let alone frequent-flier miles. Kids aged 2 to 12 are usually entitled to half-price tickets. Discounts for train and bus travel are broadly similar. Car-rental companies usually provide kids' car seats – which are required by law for children under the age of 4. You would, however, be advised to check, or bring your own; they are not always available. Recreational vehicles (RVs) are a particularly good option for families. Even the cheapest motel will offer inexpensive two-double bed rooms, which is a relief for non-US travellers used to paying a premium for a "family room", or having to pay for two rooms.

Virtually all tourist attractions offer reduced rates for kids. Most large cities have natural history museums or aquariums, and quite a few also have hands-on children's museums; in addition most state and national parks organize children's activities. All the national restaurant chains provide highchairs and special kids'

CLOTHING AND SHOE SIZES

WOMEN'S CLOTHING

American	4	6	8	10	12	14	16	18		
British	6	8	10	12	14	16	18	20		
Continental	34	36	38	40	42	44	46	48		

WOMEN'S SHOES

American	5	6	7	8	9	10	11			
British	3	4	5	6	7	8	9			
Continental	36	37	38	39	40	41	42			

MEN'S SHIRTS

American	14	15	15.5	16	16.5	17	17.5	18		
British	14	15	15.5	16	16.5	17	17.5	18		
Continental	36	38	39	41	42	43	44	45		

MEN'S SHOES

American	7	7.5	8	8.5	9	9.5	10	10.5	11	11.5
British	6	7	7.5	8	8.5	9	9.5	10	11	12
Continental	39	40	41	42	42.5	43	44	44	45	46

MEN'S SUITS

American	34	36	38	40	42	44	46	48		
British	34	36	38	40	42	44	46	48		
Continental	44	46	48	50	52	54	56	58		

menus; and the trend for more upmarket family-friendly restaurants to provide crayons with which to draw on paper tablecloths is still going strong.

For a database of kids' attractions, events and activities, check the useful site Ⓦ nickelodeonparents.com.

Travellers with disabilities

By international standards, the USA is exceptionally accommodating for travellers with mobility concerns or other physical disabilities. By law, all ˅public buildings, including hotels and restaurants, must be wheelchair accessible and provide suitable toilet facilities. Most street corners have dropped curbs (less so in rural areas), and most public transport systems include subway stations with elevators and buses that "kneel" to let passengers in wheelchairs board.

Getting around

The Americans with Disabilities Act (1990) obliges all air carriers to make the majority of their services accessible to travellers with disabilities, and airlines will usually let attendants of more severely disabled people accompany them at no extra charge.

Almost every Amtrak train includes one or more coaches with accommodation for handicapped passengers. Guide dogs travel free and may accompany blind, deaf or disabled passengers. Be sure to give 24 hours' notice. Hearing-impaired passengers can get information on 800 523 6590 (TTY/TDD).

Greyhound, however, has its challenges. Buses are not equipped with lifts for wheelchairs, though staff will assist with boarding (intercity carriers are required by law to do this), and the "Helping Hand" policy offers two-for-the-price-of-one tickets to passengers unable to travel alone (carry a doctor's certificate). The American Public Transportation Association, in Washington DC (202 496 4800, Ⓦ apta.com), provides information about the accessibility of public transport in cities.

The American Automobile Association (contact http://aaa.com for phone number access for each state) produces the Handicapped Driver's Mobility Guide, while the larger car-rental companies provide cars with hand controls at no extra charge, though only on their full-sized (ie most expensive) models; reserve well in advance.

Resources

Most state tourism offices provide information for disabled travellers (see page 43). In addition, SATH, the Society for Accessible Travel and Hospitality, in New York (212 447 7284, Ⓦ sath.org), is a not-for-profit travel-industry group of travel agents, tour operators, hotel and airline management, and people with disabilities. They pass on any enquiry to the appropriate member, though you should allow plenty of time for a response. Mobility International USA, in Eugene, OR (541 343 1284, Ⓦ miusa.org), offers travel tips and operates exchange programmes for disabled people; it also serves as a national information centre on disability.

The "America the Beautiful Access Pass", issued without charge to permanently disabled or blind US citizens, gives free lifetime admission to all national parks. It can only be obtained in person at a federal area where an entrance fee is charged; you'll have to show proof of permanent disability, or that you are eligible for receiving benefits under federal law.

Women travellers

A woman travelling alone in New England is not usually made to feel conspicuous, or liable to attract unwelcome attention. Cities can feel a lot safer than you might expect, though particular care must be taken at night: walking through unlit, empty streets is never a good idea, and, if there's no bus service, take a taxi.

In the major urban centres, if you stick to the better parts of town, going into bars and clubs alone should pose few problems.

Women should never hitchhike in the USA. Similarly, you should never pick up anyone who's trying to hitchhike. If someone is waving you down on the road, ostensibly to get help with a broken-down vehicle, just drive on by or call the highway patrol to help them.

Avoid travelling at night by public transport – deserted bus stations will do little to make you feel secure. Where possible, team up with a fellow traveller. On Greyhound buses, sit near the driver.

Should disaster strike, all major towns have some kind of rape counselling service; if not, the local sheriff's office will arrange for you to get help and counselling, and, if necessary, get you home. The National Organization for Women (202 628 8669, Ⓦ now.org) has branches listed in local phone directories and on its website, and can provide information on rape crisis centres, counselling services and feminist bookstores.

New
England

BOSTON'S FINANCIAL DISTRICT

1 New England

The states of Massachusetts, Rhode Island, Connecticut, Vermont, New Hampshire and Maine – collectively known as New England – exemplify America at its most nostalgic: country stores that brim with cider and gourds, snow-dusted hillsides, miles of blazing fall foliage, clam shacks, cranberry bogs and an unruly ocean that distinguishes and defines it all. Scratch just beneath the surface, and you'll also uncover fiercely independent locals, innovative chefs, some of the country's best contemporary art museums and a profound sense of history.

Boston especially is celebrated as the birthplace of American independence – so many seminal events took place here, or nearby at Lexington and Concord. New England was also home to many of the pre-eminent figures of American literature, from Mark Twain and Henry Thoreau to Emily Dickinson and Jack Kerouac. These days, it's home to horror-fiction writer Stephen King, whose books have sold more than 350 million copies worldwide. The **Ivy League** colleges – Harvard, Yale, Brown, Dartmouth et al – are the oldest in the country and remain hugely influential, continually channelling new life into towns like Cambridge and New Haven and setting a decidedly liberal tone throughout the region.

To the east, the peninsula of **Cape Cod** flexes off **Massachusetts** like a well-tanned arm. Here you will find three hundred miles of shoreline, sea roses, tumbling sand dunes and the fantastic isles of **Nantucket** and **Martha's Vineyard**. In the western part of the state, the tranquil **Berkshires** offer the best in summer festivals as well as fascinating art museums. The sights of **Connecticut** and **Rhode Island** tend to be urban, but away from I-95 you'll find plenty of tranquil pockets, particularly in the way of Newport and Block Island, fifty miles south of Providence. **Boston** is a vibrant and enchanting city from which to set off north, where the population begins to thin out (and the **seafood** gets better as you go). The rest of **Massachusetts** is rich in historical and literary sights, while further inland, the lakes and mountains of **New Hampshire** and **Maine** offer rural wildernesses to rival any in the nation. Maine is especially known for its coastline, dotted with lighthouses and wild blueberry bushes. The beloved country roads of **Vermont** offer pleasant wandering through rural towns and serene forests; during your travels, be sure to pick up some maple syrup, a local delicacy, for your pancakes back home. In 2020, New England celebrated the 400th anniversary of its founding – and the founding of the United States. The region is marking the quadricentennial of the *Mayflower* voyage and settlement of Plymouth Colony with a wide range of events, exhibits, the launch of a *Mayflower* replica and much more.

GREAT REGIONAL DRIVES

Rte-100, VT Vermont is famed far and wide for its spectacular fall foliage. Easy-going Rte-100 cuts through the heart of the state and skirts the perimeter of the Green Mountain Forest.

Acadia's Park Loop Road, ME Craggy granite cliffs, crisp ocean air and melancholy stands of fir and spruce are hallmarks of this breathtaking national park in the eastern corner of the country.

Kancamagus Hwy, NH Easily driven in a day, but pleasant enough to be savoured for weeks, "the Kanc" – set in the White Mountains – has enough hiking trails, campgrounds and tumbling waterfalls to satisfy the most discerning nature lover.

PEACHAM, VERMONT

Highlights

❶ Boston, MA Revolutionary history comes to life around every corner in one of America's most chronicled, walkable cities. See page 49

❷ Provincetown, MA Wild beaches, lovely flower-filled streets and an alternative vibe on the outer reaches of Cape Cod. See page 73

❸ Historic "summer cottages", Newport, RI Conspicuous consumption gone crazy in this yachtie resort. See page 86

❹ Burlington, VT In a complete contrast to Vermont's profusion of perfect villages, this

is a genuine city, with a waterfront, a vibrant downtown and the state's best restaurants and nightlife. See page 100

❺ White Mountains, NH Ski, hike, cycle or just soak up the scenery on Mount Washington or Franconia Notch. See page 105

❻ Acadia National Park, ME Remote mountains and lakes, stunning cliffs and the chance to catch the sunrise before anyone else in the USA. See page 105

HIGHLIGHTS ARE MARKED ON THE MAP ON PAGE 48

1

The best time to visit New England is in late September and October, when visitors flock to see the magnificent **fall foliage**. Particularly vivid in Vermont, it's an event that's not to be missed.

Massachusetts

The state of **MASSACHUSETTS** was established with a lofty aim: to become, in the words of seventeenth-century governor John Winthrop, a utopian "**City upon a hill**". This Puritan clarity of thought and forcefulness of purpose can be

NEW ENGLAND

HIGHLIGHTS

1. Boston, MA
2. Provincetown, MA
3. Historic "summer cottages", Newport, RI
4. Burlington, VT
5. White Mountains, NH
6. Acadia National Park, ME

0   100
miles

traced from the foundation of Harvard College in 1636, through the intellectual impetus behind the Revolutionary War and the crusade against slavery, to the nineteenth-century achievements of **writers** such as Melville, Emerson, Hawthorne and Thoreau.

Spending a few days in **Boston** is strongly recommended. Perhaps America's most historic city, and certainly one of its most elegant, it offers a great deal of modern life as well, thanks in part to the presence of **Cambridge**, the home of Harvard University and MIT (Massachusetts Institute of Technology), just across the river. Several historic towns are within easy reach – **Salem** to the north, known for its "witch" sights, **Concord** and **Lexington**, just inland, richly imbued with Revolutionary War history, and **Plymouth**, to the south, the site of the Pilgrims' first settlement (1620). Alternative **Provincetown**, a ninety-minute ferry ride across the bay at the tip of Cape Cod, is great fun, known for its LGBTQ scene, sunbathing and bike riding galore. The rest of the Cape, particularly its two islands – **Nantucket** and **Martha's Vineyard** – offers old sea-salted towns, excellent shellfish and lovely beaches. **Western Massachusetts** is best known for the beautiful **Berkshires**, which host the celebrated **Tanglewood** summer music festival and boast museum-filled towns such as **North Adams** and **Williamstown** – both in the far northwest corner of the state, at the end of the incredibly scenic **Mohawk Trail**. **Amherst** and **Northampton** are stimulating college towns in the verdant **Pioneer Valley**, with all the cafés, restaurants and bookstores you could want.

Boston

A modern American city that proudly trades on its colonial past, **BOSTON** is about as close to the Old World as the New World gets. This is not to say it lacks contemporary attractions: its restaurants, bars, museums and neatly landscaped public spaces are all as alluring as its historic sites. Boston has grown up around **Boston Common**, a utilitarian chunk of green established for public use and "the feeding of cattell" in 1634. A good starting point for a tour of the city, it is also one of the links in the string of nine parks called the **Emerald Necklace**. Another piece is the lovely **Public Garden**, across Charles Street from the Common, where Boston's iconic swan boats paddle the main pond. Grand boulevards such as Commonwealth Avenue ("Comm Ave") lead west from the Public Garden into **Back Bay**, where Harvard Bridge crosses into **Cambridge**. The beloved **North End**, adjacent to the waterfront, is Boston's Little Italy, its narrow streets chock-a-block with excellent bakeries and restaurants. Behind the Common rises the **State House** and lofty **Beacon Hill**, every bit as dignified as when writer Henry James called Mount Vernon Street "the most prestigious address in America".

THE FREEDOM TRAIL

Delineated by a 2.5-mile-long red-brick (or paint) stripe in the sidewalk, the **Freedom Trail** (ⓦ thefreedomtrail.org) stretches from Boston Common to Charlestown, linking sixteen points "significant in their contribution to this country's struggle for freedom". About half the sights on the trail are related to the Revolution itself; the others are more germane to other times and topics.

Though some of the touches intended to accentuate the trail's appeal move closer to tarnishing it (the costumed actors outside some of the sights, the pseudo-antique signage), the Freedom Trail remains the easiest way to orient yourself downtown, and is especially useful if you'll only be in Boston for a short time, as it does take in many "must-see" sights. Detailed National Park Service **maps** of the trail can be picked up from the visitor centre (see page 62). Thrifty travellers take note: most stops on the trail are either **free** or inexpensive to enter.

1

BOSTON

0 — 400 yards

■ ACCOMMODATION	
Ames Hotel	3
Charlesmark Hotel	10
Clarendon Square Inn	12
College Club	8
The Godfrey	13
The Eliot	6
Harborside Inn	1
HI-Boston	7
Hotel Commonwealth	14
Liberty Hotel	5
Marriott's Custom House	11
Newbury Guest House	4
Omni Parker House	2
Residence Inn by Marriott	16
The Revolution Hotel	9
Verb Hotel	15

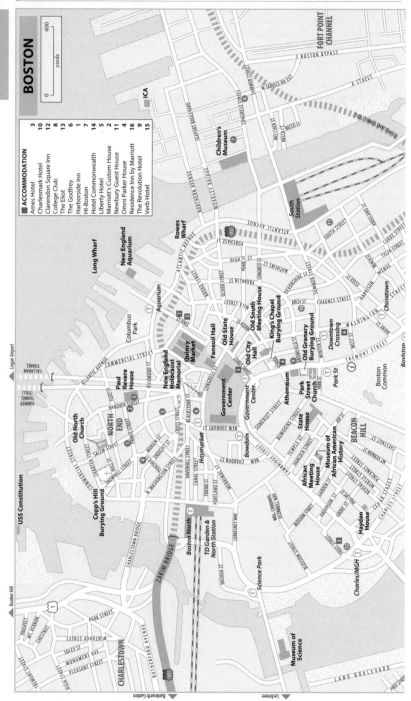

FORT POINT CHANNEL

ICA

Children's Museum

South Station

CHARLESTOWN

Bunker Hill

Logan Airport

USS Constitution

Copp's Hill Burying Ground

Old North Church

NORTH END

Paul Revere House

New England Holocaust Memorial

Long Wharf

New England Aquarium

Rowes Wharf

Columbus Park

Aquarium

Quincy Market

Faneuil Hall

Old State House

Old City Hall

Old South Meeting House

King's Chapel Burying Ground

Downtown Crossing

Government Center

Athenaeum

Old Granary Burying Ground

Park Street Church

Boston Common

State House

Museum of African American History

African Meeting House

BEACON HILL

Hayden House

Charles/MGH

Science Park

TD Garden & North Station

Boston North

Haymarket

Bowdoin

ZAKIM BRIDGE

CHARLESTOWN BRIDGE

Museum of Science

LAND BOULEVARD

Chinatown

Boylston

Park St

Charlestown

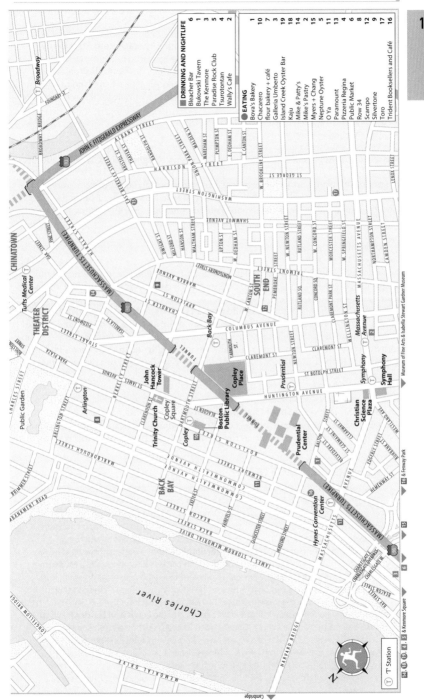

DRINKING AND NIGHTLIFE	
Bleacher Bar	6
Bukowski Tavern	1
The Kenmore	3
Paradise Rock Club	5
Tsurotontan	4
Wally's Café	2

EATING	
Bova's Bakery	1
Chacarero	10
flour bakery + café	7
Galleria Umberto	3
Island Creek Oyster Bar	19
Kaju	18
Mike & Patty's	14
Mike's Pastry	2
Myers + Chang	15
Neptune Oyster	5
O Ya	11
Paramount	13
Pizzeria Regina	4
Public Market	8
Row 34	12
Scampo	9
Silvertone	17
Toro	16
Trident Booksellers and Café	16

1

Massachusetts State House

Corner of Beacon and Park sts • Mon–Fri 8.45am–5pm, guided tours Mon–Fri 10am–3.30pm • Free • ⑩ malegislature.gov • Park St T

Behind Boston Common rises the large gilt dome of the **Massachusetts State House**, completed in 1798 and still the seat of Massachusetts' government. Its most famous fixture, a carved fish dubbed the "Sacred Cod", symbolizes the wealth Boston accrued from maritime trade. Politicos take this symbol so seriously that when Harvard pranksters stole it in the 1930s the House of Representatives didn't reconvene until it was recovered.

54th Massachusetts Regiment Monument

Beacon St, on the edge of Boston Common • Free • Park St T

Across from the State House is a majestic monument honouring the **54th Massachusetts Regiment**, the first all-black company to fight in the Civil War, and its leader, Robert Gould Shaw, scion of a moneyed Boston Brahmin clan. Isolated from the rest of the Union army, the regiment performed bravely; most of its members, including Shaw, were killed in a failed attempt to take Fort Wagner from the Confederates in 1863. Augustus Saint-Gaudens' outstanding 1897 bronze sculpture depicts the regiment's farewell march down Beacon Street.

Beacon Hill

Charles St T

No visit to Boston would be complete without an afternoon spent strolling around delightful **Beacon Hill**, a dignified stack of red brick rising over the north side of Boston Common. This is the Boston of wealth and privilege, one-time home to numerous historical and literary figures – including John Hancock, John Quincy Adams, Louisa May Alcott and Oliver Wendell Holmes. As you walk, keep an eye out for the **purple panes** in some of the townhouses' windows (such as nos. 63 and 64 Beacon St). At first an irritating accident, they were eventually regarded as the definitive Beacon Hill status symbol due to their prevalence in the windows of Boston's most prestigious homes.

Park Street Church

Corner of Park and Tremont sts • Office hours Mon–Fri 8.30am–4.30pm • Free • ⑩ parkstreet.org • Park St T

Although the 1809 **Park Street Church** is a simple mass of bricks and mortar, its 217ft-tall white telescoping **steeple** is undeniably impressive. The church's reputation rests not on its size, however, but on the events that took place inside: this is where

---

THE BLACK HERITAGE TRAIL

Massachusetts was the first state to declare slavery illegal, in 1783 – partly as a result of black participation in the Revolutionary War – and a large community of free blacks and escaped slaves swiftly grew in the North End and on Beacon Hill. The **Black Heritage Trail** traces the neighbourhood's key role in local and national black history and is the most important historical site in America devoted to pre-Civil War African American history and culture.

Pick up the trail at 46 Joy St, where the **Abiel Smith School** – the first public building in the country established for the purpose of educating black children – contains a **Museum of African American History** (Mon–Sat 10am–4pm; charge; ⑩ maah.org). Adjacent, the **African Meeting House** was built in 1806 as the country's first African American church; Frederick Douglass issued his call here for all blacks to take up arms in the Civil War. The trail continues around Beacon Hill, including a glimpse of the **Lewis and Harriet Hayden House**. Once a stop on the famous "Underground Railroad", the home was owned by the Haydens who sheltered legions of runaway slaves from bounty hunters in pursuit.

A great way to experience the trail is by taking a National Park Service guided walking tour, departing from the Robert Gould Shaw and Massachusetts 54th Regiment Memorial (generally offered from spring to fall, Mon–Sat at 1pm; free; ⑩ nps.gov/boaf; Park St T).

abolitionist William Lloyd Garrison delivered his first public address calling for the nationwide abolition of slavery, and where the song *America* ("My country 'tis of thee…") was first sung, on July 4, 1831.

Granary Burying Ground

Tremont St, between Park and Beacon sts • Daily 9am–5pm • Free • ☎ 617 523 3383 • Park St T

Adjacent to the Park Street Church, the atmospheric **Granary Burying Ground** includes the Revolutionary remains of Paul Revere, Samuel Adams and John Hancock, although, as the rangers will tell you, "the stones and the bones may not match up".

The Boston Athenæum

10½ Beacon St • Tues noon–8pm, Wed–Sat 10am–4pm; art and architecture tour Tues 5.30pm, Thurs 3pm, Sat 11am (reservations recommended; charge • Up Close tour Wed 11am (reservations recommended; free with admission) • Charge • ☎ 617 720 7612, ⓦ bostonathenaeum.org • Park St T

Around the block from the Granary Burying Ground, the venerable **Boston Athenæum** is one of Boston's most alluring and yet least-visited sights. Established in 1807, it's one of the oldest independent research libraries in the country, and counts among its holdings books from the private library of George Washington. Additionally, the library's **ornate interior** and impressive array of **artworks**, including paintings by John Singer Sargent and Gilbert Stuart, are museum calibre.

King's Chapel & King's Chapel Burying Ground

58 Tremont St • **Burying Ground** June–Sept Mon–Sat 10am–4pm, Sun 1–4pm • Free • **Music recitals** Tues 12.15–12.50pm; donations suggested • ⓦ kings-chapel.org & ⓦ thefreedomtrail.org • Park St T

The ethereal **King's Chapel Burying Ground**, one of the sites along The Freedom Trail, is the final resting place for seventeenth-century luminaries such as Mary Chilton, the first European woman from the *Mayflower* to step ashore to Plymouth, Massachusetts (see page 69), and Boston's first governor, John Winthrop. One of the chief pleasures here is examining the ancient tombstones, many beautifully etched with winged skulls and wistful seraphim. On Tuesday afternoons, stop by the **chapel** for a taste of jazz, folk or classical, including unique medieval music concerts.

Old South Meeting House

310 Washington St • Daily: 10am–5pm • Charge • ⓦ osmh.org • Downtown Crossing T

On the morning of December 16, 1773, nearly five thousand locals met at **Old South Meeting House**, awaiting word from **Governor Thomas Hutchinson** on whether he would permit the withdrawal of three ships in Boston Harbor containing taxed tea. When a message was received that the ships would not be removed, Samuel Adams announced, "This meeting can do no more to save the country!" His simple declaration triggered the **Boston Tea Party**. Considered to be the first major act of rebellion preceding the Revolutionary War, it was a carefully planned event wherein one hundred men, some dressed in Native American garb, solemnly threw enough British tea into the harbour to make 24 million cuppas.

Old State House

206 Washington St • Daily 10am–5pm • Revolutionary Characters Live tour Mon, Wed, Fri, Sun 11am, 1pm, 3pm, included with admission • Charge • ⓦ bostonhistory.org • State St T

That the graceful, three-tiered tower of the red-brick **Old State House** is dwarfed by skyscrapers amplifies rather than diminishes its colonial-era dignity. Built in 1712, this was the seat of colonial government, and from its balcony the Declaration of Independence was first publicly read in Boston on July 18, 1776; two hundred years later, Queen Elizabeth II made a speech from the same balcony. Inside is a small, diverting **museum** of Boston history that includes a dapper jacket belonging to John Hancock. Outside, a circle of cobblestones set on a traffic island at the intersection of

Devonshire and State streets marks the site of the **Boston Massacre** on March 5, 1770, when British soldiers fired on a crowd that was pelting them with stone-filled snowballs and killed five, including Crispus Attucks, a former slave.

Faneuil Hall
Faneuil Hall Square • Daily 9am–6pm • Free • ⓦ nps.gov/bost • State St T

Inside **Faneuil Hall**, a four-storey brick building and former colonial marketplace, Revolutionary firebrands such as Samuel Adams and James Otis whipped up popular support for independence by protesting British tax legislation. Head upstairs to the impressive second floor: its focal point is a massive canvas depicting an embellished version of "The Great Debate", during which Daniel Webster argued, in 1830, for the concept of the United States as one nation.

Quincy Market
In front of Faneuil Hall • Mon–Sat 10am–9pm, Sun 11am–7pm; winter Mon–Thurs 10am–7pm, Fri–Sat 10am–9pm, Sun noon–6pm • Free • ⓦ quincy-market.com • State St T

The three oblong markets just behind Faneuil Hall were built in the early eighteenth century to contain the trade that outgrew the hall. The centre building, known as **Quincy Market**, holds a super-extended corridor lined with stands vending a variety of takeaway treats – it's the mother of mall food courts.

New England Holocaust Memorial
98 Union St • Daily 24hr • Free • ⓦ nehm.org • Haymarket T

Just north of Faneuil Hall are six tall hollow glass pillars erected as a memorial to victims of the Holocaust. Built to resemble smokestacks, the columns of the **New England Holocaust Memorial** are etched with six million numbers, recalling the tattoos the Nazis gave their victims. Steam rises from grates beneath the pillars to accentuate their symbolism, an effect that's particularly striking at night.

The North End
Haymarket T

Hemmed in nearly all around by Boston Harbor, the small, densely populated **North End** is Boston's **Little Italy,** one of the oldest neighbourhoods in the city and packed with Italian restaurants and cafés. Though the above-ground highway that once separated the area from downtown has been removed (replaced by an inviting park – the Rose Kennedy Greenway), the area still has a bit of a detached feeling, making it all the more charming.

The Paul Revere House
19 North Square • Mid-April to Oct daily 9.30am–5.15pm; Nov to mid-April daily 9.30am–4.15pm • Charge • ⓦ paulreverehouse.org • Haymarket T

The little triangular wedge of cobblestones and gaslights known as **North Square** is among the most historic and attractive pockets of the city, home to **The Paul Revere House**, the oldest residential address in downtown Boston. Revere, a silversmith who fathered sixteen children, gained immortality on April 18, 1775, when he headed

---

SWEET WAVE

The granite **Copp's Hill Terrace**, on Charter Street across from the Copp's Hill Burying Ground, was the place from which British cannons bombarded Charlestown during the Battle of Bunker Hill. Just over a century later, in 1919, a 2.3-million-gallon tank of molasses exploded nearby, creating a syrupy tidal wave 30ft high that engulfed entire buildings and drowned 21 people and a score of horses. Old North Enders claim you can still catch a whiff of the stuff on exceptionally hot days.

out on his now-legendary "midnight ride" to Lexington (see page 67), successfully warning John Hancock and Samuel Adams (and anyone else within earshot) of the impending British march.

Polcari's Coffee

105 Salem St • Mon–Fri 10am–6pm, Sat 9am–6pm • Free • Ⓦ polcariscoffee.com • Haymarket T

Located on colourful Salem Street since 1932, **Polcari's Coffee** is a North End landmark and a renowned coffee bean and spice vendor; on hot days, a serving of their lemon slush – scooped into paper cups from an old barrel at the front door – is a must.

Old North Church

193 Salem St • **Church** Daily: April–Oct 9am–6pm; Nov–March 10am–4pm • Charge (combo ticket available that includes Behind the Scenes tour) • **Behind the Scenes tour** (gives access to steeple and crypt) March Sat & Sun on the hour (except noon) 10am–3pm; April, May, Nov & Dec daily on the hour (except noon) 10am–4pm; June–Oct daily on the half hour (except noon and 12.30pm) 10am–4pm • Charge • Ⓦ oldnorth.com • Haymarket T

Few places in Boston are as emblematic as the simple yet noble **Old North Church**. Built in 1723, it's easily recognized by its gleaming 191ft **steeple** – though it was a pair of lanterns that secured the structure's place in history. The church sexton, Robert Newman, is said to have hung both of them inside on the night of April 18, 1775, to signal the movement of British forces "by sea" from Boston Common (which then bordered the Charles River) to Lexington–Concord (see page 67). The interior is spotlessly white and well lit, thanks to the Palladian windows behind the pulpit. Below your feet are 37 basement-level crypts (viewable on the "Behind the Scenes" tour). The church also hosts a wide variety of events and special tours throughout the year, covering such themes as Boston's seafaring history, the art of quilting and more; check the calendar on the website for details.

Copp's Hill Burying Ground

Hull St • Daily dawn–dusk • Free

Up Hull Street from Old North Church, **Copp's Hill Burying Ground**, with eerily tilting slate tombstones and stunning harbour views, holds the highest ground in the North End. You'll notice that many gravestones have chunks missing, the consequence of British soldiers using them for target practice during the 1775 Siege of Boston; the grave of one Captain Daniel Malcolm bears particularly strong evidence of this. As you exit the cemetery, keep an eye out for the **narrowest house** at 44 Hull St; a private residence merely 10ft wide.

All Saints' Way

Between nos. 4 and 8 Battery St • Free • Haymarket T

At the northern end of Hanover Street, the North End's main byway, sits **All Saints' Way**. Squeezed in between two homes, it's a narrow brick alley decked out with reverential images of saints and serene cherubim. A celebrated neighbourhood landmark, it offers a unique bit of local flavour.

Charlestown

To get here, cross over the Charlestown Bridge (follow the Freedom Trail), or take the short ferry trip (Ⓦ mbta.com; charge) from Long Wharf to the Charlestown Navy Yard

Across Boston Harbor from the North End, historic **Charlestown** is a quiet, affluent, very pretty neighbourhood that stands fairly isolated from the city. Most visitors only make it over this way for the historic frigate the **USS Constitution** (if at all), which is a shame, because the neighbourhood's narrow, hilly byways, lined with antique gaslights and Colonial- and Federal-style rowhouses, make for pleasant exploration and offer great views of Boston. As you trek up to the **Bunker Hill Monument** – Charlestown's other big sight – look toward the water for jaw-dropping vistas.

1

USS Constitution and Museum

1 Constitution Rd • **USS Constitution** April–Sept Tues–Fri 2.30–6pm, Sat & Sun 10am–6pm; Oct Tues–Fri 2.30–5pm, Sat & Sun 10am–5pm; Nov–March Thurs & Fri 2.30–4pm, Sat & Sun 10am–4pm • Free • ⓦ navy.mil/local/constitution • **Museum** Building 22 • Daily: April–Oct 9am–6pm; Nov–March 10am–5pm • Donation • ☎ 617 426 1812, ⓦ ussconstitutionmuseum.org • North Station T

The celebrated **USS Constitution**, also known as "Old Ironsides", is the oldest commissioned warship afloat in the world. Launched in Boston in 1797, she earned her nickname during the War of 1812, when advancing cannonballs bounced off her hull; she subsequently saw 33 battles without ever losing one. Across the way, the **USS Constitution Museum** has engaging displays on the history of the ship; hands-on, sailorly exhibits test your ability to balance on a footrope and help you determine whether your comrades have scurvy or gout.

Bunker Hill Monument and Museum

43 Monument Square • Jan to mid-May & Nov–Dec 10am–5pm; mid-May to June 9.30am–5pm; July–Sept 9am–6pm; museum open 30min longer than monument • Free, timed tickets given at the museum • ⓦ nps.gov/bost

A grey, dagger-like obelisk that's visible from just about anywhere in Charlestown, the **Bunker Hill Monument** sits on Breed's Hill, the actual site of the battle fought on June 17, 1775, which, while technically won by the British, invigorated the patriots, whose strong showing felled nearly half the British troops. A spiral staircase of 294 steps leads to sweeping views at the top; the **museum** at the base has interesting exhibits on the battle as well as the history of Charlestown.

The waterfront, Fort Point and the Seaport District

Boston's **waterfront** has come a long way over the last few decades. Major revitalization efforts ushered in stylish condos and towers, new restaurants and manicured walkways making this prime strolling territory. Wisteria-laden **Columbus Park**, adjacent to the North End, is a pretty place to picnic. **Long Wharf**, just south of the park, is the base for **ferries** to the Cape, Salem, MA, and the Harbor Islands. Over the Congress Street bridge, you'll find the **Fort Point** neighbourhood and **Seaport District**. The latter, in particular, is vast; both boast warehouse galleries, tempting restaurants and compelling museums.

New England Aquarium

1 Central Wharf • July & Aug daily: 9am–6pm; Sept–June Mon–Fri 9am–5pm, Sat & Sun 9am–6pm • Charge • ⓦ neaq.org • Aquarium T

The **New England Aquarium** is the waterfront's main draw. Inside, a colossal, three-storey glass cylindrical tank is packed with giant sea turtles, moray eels and sharks as well as a range of other ocean exotica that swim by in unsettling proximity. Near the ticket counter, brave visitors can pat scratchy bonnethead sharks as they swim through a mangrove-themed touch tank. Watch frisky fur seals splash in the water at the airy Marine Mammal Center. The Aquarium also runs **whale-watching** trips and houses a **3-D IMAX theatre**.

Boston Children's Museum

308 Congress St • Mon–Thurs, Sat & Sun 10am–5pm, Fri 10am–9pm • Charge • ⓦ bostonchildrensmuseum.org • South Station T

It's hard to miss the larger-than-life 1930s-era **Hood Milk Bottle** model, across the Congress Street bridge from downtown. Just behind the bottle, the expanded **Boston Children's Museum** comprises three floors of educational exhibits craftily designed to trick kids into learning about topics from musicology to the engineering of a humungous bubble. Create arts and crafts at the colourful Art Studio, which also hosts kid-friendly workshops by visiting artists.

Institute of Contemporary Art (ICA)

25 Harbor Shore Drive • Tues, Wed, Sat & Sun 10am–5pm, Thurs & Fri 10am–9pm (first Fri of month 10am–5pm) • Charge • **The Watershed** 256 Marginal St • May–Aug Tues–Wed & Sat–Sun 11am–5pm, Thurs–Fri 11am–9pm • Free • ⓦ icaboston.org • Courthouse Station T

Looking like a tremendous, glimmering ice cube perched above Boston Harbor, the **Institute of Contemporary Art**, located in the Seaport District, offers a show before you've even crossed the threshold. Complementing the museum's collection of avant-garde artworks is the building's dramatic cantilever shape, which juts 80ft over the water. From the interior, this extended section functions as the "Founders Gallery", a meditative ledge where, if you look down, you'll find yourself standing directly above the water.

The **ICA Watershed**, in the Boston Harbor Shipyard in East Boston, opened in 2018 in a massive former warehouse, to showcase large-scale art. Getting here is part of the fun: Hop on the ICA Water Shuttle (roundtrip fare included with ICA admission) for the short ride to The Watershed.

The Museum of Science

1 Science Park • July to early Sept Mon–Thurs & Sat 9am–7pm, Fri 9am–9pm; mid-Sept to June Mon–Thurs & Sat 9am–5pm, Fri 9am–9pm • Charge • Ⓦ mos.org • Science Park T

At the northern end of the waterfront, clear across the Boston peninsula from the Children's Museum, the beloved **Museum of Science** has several floors of interactive exhibits illustrating basic principles of natural and physical science. An impressive IMAX cinema takes up the full height of one end of the building.

Back Bay and beyond

Beginning in 1857, the spacious boulevards and elegant houses of **Back Bay** were fashioned along gradually filled-in portions of former Charles River marshland. Thus a walk through the area from east to west provides an impressive visual timeline of Victorian architecture. One of the most architecturally significant of its buildings is the Romanesque **Trinity Church**, 206 Clarendon St (tours Tues–Sat 10am–5pm, Sun 1–5pm; charge; Ⓦ trinitychurchboston.org; Copley T), whose stunning interior was designed to feel like "walking into a living painting". Towering over the church is Boston's signature skyscraper, the **John Hancock Tower**, an elegant wedge designed by I.M. Pei. Nearby **Newbury Street** is famed for its swanky boutiques, cafés and art galleries.

Public Garden

Bounded by Boylston, Arlington, Beacon and Charles sts • Ⓦ boston.gov/parks/public-garden • **Swan boats** April to late June daily 10am–4pm; late June to early Sept daily 10am–5pm; early to mid-Sept Mon–Fri noon–4pm, Sat & Sun 10am–4pm • Ⓦ swanboats.com • Arlington T

Boston's most beautiful outdoor space, the 24-acre **Public Garden** was the first public botanical park in the U.S., established in 1837. Of the garden's 125 types of trees, most impressive are the weeping willows that ring the picturesque man-made **lagoon**, around which you can take a fifteen-minute ride in a **swan boat**. These elegant, pedal-powered conveyances have been around since 1877, long enough to have become a Boston institution.

Boston Public Library

700 Boylston St • Mon–Thurs 9am–9pm, Fri & Sat 9am–5pm, Sun 1–5pm • Free • Ⓦ bpl.org • Copley T

The handsome **Boston Public Library** (1895) faces Trinity Church (see page 57) and iconic Copley Square. Beyond the marble staircase and signature lions are a series of impressive murals. You can also check out the imposing **Bates Reading Room**, with its barrel-vaulted ceiling and oak panelling. Seek out the top floor's **Sargent Hall**, covered with seventeen remarkable murals painted by John Singer Sargent.

Christian Science Plaza

200 Massachusetts Ave • Mapparium is available for viewing by tour only; 20min tours run daily 10.20am–4.40pm • Charge • Ⓦ marybakereddylibrary.org • Hynes T

The **Christian Science Plaza** includes the "Mother Church" of the First Church of Christ, Scientist, and is the home of the *Christian Science Monitor* newspaper. Its campus houses the marvellous **Mapparium**, a curious, 30ft stained-glass globe through which you can walk on a footbridge. The sphere's best feature is its lack of sound absorption, which enables a tiny whisper spoken at one end of the bridge to be easily heard by someone at the other.

The Christian Science Plaza wrapped up an extensive revitalization project in 2020, which includes rebuilding the beautiful reflecting pool and expanding green spaces, from replanting lawns to creating a grass "beach area."

South End
Back Bay T

The residential **South End**, extending below Back Bay from Massachusetts Avenue ("Mass Ave") to I-93 and the Mass Pike (I-90), is both quaint and stylish in equal measure. This posh enclave boasts a spectacular concentration of **Victorian architecture**, adorned with fanciful "Rinceau" **ironwork**. Details like these have made the area quite popular with upwardly mobile Bostonians, among them a strong LGBTQ contingent. Here you will find some of the liveliest **street life**, and the best restaurants, in town.

Museum of Fine Arts
465 Huntington Ave • Mon, Tues, Sat & Sun 10am–5pm, Wed–Fri 10am–10pm • Charge; under-17s free at weekends and after 3pm weekdays • ⓦ mfa.org • Museum T

Beyond the boundaries of Back Bay is the **Museum of Fine Arts**. From its magnificent collections of Asian and ancient Egyptian art onwards, the MFA (as it's known) holds sufficient marvels to detain you all day. In 2010, the museum completed an ambitious expansion that saw the addition of a magnificent Art of the Americas wing, 53 galleries, a state-of-the-art auditorium and a glass pavilion for the central courtyard. High points include Renoir's *Dance at Bougival*; Gauguin's sumptuous display of existential angst *Where do we come from? What are we? Where are we going?*; a saxophone made by Adolphe Sax himself (Musical Instruments room); and Gilbert Stuart's George Washington portraits (one of which is famously replicated on the dollar bill).

Isabella Stewart Gardner Museum
25 Evans Way • Mon & Wed–Sun 11am–5pm, Thurs 11am–9pm; tours all week, times vary • Charge; under 17s or anyone named "Isabella" free; tours free • ⓦ gardnermuseum.org • Museum T

Less broad in its collection, but more distinctive and idiosyncratic than the MFA, the **Isabella Stewart Gardner Museum** is one of the city's jewels. Styled after a fifteenth-century Venetian villa, the Gardner brims with a dazzling collection of works meant to "fire the imagination". Best known for its spectacular central courtyard, the museum's show-stopping pieces by John Singer Sargent – including a famous portrait of Isabella – are another highlight. In 2012, the Gardner unveiled a new glass-and-copper **entrance wing**, which has greenhouses, a special exhibition gallery and an information centre called "The Living Room", dedicated to the museum's own intriguing story. Classical concerts are held on select afternoons and evenings (ticket price includes museum admission).

Fenway Park
4 Yawkey Way • 1hr tours daily 9am–5pm (opens 10am in winter), on the hour but call ahead as times vary according to game schedule • Charge • ⓦ mlb.com/redsox • Kenmore or Fenway T

Home to Boston's beloved **Red Sox** baseball team, **Fenway Park** was constructed in 1912 in a tiny, asymmetrical space just off Brookline Avenue, resulting in its famously awkward dimensions. The 37ft left-field wall, aka the **Green Monster**, is its most distinctive quirk (it was originally built because home runs were breaking local windows); that it is so high makes up for some of the park's short distances.

Tours of the ballpark are fun and deservedly popular, but your best bet is to come to see a game. The season runs from April to October, and **tickets** are reasonable, though tough to snag (Sox fans are an exceptionally devoted lot).

364.4 SMOOTS (+ 1 EAR)

If you walk from Back Bay to Cambridge via the scenic **Harvard Bridge** (which leads directly into MIT's campus), you might wonder about the peculiar marks partitioning the sidewalk. These units of measure, affectionately known as "Smoots", represent the height of **Oliver R. Smoot**, an MIT Lambda Chi Alpha fraternity pledge in 1958. As the shortest pledge, part of Smoot's initiation included the use of his body as a tape measure, all down the **Harvard Bridge** – resulting in the conclusive "364.4 Smoots (+ 1 Ear)" at the bridge's terminus. While the marks continue to be repainted each year by LCA, the "Smoot" itself has gone global and even appears on a Google conversion calculator.

Cambridge

Harvard or Central T

The excursion across the Charles River to **Cambridge** merits at least half a day, and begins with a fifteen-minute ride on the Red T line to **Harvard Square**. Walk down almost any street here and you will pass monuments and plaques honouring literati and revolutionaries who lived in the area as early as the seventeenth century. But Cambridge also vibrates with energy: it's filled with students from nearby Harvard University and MIT, and in warm weather, street musicians. Feel free to wander into **Harvard Yard** and around the core of the university, founded in 1636; its enormous Widener Library (named for a victim of the *Titanic* disaster) boasts a Gutenberg Bible and a first folio of Shakespeare.

Harvard Art Museums

32 Quincy St • Daily 10am–5pm • Charge, under-18s free • ⓦ harvardartmuseums.org • Harvard T

After a six-year hiatus, the **Harvard Art Museums** reopened in 2014 to reveal a splendid new home. Galleries here fan out beneath a radiant glass atrium, and display highlights of Harvard's substantial collection of Western art, along with a small yet excellent selection of German Expressionists and Bauhaus works, and sensuous Buddhas and gilded bodhisattvas from the school's Asian and Islamic art collection.

Harvard Museum of Natural History

26 Oxford St • Daily 9am–5pm • Charge, includes entry to the Peabody Museum • ⓦ hmnh.harvard.edu • Harvard T

A few blocks north of the Harvard Art Museums is the **Harvard Museum of Natural History**, a nineteenth-century Victorian building with curio-style exhibits. The galleries feature a number of gloriously huge dinosaur fossils as well as a stunning collection of flower models constructed entirely from glass. Prior reservation is required for admission.

MIT Museum

265 Massachusetts Ave • Daily: July & Aug 10am–6pm; Sept–June 10am–5pm • Charge • ⓦ web.mit.edu/museum • Central T

A couple of miles southeast of Harvard Square is the **Massachusetts Institute of Technology** (MIT). The small but compelling **MIT Museum**, near Central Square, has standout displays including "Holography: Dimensions of Light", a seriously cool collection of eye trickery. The best exhibit, however, is Arthur Ganson's "Gestural Engineering", a hypnotizing ensemble of imaginative mini-machines, such as a walking wishbone.

ARRIVAL AND DEPARTURE · BOSTON

By plane Just 3 miles from downtown, Logan International Airport (ⓦ massport.com), has four terminals (A, B, C and E), connected by shuttle buses. Taxis will take you downtown for a fixed fare, or you can take the subway (daily 5am–midnight; Blue or Silver lines; ⓦ mbta. com). A fun alternative is to take a Boston Harbor Cruises Water Taxi (early Sept–May Mon–Sat 6.30am–10pm, Sun 6.30am–8pm; June–early Sept Mon–Wed 6.30am–10pm, Thurs–Sat 6.30am–11pm, Sun 6.30am–10pm; ⓦ bostonharborcruises.com) across the harbour. Rowes

1

Wharf Water Transport (May–Oct Mon–Sat 7am–10pm, Sun 7am–8pm; Nov–April daily 7am–5pm; ⓦ roweswharfwatertransport.com) also offers transport to and from the airport. Additionally, they have luggage storage available for those with long layovers at the airport. The Airport Package includes transport from the airport, luggage storage for the day and transport back to the airport. Courtesy bus #66 will take you to the pier to pick up water taxis.

By bus Boston's major bus hub is South Station, in the southeast corner of downtown at Summer St and Atlantic Ave; the subway (Red Line), takes you to the centre of town or to Cambridge. Greyhound, Mega Bus (ⓦ megabus.com) and Peter Pan (ⓦ peterpanbus.com) offer national service, including frequent direct routes to New York City and Washington DC.

Destinations Concord, NH (1 daily; 1hr 45min); Hartford, CT (12 daily; 2hr 30min); New York City (15 daily; 4hr 20min); Portland, ME (2 daily; 2hr).

By train As with the buses, the main terminus is South Station. Some Amtrak services make an extra stop at Back Bay Station, 145 Dartmouth St, on the Orange subway line near Copley Square. North Station, at 135 Causeway St, is used by northerly commuter trains and Amtrak's Downeaster (ⓦ amtrakdowneaster.com), which connects New Hampshire and Maine.

Destinations Dover, NH (1hr 25min; 5 daily); Durham, NH (1hr 20min; 5 daily); Freeport, ME (3hr 10min; 2 daily); Portland, ME (2hr 30min; 5 daily).

By ferry The Inner Harbor ferry connects Long Wharf with the Charlestown Navy Yard (every 15min: Mon–Fri 6.30am–8pm, Sat & Sun 10am–6pm; ⓦ mbta.com).

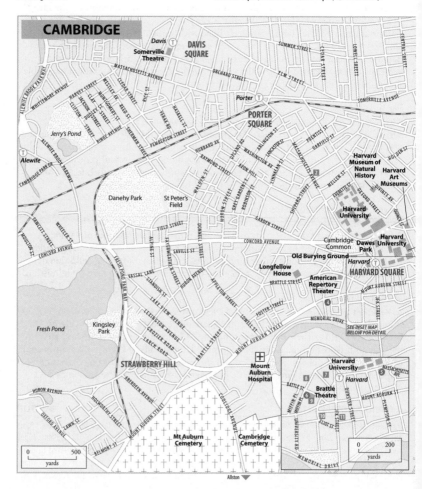

GETTING AROUND

Much of the pleasure of visiting Boston comes from being in a city that was built long before cars were invented. Walking around town can be a joy; conversely, driving is a nightmare. All **public transport** in the area is run by the Massachusetts Bay Transport Authority (wmbta.com).

BY SUBWAY

Boston's subway, known as the "T", is the oldest subway system in the United States, built in 1897. Its first station, Park Street, remains its centre (any train marked "inbound" is headed here). Four lines – Red, Green, Blue and Orange – operate daily from 5am until 12.30am, although certain routes begin to shut down earlier. The four lines are supplemented by a bus rapid transit (BRT) route, the Silver Line.

TICKETS AND FARES

Boston has a somewhat confusing system for subway fares. Within the city, the standard fare is payable by the purchase of a "CharlieTicket", bought at ATM-like machines in the station. If you pick up a "CharlieCard" – with more of a credit card thickness and a longer lifespan – from a station attendant your fare begins at only $2.40 per ride. If you're in town for a couple of days, the one-day LinkPass is a good bet, offering 24 hours of unlimited travel on the subway, bus and Charlestown Ferry. For longer stays, go for the seven-day LinkPass.

BY BUS

The MBTA manages a whopping 170 bus routes around the city. Fares are slightly cheaper with a CharlieCard than with a CharlieTicket. Most buses run from 5.30am to 1am.

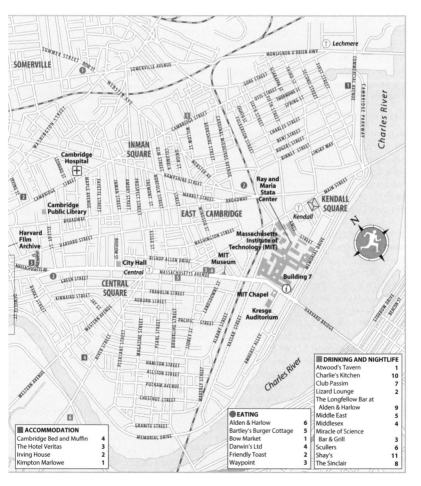

1

BY BIKE

In and around Boston are some 80 miles of bike trails. Rent from Urban AdvenTours, in the North End at 103 Atlantic Ave (w urbanadventours.com; Haymarket T) and Back Bay Bicycles, 366 Commonwealth Ave (w papa-wheelies.com; Hynes T).

INFORMATION

Boston Common Visitor Center 139 Tremont St (Mon–Fri 8.30am–5pm, Sat–Sun 9am–5pm; w bostonusa.com; Park St T). The main tourist office, with loads of maps and brochures, information on historical sights, cultural events, accommodation, restaurants and bus trips.

National Park Service visitor centre First floor of Faneuil Hall (daily 9am–6pm; w nps.gov/bost; State St T). Chock-full of maps, facts and helpful park rangers who lead fascinating free history tours.

Cambridge Office of Tourism Harvard Square (Mon–Fri 9am–5pm, Sat & Sun 9am–1pm; w cambridgeusa.org; Harvard T). Kiosk outside the subway station.

Advance information The best sources are the Greater Boston Convention & Visitors Bureau (GBCVB; w bostonusa. com) and the *Boston Globe* (w bostonglobe.com).

TOURS

Boston Duck Tours w bostonducktours.com. Popular tours that take to the streets and the Charles River in restored World War II amphibious landing vehicles. Tours (1hr 20min) depart mid-March to Nov every 30min from the Prudential Center (53 Huntington Ave) and the Museum of Science (1 Science Park); abbreviated, tours also leave from the New England Aquarium (1 Central Wharf); call for scheduling as it varies widely. Reservations advised.

Freedom Trail Foundation w thefreedomtrail.org. A variety of lively 90min tours (charge) of Freedom Trail highlights led by costumed guides.

Harvard and MIT Tours w trademarktours.com. A boisterous 70min tour of the Harvard campus (charge) led by undergrads in intentionally misspelled "Hahvahd" T-shirts; they also offer MIT tours (charge).

Urban AdvenTours (see page 62). Leisurely themed bike tours (charge) which pedal alongside the Charles River and take in sights such as Fenway Park and Back Bay.

ACCOMMODATION   SEE MAP PAGE 51

Boston has a wide array of accommodation, with prices rising the closer you get to downtown – expect to pay no less than $200 for quality digs in the centre. Note that room rates range wildly depending on the season and the day – the Boston hotel market is competitive, so it's well worth hunting around for the best deal. The city also has a number of good hostels, well-priced B&Bs and, of course, extensive Airbnb listings.

BOSTON COMMON AND DOWNTOWN

Ames Hotel 1 Court St w ameshotel.com; State St T One of Boston's "it" spots, a contemporary boutique hotel in the city's oldest skyscraper. Luxurious interiors are furnished in whites and greys (with the odd pop of colour), and enhanced by rain showerheads, sound machines for a restful sleep and great views. $$$$

The Godfrey 505 Washington St w godfreyhotelboston. com; Park T. This handsome boutique hotel in Downtown Crossing, set in two historic adjacent buildings, offers a delicious blend of past and present, from the elegant lobby and marble staircase to the bright, minimalist rooms. $$$

Marriott's Custom House 3 McKinley Square w marriott. com; Aquarium T. All the rooms at this downtown landmark-turned-hotel are high-end, one-bedroom suites with spectacular views. While the exterior embodies a bygone era, the interior is modern and plush, with luxurious linens and a small kitchen setup. $$$$

Omni Parker House 60 School St w omnihotels.com; Park T. Though the present building only dates from 1927, the lobby, decorated in dark oak with carved gilt mouldings, recalls the splendour of the original nineteenth-century property. Rooms are on the small side, but come equipped with modern amenities and thick robes. $$$

BEACON HILL

Liberty Hotel 215 Charles St w libertyhotel.com; Charles/MGH T. The *Liberty Hotel* has taken over the labyrinthine digs of an 1851 prison and fashioned it with stylish furniture and innovative design details. Prepare to be wowed by its 90ft lobby, phenomenal skyline views and unique architecture. The property also houses *Scampo* restaurant (see page 64), the trendy *Alibi* lounge and the seafood-focused Clink $$$$

THEATER DISTRICT

HI-Boston 19 Stuart St w hiusa.org; Chinatown T. Straddling the Chinatown-Theater District border, this eco-friendly hostel is set in a handsome historic building. Rooms are bright, clean and stylish, with personal charging stations, laundry facilities and a community kitchen. Dorms $, doubles $$$

THE WATERFRONT

Harborside Inn 185 State St w harborsideinnboston. com; State St T. This small hotel is housed in a renovated 1890s mercantile warehouse across from Faneuil Hall. The rooms are a bit faded but clean, with exposed brick, hardwood floors and cherry furniture. They also have an excellent sister property, the *Charlesmark Hotel*, in Back Bay. $$$

1

BACK BAY

Charlesmark Hotel 655 Boylston St ⓦ charlesmarkhotel.com; Copley T. This straightforward spot has small rooms with cosy beechwood furniture and a lively bar. Great location, across from the library. $$–$$$

★ **College Club** 44 Commonwealth Avenue ⓦ thecollegeclubofboston.com; Arlington T. Housed in a historic Victorian building which also serves as the home of Boston's first women's college club, this handsome brownstone B&B has lovely double and single rooms with a traditional Victorian decor; there's a continental breakfast included in the great price. $$

The Eliot 370 Commonwealth Ave ⓦ eliothotel.com; Hynes T. This elegant and historic – but far from stuffy – Back Bay hotel features lovely Neo-Georgian architecture and a marble-clad lobby that gives way to classic rooms and suites. The hotel offers complimentary access to the nearby Boston Sports Club, or take a stroll along the Charles River. Another bonus: The hotel's Uni restaurant – helmed by chef Ken Oringer – serves innovative Japanese cuisine, as well as creative craft cocktails. $$$

Newbury Guest House 261 Newbury St ⓦ newburyguesthouse.com; Copley T. This big, popular Victorian brownstone in a great location fills up frequently, so call ahead. Rooms range from spacious bay-windowed quarters with hardwood floors to tiny digs ideal for the discerning economic traveller. Rooms can be noisy, however. Continental breakfast included. $$$

THE SOUTH END

★ **Clarendon Square Inn** 198 W Brookline St ⓦ clarendonsquare.com; Prudential T. Gorgeous three-room B&B on a residential side street with lavish design details such as chandeliers and wainscoting, an inspired art collection and extras like limestone bathrooms, a private garden and a roof-deck hot tub. $$$

The Revolution Hotel 40 Berkeley St ⓦ therevolutionhotel.com; Back Bay T. This former YWCA is now a unique boutique hotel-hostel, with splashy murals and cool installations by local artists, and a variety of rooms – including doubles with the option of in-room bath or a bath down the hall and triple or quad dorm rooms. Doubles $$$, triples $$–$$$, quads $$–$$$

AROUND FENWAY PARK

★ **Hotel Commonwealth** 500 Commonwealth Ave ⓦ hotelcommonwealth.com; Kenmore T. Old-world charm paired with modern decor make this a top choice in Boston's luxury hotel scene, with nice touches including Malin+Goetz products, smart TVs and access to the *Island Creek* restaurant (see page 65) and the *Hawthorne* and *Eastern Standard* bars (see page 65). Some rooms face Fenway Park (see page 58). $$$

Residence Inn by Marriott 125 Brookline Ave ⓦ marriott.com; Fenway T. Ever-reliable property from Marriott's Residence Inn portfolio, with colourful, contemporary guestrooms, a fully equipped fitness centre and rooftop swimming pool, and full American breakfasts included in the price. $$$

Verb Hotel 1271 Boylston St Wtheverbhotel.com; Kenmore T. Add some rock and roll to your stay at the lively, music-themed The Verb, which is happily stuck in the 1960s. The hotel has had many colourful former lives, from a *Howard Johnsons* to the *Fenway Motor Inn*, and it mines its past with plenty of retro touches, including a vinyl library and typewriters in the comfortable rooms. Uniquely, there is also a sizeable, year-round outdoor pool – plus a fun Japanese restaurant, *Hojoko*. $$$

CAMBRIDGE   SEE MAP PAGE 60

Cambridge Bed and Muffin 267 Putnam Ave ⓦ bedandmuffin.com; Central or Harvard T. Just a block from the river and close to Harvard and Central squares, this tranquil B&B has endearing little rooms with polished pine floors. No en-suite bathrooms and no TVs, but plenty of books and quiet. $$

★ **The Hotel Veritas** 1 Remington St ⓦ thehotelveritas.com; Harvard T. A chic European-style boutique hotel in the heart of Harvard Square. The landscaped patio, silk drapes and cocktails are all welcome amenities, plus return guests are greeted with fancy chocolates. Rooms are on the small side, however. $$$

Irving House 24 Irving St ⓦ irvinghouse.com; Harvard T. Friendly, popular option near Harvard Square that falls somewhere between an inn, a hostel and a B&B. Limited parking and generous breakfasts are included. It has a sister facility, *Harding House* (ⓦharding-house.com), at 288 Harvard St. Singles $$, doubles $$$

★ **Kimpton Marlowe** 25 Edwin H Land Blvd ⓦ hotelmarlowe.com; Lechmere or Kendall/MIT T. The decor at this hotel is cosy, plush and hip with faux-leopard-print couches in the lobby and bold furniture in the guestrooms. There's an evening wine hour, fitness centre and free kayak and bicycle use. Pet friendly. $$$

EATING   SEE MAP PAGE 51

Boston is loaded with excellent **restaurants**. While boiled lobster, shucked oysters and clam chowder are ever-popular New England specialities, Boston is also blessed with a superb rainbow of other offerings. Studenty Cambridge has the best budget eats, while the historic North End is king of Italian – some of its bakeries and pizzerias are nearly a century old. Tremont Street, in the stylish South End, is known as "Restaurant Row", and beloved by foodies.

1

BOSTON COMMON

Chacarero 101 Arch St ⓦ chacarero.com; Downtown Crossing T. Fabulous and fresh, the *chacarero* is a Chilean sandwich built on warm, soft bread and filled with avocado, chicken or beef, green beans, muenster cheese and hot sauce; good veggie version, too. ₅

Silvertone 69 Bromfield St ⓦ silvertonedowntown. com; Park St T. Nostalgia runs high at this bustling basement bar and restaurant serving standout comfort foods such as a giant signature burger topped with guacamole, bacon and Swiss cheese and a super-cheesy macaroni cheese. Also has cocktails and a good selection of beer on tap. ₅₅

FANEUIL HALL

O Ya 9 East St ⓦ o-ya.restaurant; South Station T. Come here for superlative sushi that's worth the splurge. Yes, it's pricey, but there's good reason *O Ya* is showered in culinary awards – it serves one of Boston's finest sushi and sashimi feasts, with fish so fresh it's practically flopping on the plate. Try the smoked trout with wasabi vinaigrette, and the salmon belly with ginger and hot sesame oil. ₅₅₅

★ **Public Market** 100 Hanover St ⓦ bostonpublicmarket. org; Haymarket T. Opened in 2015, this marketplace quickly became a celebrated corner of downtown. Brimming with farmers and food vendors, with all produce local to New England, it's a great spot for lunch or sussing out regional gifts. ₅–₅₅

BEACON HILL

Paramount 44 Charles St ⓦ paramountboston.com; Charles/MGH T. Dating from 1937, the Hill's neighbourhood diner serves banana and caramel French toast and omelettes to brunch regulars by day, and American standards such as hamburgers and steak tips. Expect long queues at weekends. ₅

Scampo 215 Charles St (in the Liberty Hotel) ⓦ scampoboston.com; Charles/MGH T. At this Italian restaurant helmed by star chef Lydia Shire, the imaginative menu includes a "mozzarella bar", hand-made pasta dishes and eclectic pizzas – try the one topped with truffle cheese, mushrooms and honey. ₅₅₅

NORTH END

★ **Bova's Bakery** 134 Salem St ⓦ bovabakeryboston. net; Haymarket T. The best pastries in the North End. The chocolate *cannoli* with fresh ricotta filling will make your day. ₅

Galleria Umberto 289 Hanover St ☎ 617 227 5709; Haymarket T. North End nirvana. There are fewer than a dozen items on the menu, including perfect pizza slices and savoury *arancini* (fried and stuffed rice balls). Lunch only, and get there early as they almost always sell out. Cash only. ₅

Mike's Pastry 300 Hanover St ⓦ mikespastry.com; Haymarket T. In many ways *Mike's* is the North End, and lining up for its twine-wrapped boxes of eclairs, *cannoli*, marzipan and the like is a quintessential Boston experience. ₅

★ **Neptune Oyster** 63 Salem St ⓦ neptuneoyster. com; Haymarket T. Snazzy little raw bar serving excellent shucked shellfish and best-in-town lobster rolls (served hot with butter or cold with mayo; market price). If you can only make it to one of Boston's seafood restaurants, let this be the one. ₅₅₅

Pizzeria Regina 11½ Thacher St ⓦ reginapizzeria.com; Haymarket T. Visit this North End legend for tasty, cheap pizza, served in a neighbourhood feed station where the wooden booths haven't budged since the 1920s. Don't be fooled by spin-offs bearing the *Regina* label in other parts of town – this is the original, vastly superior location. Be prepared for a wait. ₅–₅₅

THE WATERFRONT AND FORT POINT

flour bakery + café 12 Farnsworth St ⓦ flourbakery. com; South Station T. This first-rate café is just around the corner from the Children's Museum (see page 56). Bursting with fantastic pastries, sandwiches and salads, it's best known for its BLTs and raspberry seltzer. Top off your meal with a chocolate cream tartlette or a dark-chocolate Oreo cookie. Other branches. ₅

★ **Row 34** 383 Congress St ⓦ row34.com; South Station or World Trade Center T. Over the water in Fort Point, and a fair walk from the subway, this oyster lover's dream rewards patrons with a stellar bivalve line-up and an excellent beer selection. The setting is a raw industrial space with brick walls, high ceilings and dangling light fixtures. Reservations recommended. ₅₅₅

BACK BAY

Mike & Patty's 12 Church St ⓦ mikeandpattys.com; Arlington T. Located in Bay Village, a residential satellite of Back Bay, this teensy breakfast and lunch spot serves the best sandwiches in Boston. While it's not on the road to any major sights, those who make the trek out will feel amply rewarded by the breakfast torta – fried eggs, cheddar cheese, black beans, salsa and avocado on a sesame roll. ₅

Trident Booksellers & Café 338 Newbury St ⓦ tridentbookscafe.com; Hynes T. Divine bookshop-café, with a "perpetual breakfast" and tasty, vegetarian-friendly lunches and dinners. ₅

SOUTH END

★ **Myers + Chang** 1145 Washington St ⓦ myersandchang. com; Broadway T. This "indie diner" with an open kitchen serves Asian fusion dishes such as twice-cooked lamb belly stir-fry, pork and chive dumplings and fried chicken with ginger waffles, and vacation-in-a-glass style tropical cocktails. Bonus: your bill comes with coconut macaroons. ₅₅

★ **Toro** 1704 Washington St ⓦ toro-restaurant.com; Back Bay T. This superlative tapas bar shakes up hibiscus-

1

ginger cocktails, and serves grilled octopus with warm potatoes and cured Spanish ham to a buzzing, stylish crowd. On weekend nights, waiting times can be obscene (no reservations are taken); get there as early as possible. $\overline{55}$

AROUND FENWAY PARK
Island Creek Oyster Bar 500 Commonwealth Ave, in the Hotel Commonwealth ⓦislandcreekoysterbar. com; Kenmore T. Swish shellfish restaurant busy with plates of lobster roe noodles, salt cod buttermilk biscuits and the region's freshest oysters. The ultra-modern interior is distinguished by high ceilings and walls of discarded seashells. Extremely popular; reservations recommended. $\overline{55}$

CAMBRIDGE   SEE MAP PAGE 60
Alden & Harlow 40 Brattle St, ⓦaldenharlow.com; Harvard T. This new American favourite has a stylish interior of exposed beams and brick and tile-lined walls. Locals swear by the "secret burger" (so-called because you need to ask if it's available – it frequently sells out). Also renowned for brunch (try the corn pancakes with cherries and black pepper cream cheese). Reservations recommended. $\overline{55}$
Bartley's Burger Cottage 1246 Massachusetts Ave ⓦmrbartley.com; Harvard T. A must-visit since 1960: Boston's best burgers, washed down with raspberry lime rickeys. The names of the dishes poke fun at politicians of the hour, and noisy servers shout out your order. Good veggie burgers, too. Sometimes they close on a whim. Cash only. $\overline{5}$–$\overline{55}$
★ **Bow Market** 1 Bow Market Way, in Somerville, just east of Cambridge ⓦbowmarketsomerville.com; from Harvard Square, bus #86 or #87. Graze on the best of local Boston at the innovative Bow Market, which

opened in 2018, and has become a signature stop on the Somerville culinary trail. Formerly a storage building, this Union Square market features a colourful variety of small-scale food, drink, art and retail shops. Sample natural wines at Rebel Rebel and microbrews at Remnant Brewing; try South American goodies like warm empanadas at Buenas; pick up fresh fish from Hooked; and more. Plus, Bow Market features a lively events calendar, including a summer music series, comedy and movie nights. Hours vary depending on retailer. $\overline{5}$–$\overline{555}$
Darwin's Ltd 148 Mt Auburn St (ⓦdarwinsltd.com), 1629 Cambridge St, 313 Massachusetts Ave; Harvard and Central T. Three locations, each offering wonderfully inventive sandwich combinations (such as roast beef, sprouts and apple slices) on freshly baked bread. A Cambridge institution. $\overline{5}$–$\overline{55}$
Friendly Toast 1 Kendall Square ⓦthefriendlytoast. net; Kendall/MIT T. A riot of 1950s kitsch, vinyl seating and lime-green walls, this breakfast-all-day funhouse serves lemon-curd pancakes with whipped cream and "King Cakes" in honour of Elvis (banana and chocolate-chip pancakes with peanut butter in between). Expect a long wait at weekends. Second location at 35 Stanhope St, Back Bay. $\overline{5}$–$\overline{55}$
Waypoint 1030 Massachusetts Ave ⓦwaypointharvard. com; Harvard T. Chef Michael Scelfo (of the perennially popular Alden & Harlow, see page 65) scores again with this lively seafood-focused eatery in Harvard Square. Sample from the top-notch raw bar – oysters, clams, striped bass and more – plus an array of pastas and other dishes, from lobster Cacio e Pepe to whole roasted branzino. The cocktails rival the food, and include a unique line-up of absinthe drinks. $\overline{555}$

DRINKING AND NIGHTLIFE   SEE MAP PAGE 51
Boston's vibrant nightlife scene offers everything from tried-and-true neighbourhood taverns to young, trendy lounges. The live music is dominated by the very best local and touring indie bands. The free weeklies *Boston Phoenix* (ⓦthephoenix.com) and *Dig Boston* (ⓦdigboston.com) are the foremost sources for up-to-date listings. Note that most establishments are officious in demanding ID.

BARS
Bleacher Bar 82A Lansdowne St, Kenmore Square ⓦbleacherbarboston.com; Kenmore T. Beneath the bleachers in centre field is this popular addition to Fenway Park, and you don't need a ticket to get in. Here, you'll find a pub festooned with vintage memorabilia and a window with a direct view of the diamond – quite thrilling on game night. $\overline{55}$
Bukowski Tavern 50 Dalton St, Back Bay ⓦbukowski-tavern.com; Hynes T. Arguably Boston's best dive bar, with views over the Mass Pike and such a vast beer selection that

a home-made "wheel of indecision" is spun by staff when patrons can't decide. Cash only. $\overline{5}$
Charlie's Kitchen 10 Eliot St, Cambridge ⓦcharlieskitchen. com; Harvard T. Downstairs is a well-loved burger joint, upstairs is a buzzing bar – with eighteen beers on tap, a rocking jukebox and a good mix of patrons – at its rowdiest on Tuesday karaoke nights. There's an outdoor beer garden, too. $\overline{55}$
Kaju 636 Beacon St ⓦfacebook.com/kajukenmore; Kenmore T. Cheap and cheerful Korean joint always popular with students, where the menu includes hearty bowls of bibimbap tofu soups with kimchi, and beef bulgogi. $\overline{5}$–$\overline{55}$
The Kenmore 476 Commonwealth Ave, Kenmore Square ⓦthekenmorebar.com; Kenmore T. A down-home addition to the ballpark scene, this attractive pub is known for its extensive beer selection and for its hearty bar food. $\overline{5}$
★ **The Longfellow Bar at Alden & Harlow** 40 Brattle St ⓦlongfellowharvard.com; Harvard T. Toast the night at this handsome bar – awash in brick walls, oak floors and

1

dark woods – which sits atop *Alden & Harlow*. Potent craft cocktails include concoctions like Temptation – bananas, rum, manzanilla. Chef Michael Scelfo's prowess shines in the small plates menu, like a creamy eggplant and white bean dip with fried garlic. $$$

Middlesex 315 Massachusetts Ave, Cambridge ⓦ middlesexcambridge.com; Central T. A slightly hipper-than-thou vibe, but the gorgeous space (exposed brick, pale wood panelling) makes you want to dress to impress. There are queues out the door for its nights of electro-retro dance. $$

★ **Miracle of Science Bar & Grill** 321 Massachusetts Ave, Cambridge ⓦ miracleofscience.us; Central T or #1 bus. Surprisingly hip despite its status as an MIT hangout, this popular bar has a science-themed decor and a laidback, unpretentious crowd, though it can get quite crowded on weekend nights. The bar stools will conjure up memories of high-school chemistry class. $$

Shay's 58 JFK St, Cambridge ⓦ shayspubwinebar.com; Harvard T. Unwind with grad students over wine and quality beer at this relaxed hideaway with a welcome little outdoor patio and plates overflowing with nachos. $$

Tsurutontan 500A Commonwealth Ave, in the Hotel Commonwealth, Kenmore Square ⓦ hotelcommonwealth. com; Kenmore T. Superb Japanese restaurant, open for lunch and dinner, which specialises in rich udon noodle dishes. Pair a meal here with a game at Fenway Park (see page 58) and you'll have a Boston evening for the memory books. $$

LIVE MUSIC VENUES

Atwood's Tavern 877 Cambridge St, Cambridge ⓦ atwoodstavern.com; Lechmere T. Great neighbourhood bar showcasing plenty of superb, rootsy Americana tunes. Nightly live performances. $$

Club Passim 47 Palmer St, Cambridge ⓦ passim.org; Harvard T. Legendary folkie hangout where Joan Baez and Suzanne Vega got their starts. Acoustic music, folk, blues and jazz in a windowed basement setting. *Passim* also hosts a great variety of music events and festivals around Cambridge – check the calendar on the website. $$

Lizard Lounge 1667 Massachusetts Ave, Cambridge ⓦ lizardloungeclub.com. Looking to catch up-and-coming performers in rock, blues and jazz? Come by this low-lit, welcoming bar that celebrates new voices in song, as well as poetry, and pours from a wonderfully varied array of brews. Come by for the lively Poetry Jam and Slam every Sunday at 7.30pm. $$

Middle East 472 Massachusetts Ave, Cambridge ⓦ mideastclub.com; Central T. Local and regional bands of every sort – rock to mambo to hardcore – stop in regularly at this Cambridge institution. Bigger acts are hosted downstairs; smaller ones ply their trade in a tiny upstairs space. A third venue, *Corner*, has shows nightly that are usually free, with belly dancing every Sunday. $$

Paradise Rock Club 967 Commonwealth Ave, Allston ⓦ crossroadspresents.com; Pleasant St T. One of Boston's classic venues – it has hosted Blondie, Elvis Costello and Tom Waits, to name a few – and as popular as it was 35 years ago. $$

Scullers DoubleTree Hotel, 400 Soldiers Field Rd, Allston ⓦ scullersjazz.com; Central T. Genteel jazz club that draws five-star acts. You'll need to hop in a taxi to get here, as the walk along the river at night can be dodgy. Cover varies wildly. $$–$$$

The Sinclair 52 Church St, Cambridge ⓦ sinclaircambridge.com; Harvard T. This industrial-style gem books bands at the top of the indie list but presents them in an intimate standing-room setting. There's a solid restaurant here too, serving sophisticated takes on comfort food like pork ribs, hefty burgers and house-made gnocchi. $$

Wally's Cafe 427 Massachusetts Ave, Roxbury ⓦ wallyscafe.com; Massachusetts Ave T. Founded in 1947, this jazz club is a Boston legend. Refreshingly unhewn, it hosts lively jazz and blues shows nightly, drawing a diverse crowd. Drinks are pricey; come for the music. $$

ENTERTAINMENT

Boston prides itself on being a sophisticated city, and nowhere does that show up more than in its proliferation of **orchestras** and **choral groups**. The city's **theatre scene** divides into the traditionally mainstream productions of the Theater District (often Broadway offshoots) and more experimental companies in Cambridge. There is also a healthy independent film scene, largely clustered in Cambridge.

BosTix Half-price, day-of-show ticket booth with two outlets: Copley Square (Sat–Sun 10am–4pm), at the corner of Dartmouth and Boylston sts, and Faneuil Hall Marketplace (Tues–Sun 10am–4pm; ⓦ artsboston.org).

Boch Center 270 Tremont St ⓦ bochcenter.org; Boylston T. Formerly the Citi Performing Arts Center, this epic space includes two classic venues: the Wang is the biggest performance centre in Boston, a movie house of palatial proportions; and the Shubert, dubbed the "Little Princess", which has been restored to its pretty, early 1900s appearance. Both host large-scale dance performances, theatre productions and rock shows.

Brattle Theatre 40 Brattle St, Cambridge ⓦ brattlefilm.org; Harvard T. A historic indie cinema that pleasantly looks its age. Hosts themed film series plus occasional author appearances and readings; beer and wine are served alongside hot popcorn.

Symphony Hall 301 Massachusetts Ave ⓦ bso.org; Symphony T. The dignified, acoustically perfect venue for the prestigious Boston Symphony Orchestra. The famous Boston Pops concerts happen in May and June (as well as their signature show on July 4); in July and Aug, the BSO retreats to Tanglewood, in the Berkshires (see page 81).

BOSTON SPECTATOR SPORTS

Boston is undeniably a sports town. Ever since the Boston Red Stockings scored their first run in 1871, the city's devotion to baseball has raged to a nearly religious fervour. There's no shortage of **Patriots** football (Ⓦ patriots.com), **Bruins** ice hockey (Ⓦ bruins.nhl.com) or **Celtics** basketball (Ⓦ nba.com/celtics) fans either. Baseball is treated with reverence in Boston, so it's appropriate that the city's team, the **Red Sox** (Ⓦ redsox.com), plays in one of the country's most celebrated ballparks, **Fenway Park** (see page 58). Though they compete in a stadium a long drive away, seeing a Patriots game live is a rare treat for non-season ticket holders. Both the Celtics and Bruins light up massive TD Garden, a stadium in Boston's West End.

Lexington and Concord

On the night of April 18, 1775, **Paul Revere** rode down what is now Massachusetts Avenue from Boston, racing through Cambridge and Arlington on his way to warn the American patriots gathered at **Lexington** (14 miles to the west) of an impending British attack. Close behind him was a force of more than seven hundred British soldiers, intent on seizing supplies hoarded by the local militia. Today, Revolutionary War history is evoked here in the **Minute Man National Historical Park**. **Concord** (where the Patriots' supplies were held) continues the Independence theme, though the town's literary associations are just as much, if not more, of a draw.

National Historical Park

Buckman Tavern 1 Bedford St • March–Nov daily 9.30am–4pm • ☏ 781 862 5598 • **Hancock-Clarke House** 36 Hancock St • April & May call for hours; June–Oct daily 10am–4pm, guided tours on the hour • ☏ 781 861 0928 • **Munroe Tavern** 1332 Massachusetts Ave • April & May, call for hours; June–Oct daily noon–4pm • ☏ 781 862 0295 • Charge • Ⓦ lexingtonhistory.org

Although much of Revere's route has been turned into major thoroughfares, the various settings of the first military confrontation of the Revolutionary War – "the shot heard 'round the world" – remain much as they were then. The triangular **Town Common** at Lexington was where the British encountered their first opposition. Captain John Parker ordered his 77 American "**Minutemen**" to "stand your ground. Don't fire unless fired upon, but if they mean to have a war let it begin here". No one knows who fired the first shot, but the eight soldiers who died are buried beneath an affecting memorial at the northwestern end of the park. Guides in period costume lead tours of the **Buckman Tavern**, where the Minutemen waited for the British to arrive; the **Hancock-Clarke House**, a quarter of a mile north, where Samuel Adams and John Hancock were awakened by Paul Revere, is now a museum. The **Munroe Tavern** served as a field hospital for British soldiers, though only for ninety minutes. It now houses the **Museum of the British Redcoats**, which gives a British perspective on the events of April 19, 1775.

By the time the British soldiers marched on Concord, on the morning after the encounter in Lexington, the surrounding countryside was up in arms, and the Revolutionary War was in full swing. In running battles in the town itself, and along the still-evocative **Battle Road** leading back toward Boston, 73 British soldiers and 49 colonials were killed over the next two days.

Orchard House

399 Lexington Rd, Concord • Tours: April–Oct Mon–Sat 10am–4.30pm, Sun 11–4.30pm; Nov–March Mon–Fri 11am–3pm, Sat 10am–4.30pm, Sun 1–4.30pm • Charge • Ⓦ louisamayalcott.org

The region's rich **literary heritage** is the focus at **Orchard House**, where Louisa May Alcott lived from 1858 to 1877 and wrote *Little Women*. The guided tour is well worth your time; although it focuses heavily on the differences between Alcott's life and her most famous book, it is also the best way to get a good understanding of the area's strong nineteenth-century literary, intellectual and liberal activist community.

1

Walden Pond State Reservation

Southern Concord, on Rte-126 • Daily sunrise to sunset • Parking charge • ⓦ mass.gov

Walden Pond was where Henry David Thoreau conducted the experiment in solitude and self-sufficiency described in his 1854 book *Walden*. The site where his log cabin once stood is marked with stones, and at dawn you can still watch the pond "throwing off its nightly clothing of mist" (at midday, it's a great spot for swimming and hiking). Thoreau is interred, along with Ralph Waldo Emerson, Nathaniel Hawthorne and Louisa May Alcott, atop a hill in **Sleepy Hollow Cemetery**, just east of the centre of Concord.

ARRIVAL, INFORMATION AND TOURS

LEXINGTON AND CONCORD

By bus Buses run to Lexington from Alewife Station (15min), at the northern end of the Red T line.

By train Trains from Boston's North Station pull in at Concord Depot (40–45min), a stiff 1.5-mile walk from the centre.

Visitor centre 250 North Great Rd, Lincoln (April–Oct daily 9am–5pm; ⓦ nps.gov/mima). The headquarters for the Minuteman National Historical Park offers the best orientation on the area.

Tours Liberty Ride (June–Oct daily 10am–4pm; April & May Sat & Sun only; charge; ⓦ libertyride.us) operates a hop-on, hop-off service, stopping at all the main sights.

EATING AND DRINKING

80 Thoreau 80 Thoreau St, Concord ⓦ 80thoreau.com. While Concord may be long on Revolutionary War heroes, historically it has been short on culinary trailblazers. Enter *80 Thoreau*, an epicurean favourite, with simple yet alluring dishes like beet salad with sunflower seeds and blue cheese, and roast halibut with snap peas and bacon. $\overline{\$\$\$}$

Royal India Bistro 7 Meriam St, Lexington ⓦ bistroroyalindia.com. Top-notch Indian food and stellar service in a cosy, central, family-run place near the Town Common. $\overline{\$\$}$

Salem

SALEM is remembered less as the site where the colony of Massachusetts was first established than as the place where, sixty years later, Puritan self-righteousness reached its apogee in the horrific **witch trials** of 1692. Nineteen Salem women were hanged as witches (and one man, Giles Corey, was pressed to death with a boulder), after fireside tales heard by teenage girls metastasized into community hysteria. Less known is Salem's eighteenth- and nineteenth-century role as a flourishing seaport, and the remnants from this era add to the town's ample historic ambience – with abandoned wharves, rows of stately sea captains' homes and an astounding display of riches at the **Peabody Essex Museum**.

Salem Witch Museum

19½ Washington Square N • Daily: July & Aug 10am–7pm; Sept–June 10am–5pm • Charge • ⓦ salemwitchmuseum.com

The **Salem Witch Museum** provides some entertaining, if kitschy, orientation on the witch trials. Really just a sound-and-light show that uses wax figures to depict the events, it's still better than the other "museums" in town. In front of the house is an imposing statue of a caped **Roger Conant**, founder of Salem's first Puritan settlement.

Peabody Essex Museum

161 Essex St • Tues–Sun 10am–5pm • Charge • ⓦ pem.org

Salem's crown jewel is the **Peabody Essex Museum**, whose vast, modern space incorporates more than thirty galleries filled with remarkable *objets* brought home by voyaging New Englanders. Founded by a ship captain in 1799, the museum has stellar Oceanic, African, contemporary art and Asian displays, most notably the **Yin Yu Tang** ($6 extra), a stunning sixteen-room Qing dynasty merchant's house reassembled here in Salem.

Salem Maritime National Historic Site

Main visitor centre 2 New Liberty St • Wed–Sun 10am–5pm • **Charge** • ⓦ nps.gov/sama

The remnants of Salem's original waterfront have been preserved as the **Salem Maritime National Historic Site**. The chief sights – opulent Derby House and the imposing

Custom House, where writer Nathaniel Hawthorne once worked as a surveyor – can only be visited on one-hour tours.

House of Seven Gables

115 Derby St • Daily: mid-Jan to June 10am–5pm; July–Oct 10am–7pm; Nov & Dec 10am–5pm; closed first half of Jan • Charge • ⓦ 7gables.org

The **House of Seven Gables**, the star of Hawthorne's eponymous novel, is a rambling old mansion beside the sea. Tours of the 1668 house – the oldest surviving wooden mansion in New England – cover the building's history and architecture. The author's birthplace, a small, burgundy, c.1750 structure, was moved here from Union Street in 1958.

ARRIVAL AND DEPARTURE   SALEM

By bus There's a regular MBTA bus (50min) from Haymarket in Boston.

By train MBTA commuter trains run hourly (30min) between Boston's North Station and Salem.

By ferry A high-speed ferry (late May to Oct; ⓦ bostonharborcruises.com) runs from Long Wharf in Boston to Salem's Blaney Street dock. Advance purchase is recommended. It's advisable to take the ferry or train in October, as the roads get very congested due to Halloween festivities.

ACCOMMODATION AND EATING

★ **A&J King Artisan Bakers** 48 Central St ⓦ ajkingbakery.com. Hidden on a side street, this to-die-for bakery has gooey sticky buns, crusty loaves of bread and plump little carrot cakes. You can also pick up artisanal sandwiches, such as smoked salmon with crème fraîche and alfalfa sprouts and roast beef with house pickled onions and cheddar. $

Hawthorne Hotel 18 Washington Square W ⓦ hawthornehotel.com. Right in the heart of things, this full-service hotel is a Salem landmark with reasonable prices and a respectable restaurant and pub. Built in 1925, it has 89 rooms furnished with eighteenth-century reproduction furniture and flatscreen TVs. $$

Life Alive Organic Cafe 281 Essex St ⓦ lifealive.com. A few blocks from the train station, this regional favourite is part café and part health store, with a huge range of smoothies and tasty organic and vegetarian meals such as "The Goddess" wrap, a blend of carrots, beets, broccoli, tofu, ginger sauce and brown rice. $$

★ **Northey Street House Bed and Breakfast** 30 Northey St ⓦ northeystreethouse.com. Big, blue 1809 Federal house with three comfortable rooms for four. The Garden Room has modern, Asian-inspired decor and opens onto a garden with raspberries, Japanese maples and a little koi fishpond. The affable host encourages a no-indoor-shoes policy, with slippers provided. $$

Plymouth

PLYMOUTH, America's so-called "hometown", is best known for being the first permanent settlement established by the English **Pilgrims** in 1620. The town is mostly given over to commemorating their landing, and needs only be visited by people with a real interest in the story. Its attractions lie in the centre, along the waterfront or in the historic district.

WHALE-WATCHING ON CAPE ANN

As you head north out of Boston, you pass through a succession of rich little ports that have been all but swallowed up by the suburbs. One of the most popular and exhilarating activities along this stretch of coast is **whale-watching**: trips depart from Gloucester, Salem and Newburyport to whale feeding grounds, where an abundance of plankton and small fish provide sufficient calories (around one million a day) to keep 50ft, 25-ton **humpbacks** happy. Gloucester whale-watching companies include Captain Bill & Sons (ⓦ facebook.com/captbillswhalewatch) at 24 Harbor Loop; and Cape Ann Whale Watch, at 415 Main St (ⓦ seethewhales.com). During July and August, each company offers two daily trips (second half of April, May, June & Sept Mon–Fri 1 daily, Sat & Sun 2 daily; Oct 1 daily).

1

Plymouth Rock

The most famous sight in town is **Plymouth Rock**, on the waterfront at North and Water streets, and sheltered by a pseudo-Greek temple on the seashore where the Pilgrims are said to have first touched land. It is really of symbolic importance only: the rock was identified in 1741, no one can be sure where exactly they did land, and the Pilgrims had in fact already spent several weeks on Cape Cod before coming here.

Mayflower II

Docked at the State Pier on Water St • Daily 9am–5pm • Charge • ⓦ plimoth.org

The best sight in Plymouth is the **Mayflower II**, a replica of the original *Mayflower*. This version meticulously reproduces the brown hull and red strapwork that were typical of a seventeenth-century merchant vessel – which is what the original was, before being "outfitted" for passengers prior to its horrendous 66-day journey across the Atlantic. On board, role-playing "interpreters" in period garb, meant to represent the Pilgrim passengers, field questions.

Following a multi-year restoration project, the *Mayflower*'s debut sail took place to Boston May 2020 – commemorating the 400th anniversary of the Pilgrim landing.

Plimoth Plantation

137 Warren Ave • Daily 9am–5pm Charge • ⓦ plimoth.org

Similar to the *Mayflower II* in approach and authenticity is the **Plimoth Plantation**, three miles south of town off Rte-3. Here, a recreation of "Plimoth" c.1627, as well as a Wampanoag settlement, have been built using traditional techniques. At the English village, visitors are expected to participate in a charade and pretend to have stepped back into the seventeenth century – which, depending on your mood, can be quite enjoyable. Exchanges in the Wampanoag village are less structured, with the Native American staff wearing traditional clothes (but not role-playing) and happy to chat about native customs.

ARRIVAL AND INFORMATION   PLYMOUTH

By bus Plymouth & Brockton buses (ⓦ p-b.com) run from Boston, stopping at the Park and Ride lot at exit 5 off Rte-3, where a local shuttle makes stops around town before heading to Plimoth Plantation (May–Aug Fri–Sun).

Visitor centre 130 Water St (daily: April & May 9am–5pm, June–Aug 8am–8pm; Sept–Nov 9am–5pm; ⓦ seeplymouth.com).

ACCOMMODATION AND EATING

Best Western Cold Spring 180 Court St ⓦ bestwestern. com. This appealing hotel, comprised of a set of small buildings on a leafy campus, has clean, modern rooms with flatscreen TVs, a swimming pool with views of Cape Cod Bay, laundry facilities and a complimentary breakfast. $\overline{\underline{\$\$}}$

Blue-Eyed Crab 170 Water St ⓦ blue-eyedcrab.com. This merry seafood favourite has a cheerful, tropical-themed menu and ambience. The grilled calamari are

tossed in plantain butter, while the Cuban Pork Bowl is filled with coconut rice and cotija cheese. $\overline{\underline{\$\$}}$

By the Sea 22 Winslow St ⓦ bytheseabedandbreakfast. com. Close to Plymouth Rock, this B&B offers three spacious, newly renovated suites with harbour views. The hosts serve a "jumpstart" in the morning (coffee and pastries), and give breakfast vouchers redeemable at area businesses. $\overline{\underline{\$\$}}$

New Bedford

The old whaling port of **NEW BEDFORD**, 55 miles due south of Boston, was immortalized at the start of Herman Melville's *Moby Dick*, and is still home to one of the nation's most active fishing fleets. Much of the downtown and working waterfront area is preserved within the **New Bedford Whaling National Historic Park** (visitor centre at 33 Williams St; daily 9am–5pm; ⓦ nps.gov/nebe), the centrepiece of which is the impressive **New Bedford Whaling Museum** at 18 Johnny Cake Hill (April–Dec daily 9am–5pm; Jan–March Tues–Sat 9am–4pm, Sun 11am–4pm; every second Thurs of the month till 8pm; charge; ⓦ whalingmuseum.org), featuring a 66ft blue whale skeleton, collections of scrimshaw and harpoons, and an evocative half-sized whaling vessel replica. More affecting is the **Seamen's Bethel** directly opposite (late May to mid-Oct daily 10am–4pm; free; ⓦportsociety.org); the chapel really does have the ship-shaped pulpit described in *Moby Dick*, though this one was rebuilt after a fire in 1866.

New Bedford Art Museum/Artworks!
608 Pleasant St • Wed–Sun noon–5pm. Thurs until 9pm • Charge • ⓦ newbedfordart.org

This colourful art **museum** celebrates the best of local artists and sculptors with changing exhibits, as well as a variety of events, including artist panels, lectures, art-focused garden parties and more. The museum also features art classes and workshops for children and adults.

ACCOMMODATION AND EATING   **NEW BEDFORD**

Antonio's 267 Coggeshall St ⓦantoniosnewbedford. com. Authentic Portuguese dishes, from shrimp croquettes to chicken with mushrooms and port wine sauce, at a popular restaurant a mile outside downtown. $\overline{\underline{\$}}$–$\overline{\underline{\$\$}}$

Brick Pizzeria Napoletana 163 Union St ⓦpizzeriabrick.com. Sumptuous brick-oven pizzas sprinkled with toppings such as hot salami and mushrooms or prosciutto, artichokes and goat's cheese. $\overline{\underline{\$}}$–$\overline{\underline{\$\$}}$

New Bedford Harbor 222 Union St

ⓦnewbedfordharborhotel.com. Modern place close to the waterfront and the whaling museum, with an American restaurant decked out with nautical decor and rooms with exposed brick walls and wooden ceilings. $\overline{\underline{\$\$}}$

No Problemo 813 Purchase St ⓦfacebook.com/No-Problemo-116233961733531. Whale-sized burritos, *taquitos* and zesty sangria are served up by tattooed staff at this hip taqueria and bar with Day of the Dead decor. Cash only. $\overline{\underline{\$}}$

Cape Cod and the islands

One of the most celebrated slices of real estate in America, **Cape Cod** boasts a dazzling, three-hundred-mile coastline with some of the best beaches in New England. A slender, crooked peninsula, it's easily accessed from the region's snug villages, many of which have been preserved as they were a hundred or more years ago.

Cape Cod was named by Bartholomew Gosnold in 1602, on account of the prodigious quantities of cod caught by his crew off Provincetown. Less than twenty years later the Pilgrims landed nearby, before moving on to Plymouth. Today, much of the land on the Cape, from its salt marshes to its ever-eroding dunes, is considered a fragile and endangered ecosystem, and once you head north to the **Outer Cape**, past the spectacular dunes of **Cape Cod National Seashore**, you get a feeling for why this narrow spit of land still has a reputation as a seaside wilderness. **Provincetown**, at the very tip of Cape Cod, is a popular LGBTQ resort and summer destination for bohemians, artists and fun-seekers lured by the excellent beaches, art galleries and welcoming atmosphere.

Just off the south coast of Cape Cod, the relatively unspoiled islands of **Martha's Vineyard** and **Nantucket** have long been some of the most popular and prestigious vacation destinations in the USA. Both mingle an easy-going cosmopolitan atmosphere and some of the best restaurants and B&Bs on the East Coast. Nantucket is considered the more genteel of the pair, teased for its preppy fashions; Martha is more expansive and laidback, known for its elaborate gingerbread-style houses, wild moorlands and perfect beaches.

ARRIVAL AND DEPARTURE   **CAPE COD AND THE ISLANDS**

By car The most direct way to reach the Cape is by car. On a fairly quiet day it takes under 2hr to get from Boston to the Sagamore Bridge via Rte-3, but expect this to double on summer weekends and holidays.

By plane A number of airlines go direct to Cape Cod, including Cape Air (ⓦcapeair.com), which flies to Hyannis and Provincetown from Boston several times a day, and JetBlue (ⓦjetblue.com) which has services from New

York City and Boston to Hyannis, Nantucket and Martha's Vineyard.

By bus Peter Pan Bus Lines subsidiary Bonanza (ⓦpeterpanbus.com) operates services from Boston, Woods Hole and Falmouth, while Plymouth & Brockton (ⓦp-b.com) has a more complete set of Cape destinations.

By ferry Ferries from Boston take 90min to cross to Provincetown; there are boats to the various islands.

1

The Cape's southern coast

From the Bourne Bridge, **Rte-28** runs south to Falmouth then hugs the Nantucket Sound until it merges with routes 6 and 6A in Orleans. Pleasant Falmouth makes a diverting jump-off point for ferries to Martha's Vineyard. Further up, Hyannis, the commercial hub of Cape Cod, is quite commercialized and ferry-oriented, although it does have a number of good beaches and watering holes.

Falmouth and Woods Hole

Boasting more coastline than any other Cape Cod town, **Falmouth** has no fewer than fourteen harbours among its eight villages. At the centre of these is **Falmouth Village**, with a prim central green surrounded by Federal and Greek Revival homes. The small town of **Woods Hole**, four miles southwest, owes its name to the water passage, or "hole", between Penzance Point and Nonamesset Island. Most people come here for the ferry to Martha's Vineyard (see box, page 77), as it's little more than picture-perfect Nobska Point Lighthouse and a few restaurants.

Hyannis

It stands to reason that **HYANNIS** – the largest port on the Cape, and its main commercial hub – would be a little less charming than Falmouth and Woods Hole. Nevertheless, it still sparkles a bit from the glamour it earned when the **Kennedy compound** at Hyannisport placed it at the centre of world affairs. Hence the existence of the **John F. Kennedy Museum** (mid-April to late May Mon–Sat 10am–4pm, Sun noon–4pm; June– Oct Mon–Sat 9am–5pm, Sun noon–5pm; Nov Mon–Sat 10am–4pm, Sun noon–4pm; charge; ⊛ jfkhyannismuseum.org), which shows photographs, news clippings and film footage of the days JFK spent on the Cape.

ACCOMMODATION AND EATING   **THE CAPE'S SOUTHERN COAST**

FALMOUTH

Captain's Manor Inn 27 W Main St ⊛ captainsmanorinn. com. Dating from 1849, this gorgeously restored sea captain's home is done up with Greek Revival accents – intended to please the original owner's Southern bride. The obliging hosts provide pampering perks including home-made snacks and a nightly turndown service. $\overline{S}\overline{S}\overline{S}$

The Glass Onion 37 N Main St ⊛ theglassoniondining. com. Swish New American restaurant firing off some of the Cape's best cuisine. Order the seared scallops with polenta cake and carrot purée, or the poached lobster and shrimp with spinach risotto for entry into seafood heaven. $\overline{S}\overline{S}\overline{S}$

Inn on the Sound 313 Grand Ave ⊛ innonthesound. com. A stunning location (45ft above the bay), mesmerizing views and gourmet food make this posh B&B a real treat, with luxury linens and a well-stocked library. Ask for a room with a balcony. $\overline{S}\overline{S}\overline{S}$

★ The Pickle Jar 170 Main St ⊛ picklejarkitchen. com. They cure their pastrami, smoke their salmon and spice their own pickles at this superb breakfast and lunch spot. Breakfast sees griddle cakes and granola and yogurt parfaits, lunch has chili-rubbed pork with smoked Gouda. Don't miss the fried pickle chips. $\overline{S}$

WOODS HOLE

Pie in the Sky Bakery 10 Water St ⊛ piecoffee.com.

Right by the ferry terminal. Stock up here before heading over to Martha's Vineyard: puffy popovers, "wonder bars" baked with chocolate, giant cookies, fresh sandwiches, soups and salads are all on offer. It's a tiny place, packed with colourful glass bottles and art in a wooden alcove overlooking the harbour. $\overline{S}$

Woods Hole Inn 28 Water St ⊛ woodsholeinn.com. In an unbeatable location just steps from the ferry terminal, this eco-friendly inn has fourteen colourful quarters artfully done up with luxury linens and iPod docks. Parking and home-made breakfast is included. $\overline{S}\overline{S}\overline{S}$

HYANNIS

Brazilian Grill 680 Main St ⊛ braziliangrill-capecod. com. Be sure to indulge in the full *rodizio* at this *churrascaria* – a carnivore's paradise where mouth-watering meats are delivered straight from hand-held skewers to diners' plates. There's also an overflowing buffet with plenty of vegetarian options. $\overline{S}\overline{S}\overline{S}$

Common Ground 360 S Main St ⊛ hyanniscommon ground.com. This dimly lit, wood-panelled café resembles a hobbit's home and serves healthful fare like banana smoothies, tangy hibiscus coolers, big salads and sandwiches on home-made bread – try the chicken Caesar with grated parmesan. Centrally located too, right on the main drag. $\overline{S}$

Four Seas Ice Cream 360 S Main St, Centerville ⓦ fourseasicecream.com. Since 1934, this scoop shop near Craigville Beach has been the place to go for unbeatable ice-cream cones. $

HI-Hyannis 111 Ocean St ⓦ hiusa.org/hyannis. Directly across from the ferry docks, this superb hostel has 37 beds (mainly dorms) in a spacious shingled house. Free continental breakfast and internet access. Open late May to mid-Oct. Dorms $

★ **The Naked Oyster** 410 Main St ⓦ nakedoyster. com. Enjoy the fruits of the sea made with French flair at this welcoming Main Street joint. Start at the raw bar – try the sample of littleneck clams, oysters and shrimp – and then dig into creative main dishes like scallops and bone marrow, seared ahi tuna with a delectable edamame puree and lobster risotto. $$$

SeaCoast Inn 33 Ocean St ⓦ booking.com. Clean and functional motel-style accommodation close to the ferry docks; the helpful owners throw in free breakfast. Open May–Oct. $$

The Mid-Cape

The middle stretch of Cape Cod holds some of its prettiest, most unspoiled places. Timeworn fishing communities such as Wellfleet and Chatham, along with dozens of carefully maintained, mildly touristy hamlets along the many winding roads, are what most people hope to find when they come to the Cape. Cutting across the middle, the **Cape Cod Rail Trail** follows a paved-over railroad track from Dennis to Eastham, through forests and cranberry bogs. It makes an excellent **cycling** trip; bikes can be rented in all the main towns.

The genteel, whitewashed town of **CHATHAM** is tucked away in a protected harbour between Nantucket Sound and the open Atlantic Ocean. Hang out at the **Fish Pier** on Shore Road and wait for the fleet to come in during the mid-afternoon, or head a mile south to **Chatham Light**, one of many lighthouses built to protect mariners from the treacherous shoals.

ACCOMMODATION AND EATING   THE MID-CAPE

The Captain's House Inn 369–377 Old Harbor Rd, Chatham ⓦ captainshouseinn.com. Sumptuously renovated 1839 Greek Revival whaling captain's home; most rooms have fireplaces, and rates include delicious breakfasts and afternoon tea with freshly baked scones. $$$

Chatham Pier Fish Market 45 Barcliff Ave Ext, Chatham ⓦ chathampierfishmarket.com. Order lobster rolls and inexpensive plates of delectable fried seafood while fishermen unload their catch and seals bob just beyond. $$–$$$

★ **Marion's Pie Shop** 2022 Main St, Chatham ⓦ marionspieshopofchatham.com. Delicious sweet apple pies, savoury chicken pies and yummy breakfast cinnamon rolls. Note that "misbehaving children will be made into pies". $

Pleasant Bay Village Resort Motel 1191 Orleans Rd, Chatham ⓦ pleasantbayvillage.com. Among the more affordable digs in town, with spacious, clean motel rooms (suites available), a pool and jacuzzi, and stunning gardens tucked inside six acres of woodlands. Open May–Oct. $$

Cape Cod National Seashore

After the bustle of Cape Cod's towns, the **Cape Cod National Seashore** really does come as a proverbial breath of fresh air. These protected lands, spared by President Kennedy from the development further south, take up virtually the entire Atlantic side of the Cape, from Chatham north to Provincetown. Most of the way you can park by the road, and strike off across the dunes to windswept, seemingly endless beaches.

Displays and movies at the main **Salt Pond Visitor Center**, on US-6 just north of Eastham (daily 9am–4.30pm, till 5pm July & Aug; ⓦ nps.gov/caco), trace the geology and history of the Cape. A road and a hiking and cycling trail head east to the sands of **Coast Guard Beach** and **Nauset Light Beach**, both of which offer excellent swimming.

ACCOMMODATION   CAPE COD NATIONAL SEASHORE

HI-Truro 111 N Pamet Rd, Truro ⓦ hiusa.org. One of the East Coast's best hostels: 42 dorm beds in a capacious former Coast Guard station that's a stone's throw from the beach. Dorms $, three-bed room $$

Provincetown

The compact fishing village of **PROVINCETOWN** (or, as it's popularly known, "P-Town") is a gorgeous place, with silvery clapboard houses and gloriously unruly gardens lining

1

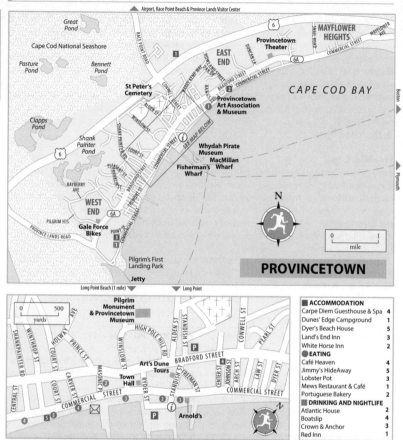

■ ACCOMMODATION	
Carpe Diem Guesthouse & Spa	4
Dunes' Edge Campground	1
Dyer's Beach House	5
Land's End Inn	3
White Horse Inn	2
● EATING	
Café Heaven	4
Jimmy's HideAway	5
Lobster Pot	3
Mews Restaurant & Café	1
Portuguese Bakery	2
■ DRINKING AND NIGHTLIFE	
Atlantic House	2
Boatslip	4
Crown & Anchor	3
Red Inn	1

the town's tiny, winding streets. Bohemians and artists have long flocked here for the quality of light and vast beaches; in 1914 Eugene O'Neill (see page 90) established the Provincetown Playhouse here in a small hut. Since the beatnik 1950s, the town has also been a **gay** centre, and today its population of five thousand rises tenfold in the summer. Commercialism, though quite visible along the main drags, tends to be countercultural: LGBTQ, environmental and feminist gift shops join arty galleries, restaurants and bars on the aptly named **Commercial Street**. However, strict zoning ensures that there are few new buildings in town. Albeit crowded and raucous from July through to September, P-Town remains a place where history, natural beauty and, above all, difference, are respected and celebrated.

Provincetown lies 120 miles from Boston by land, but less than fifty miles by sea, nestled in the New England coast's largest natural harbour. Its tiny core is centred on the three narrow miles of **Commercial Street. MacMillan Pier**, always busy with charters, yachts and fishing boats (which unload their catch each afternoon), splits the town in half. East of the centre (but still on Commercial St), are scores of quaint art galleries, as well as the delightful **Provincetown Art Association and Museum** (late May to Sept Mon–Thurs & Sat 11am–6pm, Fri 11am–10pm, Sun 11am–5pm; Oct to mid-May Thurs–Sun noon–5pm; charge; ⓦpaam.org), which rotates works from its two-thousand-strong collection.

1

Pilgrim Monument and Provincetown Museum

High Pole Hill Rd • Daily: April to mid-May & mid-Sept to Nov 9am–5pm; late May to early Sept 9am–7pm • Charge • ⓦ pilgrim-monument.org

Looming above the centre of P-Town, the **Pilgrim Monument and Provincetown Museum** has permanent exhibits giving a fairly romantic account of the Pilgrim story and subsequent history of the town, along with a 252ft granite tower with an observation deck (accessible by 116 stairs) that looks out over the whole of the Cape.

The beaches

A little way beyond the town's narrow strip of sand, undeveloped **beaches** are marked only by dunes and a few shabby beach huts. You can swim in the clear water from the uneven rocks of the two-mile breakwater, or find blissful isolation on undeveloped beaches nearby. West of town, **Herring Cove Beach**, easily reached by bike or through the dunes, is more crowded, but never unbearably so. In the wild **Province Lands**, at the Cape's northern tip, vast sweeping moors and bushy dunes are buffeted by Cape Cod's deadly sea, the site of one thousand known shipwrecks. The **visitor centre** (May–Oct daily 9am–5pm; ☎ 508 487 1256), in the middle of the dunes on Race Point Road, has videos and displays highlighting the exceptionally fragile environment here.

ARRIVAL AND DEPARTURE   PROVINCETOWN

By ferry By far the nicest way to arrive is on one of the passenger ferries. Bay State Cruise Company (ⓦ baystatecruisecompany.com) runs an express ferry in the summer three times a day from Boston's World Trade Center pier (90min express return), and a standard ferry (Sat only; 3hr), while Boston Harbor Cruises (ⓦ bostonharborcruises.

com) offers express service from Boston's Long Wharf (May–Oct; 1hr 30min).

By bus A slower option is the Plymouth & Brockton bus, which runs to Provincetown four times daily from Boston via Hyannis (3hr 45min; ⓦ p-b.com).

GETTING AROUND

By bike It couldn't be easier to walk around tiny P-Town, though many visitors prefer to cycle the narrow streets, hills and the undulating Province Lands bike trail, an enchanting 6-mile route with great vistas. For rentals, Arnold's, 329 Commercial St (ⓦ provincetownbikes.com), right in the centre of town, is open from mid-April to mid-Oct, as is Gale Force Bikes, close to the bike trail at 144 Bradford St Ext

(ⓦ galeforcebikes.com).

By bus The Cape Cod Regional Transit Authority (ⓦ capecodtransit.org) runs frequent Flex route buses (daily 6.30am–10pm) connecting P-Town with other villages on the Cape; simply flag them down on the side of the road (except for Rte-6, for safety reasons).

INFORMATION AND TOURS

Dune tours Art's Dune Tours amble about the sand in 4WD vehicles, and include sunset tours, art and lighthouse tours and more (4 Standish St; April–Oct 10am–dusk; charge; ⓦ artsdunetours.com).
Visitor centre In the Chamber of Commerce at the end of the wharf, 307 Commercial St (May–Oct daily 9am–5pm;

Nov–April limited hours; ⓦ ptownchamber.com).
Whale-watching tours Dolphin Fleet, 307 Commercial St (April–Oct; charge; ⓦ whalewatch.com), is the best company for whale-watching, with 3–4hr cruises leaving frequently from MacMillan Pier.

ACCOMMODATION   SEE MAP PAGE 74

Many of the most picturesque cottages in town are **guesthouses**, some with spectacular bay views – unsurprisingly, many are run by LGBTQ couples, and all are **LGBTQ-friendly**. The best area to be is the quiet West End, though anything on Bradford Street will also be removed from the summertime racket.
Carpe Diem Guesthouse & Spa 12–14 Johnson St ⓦ carpediemguesthouse.com. You'll find friendly, accommodating owners, beautifully appointed rooms with

a bit of an Eastern vibe, a superb spa and an afternoon wine and cheese hour at this B&B on a quiet side street. $\overline{\underline{\$\$\$}}$
Dunes' Edge Campground Rte-6 just east of the central traffic lights ⓦ bit.ly/29avyMi. Close to the beach and near to town, this campground has wooded sites, laundry facilities and hot showers. Open May–Sept. $\overline{\underline{\$}}$
Dyer's Beach House 173 Commercial St ⓦ dyersbeachhouse.com. With just five rooms, this wood-panelled beach house has an intimate feel and a traditional

1

vibe, with deep pile carpets and a courtyard hung with flowers. $\overline{\$\$}$

★ **Land's End Inn** 22 Commercial St ⓦ landsendinn. com. Every inch of this turreted house has been imaginatively decorated in an extravagant Art Nouveau style. Many of the rooms and suites have sweeping ocean views, and a continental breakfast and daily wine and cheese hour is included. A truly original and very special place. $\overline{\$\$\$}$

White Horse Inn 500 Commercial St ⓦ whitehorseinn provincetown.com. An eclectic art-strewn space in the quiet East End neighbourhood; some rooms have shared bathrooms. There are also family-sized apartments with kitchens. It's bygone-era Provincetown: no TVs or wi-fi, but there's a private strip of beach, a delightful owner and a beatnik vibe. Cash or cheque only. Open May–Sept. Doubles $\overline{\$}$, apartments $\overline{\$\$\$}$

EATING

SEE MAP PAGE 74

Café Heaven 199 Commercial St ⓦ cafeheavenptown. com. Massive breakfast plates (served through the afternoon), baguette sandwiches and local art make this a popular daytime choice, but it's the juicy hamburgers that really stand out. Just like heaven, there's often a wait to get in. $\overline{\$}$

Jimmy's HideAway 179 Commercial St ⓦ jimmys hideaway.com. Aptly named, this subterranean, low-lit restaurant serves a menu that's both simple and divine, including a delectable seafood stew with scallops, shrimp, mussels and chorizo and littleneck clams with artichoke hearts tossed with spaghetti. Top it off with enjoying the gorgeous water views from the back. $\overline{\$\$}$–$\overline{\$\$\$}$

Lobster Pot 321 Commercial St ⓦ ptownlobsterpot. com. Its landmark neon sign is like a beacon for those who

come from far and wide for the ultra-fresh crustaceans. Order the lobster ravioli and enjoy it on the great outdoor deck. $\overline{\$}$–$\overline{\$\$}$

Mews Restaurant & Café 429 Commercial St ⓦ mewsptown.com. Since opening in 1964, this unassuming restaurant has served everyone from Judy Garland to Marc Jacobs, garnering rave reviews for its rotating fusion cuisine – think lobster vindaloo or almond-crusted cod – and extensive vodka bar (286 and counting). $\overline{\$\$}$

Portuguese Bakery 299 Commercial St ⓦ provincetownportuguesebakery.com. This old stand-by is the place to come for cheap breakfasts and baked goods, particularly the tasty *malasadas* (fried dough) and *rabanada*, akin to French toast. $\overline{\$}$

DRINKING AND NIGHTLIFE

SEE MAP PAGE 74

On summer weekends, boatloads of revellers come to P-Town in search of its notoriously **wild nightlife**, which is heavily geared towards an **LGBTQ** clientele. Some establishments have terrific waterfront locations, making them ideal for a drink at sunset.

Atlantic House 6 Masonic Place, behind Commercial St ⓦ ahouse.com. The "A-House" – a dark drinking hole favoured by Tennessee Williams and Eugene O'Neill – now has a trendy, mainly gay men's, dance club and bar. Get ready to party on the Friday themed nights. $\overline{\$\$}$

Boatslip 161 Commercial St ⓦ boatslip.com. The daily

tea dances (4–7pm) at this resort are legendary; you can either dance on a long wooden deck overlooking the water, or cruise inside under a disco ball and flashing lights. $\overline{\$\$}$

Crown & Anchor 247 Commercial St ⓦ onlyatthecrown. com. A massive complex housing several bars, including *The Vault*, a leather bar, *Wave*, a video-karaoke bar and *Paramount*, a massive nightclub. $\overline{\$\$}$

Red Inn 15 Commercial St ⓦ theredinn.com. For a complete change of nightlife pace, head to the *Red Inn*'s teensy wooden bar, where you can sip martinis on the porch of a historic house by the sea. Plus, they feature lively Jazz Sundays. $\overline{\$\$}$

Martha's Vineyard

The largest offshore island in New England, twenty-mile-long **MARTHA'S VINEYARD** encompasses more physical variety than its smaller sister Nantucket (see page 78), with hills and pastures providing scenic counterpoints to the beaches and wild, windswept moors on the separate island of **Chappaquiddick**.

Martha's Vineyard's most genteel town is **Edgartown**, all prim and proper with its freshly painted, white clapboard colonial homes, museums and manicured gardens. The other main settlement, **Vineyard Haven**, is more commercial and one of the island's ferry ports. **Oak Bluffs**, in between the two (and the other docking point for ferries), has an array of fanciful wooden gingerbread cottages and inviting restaurants. Be aware of island terminology: heading "Up-Island" takes you southwest to the cliffs at **Aquinnah** (formerly known as Gay Head); conversely, "Down-Island" refers to the triumvirate of easterly towns mentioned above.

Aquinnah lighthouse

9 Aquinnah Circle • Mid-June to mid-Oct daily 11am–4pm • Charge • ⓦ mvy.com/aquinnah

FERRIES TO MARTHA'S VINEYARD AND NANTUCKET

Unless otherwise specified, all the **ferries** below run several times daily in midsummer (mid-June to mid-Sept). Most have fewer services from May to mid-June, and between mid-September and October. There is at least a skeleton service to each island year-round, though not on all routes. To discourage clogging of the roads, round-trip costs for cars are prohibitively high in the peak season (mid-May to mid-Sept; Woods Hole ferry only), while costs for bikes are generally much cheaper. Be sure to make reservations in advance as spaces do sell out. Prices below are for round-trip tickets, unless otherwise stated.

TO MARTHA'S VINEYARD

Falmouth to Oak Bluffs (about 35min). The *Island Queen* (wislandqueen.com). Passengers, bikes or kayaks.

Falmouth to Edgartown (1hr). Falmouth Ferry Service (wfalmouthedgartownferry.com).

Hyannis to Oak Bluffs (50min). Hy-Line (whylinecruises.com). High-speed passenger ferry.

New Bedford to Oak Bluffs (1hr). Seastreak (wseastreak.com). Passengers only. Seastreak runs a connecting bus service from Boston (1hr 15min).

Woods Hole to both Vineyard Haven and Oak Bluffs (45min). Steamship Authority (wsteamshipauthority.com). Car ferry, year-round. Reservations required to bring a car on summer weekends and holidays – you can bring a car stand-by all other times, though the wait can be long.

Manhattan, New York City to Oak Bluffs (5hr 15min). Seastreak. Passengers only. Leaves from E 35th St; also has a pick-up in Highlands, New Jersey.

Quonset Point, Rhode Island, to Oak Bluffs (1hr 30min). Vineyard Fast Ferry (wvineyardfastferry.com). Passengers only. Good for those travelling from Connecticut or New York; Quonset is south of Providence and Warwick. Shuttles are provided to Kingston Amtrak station and Providence airport.

TO NANTUCKET

From Hyannis (1hr or 2hr 15min). Steamship Authority. Also Hy-Line Cruises, pedestrians only; 2hr journey.

From New Bedford (1hr 55min). Seastreak.

From Manhattan, New York City (6hr 15min). Seastreak. Pedestrians only. Leaves from E 35th St; also has a pick-up in Highlands, New Jersey.

In summer, the Hy-Line ferry company runs a **connecting service** between Oak Bluffs, Martha's Vineyard and Nantucket (three departures daily; pedestrians only). The trip takes around 1hr 10min.

Trips around the west side of the island are decidedly bucolic, with nary a peep of the water beyond the rolling hills and private estates; however, you do eventually come to the **lighthouse** at **Aquinnah**, where the multicoloured clay was once the main source of paint for the island's houses – now, anyone caught removing any clay faces a sizeable fine. From Moshup beach below, you can get great views of this spectacular formation.

The beaches

Martha's Vineyard is clustered with beautiful **beaches**. Highlights include the secluded, gorgeous Wasque, at the end of Wasque Road in Chappaquiddick, and South Beach, at the end of Katama Road south of Edgartown, known for its "good waves and good bodies". The gentle State Beach, along Beach Road between Oak Bluffs and Edgartown, is more family-oriented.

GETTING AROUND AND INFORMATION   MARTHA'S VINEYARD

By bus The island has a bus system that connects the main towns and villages (daily 7am–12.45am; wvineyardtransit.com).

By car Bringing a car over on the ferry is expensive, and often impossible on summer weekends without reserving well in advance. Another alternative is to rent

1

a car from Budget, in Vineyard Haven, Oak Bluffs or the airport (◍budget.com), Sun 'N' Fun in Oak Bluffs (◍sunnfunrentals.com), or A-A Island Rentals in Vineyard Haven and Oak Bluffs (◍mvautorental.com).

By bike You can easily get around by bike; pick one up at the rental places lined up by the ferry dock. The best bike ride is along the State Beach Park between Oak Bluffs and Edgartown, with the dunes to one side and marshy Sengekontacket Pond to the other; purpose-built cycle routes continue to the youth hostel at West Tisbury.

Chamber of Commerce 24 Beach St, Vineyard Haven (Mon–Fri 9am–5pm; ◍mvy.com).

ACCOMMODATION

HI-Martha's Vineyard 525 Edgartown–West Tisbury Rd, West Tisbury ◍hiusa.org; easily accessed by the #6 bus route. Pleasant setting, 67 dorm beds and a full kitchen. It is a bit off the beaten track, but there are bike rental deals and free bike delivery. Open mid-May to mid-Oct. Dorms $\overline{\underline{S}}$, 5-person room $\overline{\underline{SS}}$

Madison Inn 18 Kennebec Ave, Oak Bluffs ◍madisoninnmv.com. Run by the masterminds behind the landmark *Nashua House*, this fourteen-room inn is gussied up with floral linens, flatscreen TVs and cheerfully painted chambers. Within easy walking distance of the beach, the ferry terminal and restaurants. $\overline{\underline{SS}}$

Martha's Vineyard Family Campground 569 Edgartown Rd, Vineyard Haven ◍campmv.com. Come nightfall, you can roast s'mores on an open fire at this full-shade campground tucked inside an oak forest. Open late May to mid-Oct. $\overline{\underline{S}}$

Menemsha Inn & Cottages and Beach Plum Inn North Rd, Menemsha ◍menemshainn.com, ◍beachpluminn. com. Beautifully maintained adjacent properties within walking distance of the Menemsha beach, but also with access to private town beaches on the north shore. The *Beach Plum Inn* is better for young adults, while the cottages at *Menemsha* suit families. Open May–Nov; book early. $\overline{\underline{SSS}}$, cottages/week $\overline{\underline{SSSS}}$

Summercamp Hotel 70 Lake Ave ◍summercamphotel. com. This bright and colourful oceanfront boutique hotel is in the very thick of things, facing the breezy harbour. The hotel is filled with quirky, retro touches that hark back to the summer camp, like rope swings and vintage board games. The welcoming rooms are done up a soft pastels and blues. $\overline{\underline{SSS}}$

EATING AND DRINKING

Eating is one of the principal pleasures of Martha's Vineyard; fresh lobster, fish and quahogs (large clams) are particularly abundant. Note that Chilmark is a "dry" town, meaning you will have to bring your own alcohol if you'd like to drink at a restaurant. West Tisbury, Aquinnah and Vineyard Haven serve only beer and wine, and these must be ordered with a meal.

★ **7a Foods** 1045 State Rd, West Tisbury ◍7afoods. com. Popularly called the island's best farm-to-takeout spot, 7a Foods turns out stellar breakfast sandwiches, made with local eggs and bacon or homemade sausage on a fresh warm muffin or bread. Lunchtime concoctions are equally delicious, like chunky chicken salad with roast garlic mayonnaise on a brioche bun. Grab your goodies and devour them at the outside bench or a nearby park – the grand outdoors is, after all, what MV is famous for. $\overline{\underline{S}}$

Back Door Donuts 5 Post Office Square, behind MV Gourmet Café and Bakery, Oak Bluffs ◍backdoordonuts.

com. Local institution knocking out crispy doughnuts in honey-dipped, Boston cream and cinnamon and sugar varieties – all warm, delicious and well-priced. $\overline{\underline{S}}$

Détente 15 Winter St, Edgartown ◍detentemv.com. Of the fancier restaurants on the island, this one's your best bet. Seasonal menus use local ingredients, ranging from halibut to lamb shank to roast octopus – it also has a fabulous wine list. Don't miss the crispy corn bread, with tangy tomato marmalade. Dinner only. $\overline{\underline{SS}}$–$\overline{\underline{SSS}}$

Larsen's Fish Market 56 Basin Rd, Menemsha ◍larsensfishmarket.com. Primarily selling fresh fish and lobster to take away (great for picnics), this much-loved shack also knocks out excellent lobster rolls – freshly caught, boiled and crammed into a hot-dog bun. $\overline{\underline{S}}$–$\overline{\underline{SS}}$

Offshore Ale Company 30 Kennebec Ave, Oak Bluffs ◍offshoreale.com. This friendly local brewpub has wooden booths and walls, frequent live shows in season, great pizzas and comfort food. $\overline{\underline{S}}$–$\overline{\underline{SS}}$

Nantucket

The thirty-mile, two-hour sea crossing to **NANTUCKET** may not be an ocean odyssey, but it does set the "Little Gray Lady" apart from her larger, shore-hugging sister, Martha. Nantucket's smaller size adds to its palpable sense of identity, as does the architecture; the "gray" epithet refers not only to the winter fogs, but to the austere grey clapboard and shingle applied uniformly to buildings across the island. The tiny cobbled carriageways of **Nantucket Town** itself, once one of the largest cities in Massachusetts, were frozen in time by economic decline 150 years ago. Today, this area of delightful old restored houses – the town has more buildings on the National

1

Register of Historic Places than Boston – is very much the island hub. Surrounding the ferry exit is a plethora of bike rental places and tour companies. **Straight Wharf** leads directly onto **Main Street**, with its shops and restaurants.

Whaling Museum

13 Broad St, at the head of Steamboat Wharf • June to mid-Oct daily 9am–5pm, mid-Oct to Dec 10am–4pm• Charge • Ⓦ nha.org

The excellent **Whaling Museum** houses an outstanding collection of seafaring *objets*, including a gallery of delicately carved scrimshaw and a 46ft sperm whale skeleton that washed ashore in 1998. Look for the rotted tooth on its jaw; officials believe it was an infection that brought about the whale's demise. In the museum lobby, check out the impressive Fresnel lens, used in the Sankaty Head Light, built on the Siasconset bluff in 1849, which beamed its guiding light to sailors up to 24 miles away.

The beaches

Beyond the town, Nantucket remains surprisingly wild, a mixture of moors, marshes and heathland, though the main draw remains its untrammelled sandy **beaches**. One of the best can be found at **Siasconset** (pronounced "Sconset"), seven flat, bike-friendly miles east of the town, where venerable cottages stand covered with roses and literally encrusted with salt.

INFORMATION   NANTUCKET

Chamber of Commerce Zero Main St, second floor (Mon–Fri 9am–5pm; Ⓦ nantucketchamber.org).

Nantucket Visitor Services 25 Federal St (daily 9am–5pm, Jan–March closed Sun; Ⓦ nantucket-ma.gov).

ACCOMMODATION

HI-Nantucket Surfside Beach 31 Western Ave Ⓦ hiusa.org. Dorm beds a stone's throw from Surfside Beach in an 1873 lifesaving station, just over 3 miles south of Nantucket Town. Very close to a summertime bus stop. Dorms $̄

Martin House Inn 61 Centre St Ⓦ martinhouseinn.net. Lovely rooms, some with working fireplaces, offer good value in this romantic 1803 seaman's house, with inviting common areas and a spacious veranda – local art and antiques feature throughout. Enjoy the complimentary wine and sherry on Friday evenings. A tasty continental breakfast is included. Singles $̄$̄, doubles $̄$̄$̄

Union Street Inn 7 Union St Ⓦ unioninn.com. This luxurious B&B boasts a central location, hearty breakfasts and dazzling rooms, with stylish rugs, drapes and patterned wallpaper – it's pricey, and much better value off-season. Also on offer is the Garden Suite, an elegant one-bedroom suite with private patio, galley kitchen and glass-enclosed shower. $̄$̄$̄, suite $̄$̄$̄$̄

Veranda House 3 Step Lane Ⓦ theverandahouse.com. The theme at this boutique hotel is "retro chic", bringing a refreshingly contemporary addition to the island's traditional Victorian-style B&Bs; rooms are stylishly designed, most with harbour views, and come with gourmet breakfast. $̄$̄$̄

EATING AND DRINKING

Nantucket abounds in first-rate restaurants, most of them located in or around Nantucket Town. If you're having dinner out, though, be prepared for the bill: **prices** are often comparable to those in Manhattan.

Black-Eyed Susan's 10 India St Ⓦ black-eyedsusans.com. Popular Southern-influenced breakfast and brunch place (plus dinner Mon–Sat), serving big, delicious omelettes and grits with cheese. Cash only. $̄–$̄$̄

Cisco Brewers 5 Bartlett Farm Rd Ⓦ ciscobrewers.com. This friendly spot is as much an alfresco bar as a tour-giving brewery (generally one a day in summer, less so in winter, and includes sampling wine, beer and spirits, as well as a complimentary tasting glass). *Cisco* peddles sample flights of home-made beer, wine and liquor in a leafy courtyard; patrons are encouraged to bring along food. The location, 2.5 miles from town, is the only drawback – take their free shuttle service, or a cab, as getting here by bike is a little hairy. $̄

The Gaslight 3 N Union St Ⓦ gaslightnantucket.com. Live music seven nights a week heats up Nantucket at this rocking venue, with a patio and main stage. A Japanese-accented menu is also served, including sushi, sashimi and small plates like chicken in a soy glaze. Music cover varies. $̄–$̄$̄

★ **The Proprietors Bar and Table** 9 India St Ⓦ proprietorsnantucket.com. Eat your way around the world, without leaving Nantucket. This jaunty restaurant – with beamed ceilings, and a summery, rustic vibe – serves a richly flavoured global menu. Try the crispy broccoli with peanuts and sambal; seared scallops tossed in miso and bok choy; green pea falafel with cucumber; and pork belly with smoked tomato grits. $̄$̄

OLD STURBRIDGE VILLAGE

Halfway between Worcester and Springfield on US-20, near the junction of I-90 and I-84, the restored and reconstructed **Old Sturbridge Village** (June–Aug daily 9.30am–5pm; Sept–Nov & Feb–May Wed–Sun 9.30am–4pm; charge; ⱳosv.org), made up of preserved buildings brought from all over the region, gives a somewhat idealized but engaging portrait of a small New England town in the 1830s. Costumed interpreters act out roles – working in blacksmiths' shops, planting and harvesting vegetables, tending cows and the like – but they pull it off in an unusually convincing manner. The 200-acre site itself, with mature trees, ponds and dirt footpaths, is very pretty, and worth a half-day visit.

Sayle's Seafood 99 Washington St Ext ⱳsaylesseafood. com. The closest thing in town to a classic clam shack, serving chowder, fresh lobster and fried clams (at market prices) – take out for a picnic or enjoy on the porch. $–$$
Something Natural 50 Cliff Rd ⱳsomethingnatural. com. Handy deli-bakery on the way to Madaket, with home-made bread stuffed with the likes of avocado, cheddar and chutney. Find a spot at a picnic table and wash down your meal with Nantucket Nectar's "Matt Fee Tea" – named after the owner. $
Straight Wharf 6 Harbor Square ⱳstraightwharfrestaurant.com. Superb New American restaurant serving bluefish pâté and watermelon salad in an airy, waterfront dining room. The bar shifts to more of an Animal House vibe come nightfall. Reservations recommended. $$

Amherst and Northampton

North of Springfield, the **Pioneer Valley** is a verdant corridor created by the Connecticut River, home to the college towns of **AMHERST** and **NORTHAMPTON**. The region is an excellent choice for those who like to hike, bike, hang out in cafés and browse bookshops.

Emily Dickinson Museum

280 Main St, Amherst • March–May & Sept–Dec Wed–Sun 11am–4pm; June–Aug daily except Tues 10am–5pm • Full tours (hourly according to season; 1hr 30min); charge • ⱳemilydickinsonmuseum.org

As the former home of one of America's greatest poets, the **Emily Dickinson Museum** acts as a poignant tribute to the writer and throws light on her famously secluded life here in the nineteenth century. The museum comprises **The Homestead**, Dickinson's birthplace and home, and **The Evergreens** next door, home of her brother Austin and his family. The two beautifully preserved houses can only be visited on **guided tours**.

ARRIVAL AND DEPARTURE
AMHERST AND NORTHAMPTON

By bus Greyhound and Peter Pan buses from Amherst and Springfield arrive at 1 Roundhouse Plaza (☎413 586 1030) in Northampton; in Amherst, buses from Northampton and Springfield drop off at 8 Main St (at Amherst Books).

By train Amtrak's Vermonter train runs once a day between Burlington, VT and New York via Northampton, pulling into town at 170 Pleasant St, just off Main St.

ACCOMMODATION AND EATING

Black Walnut Inn 1184 N Pleasant St, Amherst ⱳblackwalnutinn.com. This attractive 1821 Federal-style B&B is shaded by tall black walnut trees, its gorgeous rooms decorated with period antiques and super-comfy beds. It's the huge, scrumptious breakfasts, though, that really win five stars. $$
★ **Herrell's Ice Cream** 8 Old South St, Northampton ⱳherrells.com. Home base for a small but illustrious regional chain of ice-cream stores; original owner Steve Herrell was apparently the first to grind up candy bars and add them to his concoctions. $
Sylvester's 111 Pleasant St, Northampton ⱳsylvestersrestaurant.com. Housed in the former home of Sylvester Graham, inventor of the graham cracker, *Sylvester's* serves up delightful treats such as waffles topped with crunchy graham cracker streusel, a hefty burger with mango salsa and cheddar cheese and steak and gorgonzola salad. $–$$

The Berkshires

1

A rich cultural history, world-class summer arts festivals and a bucolic landscape of forests and verdant hills make the **Berkshires**, at the extreme western edge of Massachusetts, an especially enticing region.

Stockbridge

Just south of I-90 and fifty miles west of Springfield, the spotless main street of **STOCKBRIDGE** is classic Berkshires, captured by the work of artist **Norman Rockwell**, who lived here for 25 years until his death in 1978.

Magnificent houses in the hills around Stockbridge include **Chesterwood**, at 4 Williamsville Rd (daily: late May to mid-Oct 10am–5pm; charge; ⓦchesterwood.org), the Colonial Revival mansion and studio of Daniel Chester French, sculptor of the Lincoln Memorial, and the gorgeously whimsical **Naumkeag**, at 5 Prospect Hill Rd, Rte-7 (April–May Fri–Sun 10am–5pm, June–Oct daily 10am–5pm; charge; ⓦthetrustees.org), built in 1886 as a summer home for the prosperous attorney Joseph Hodges Choate.

Norman Rockwell Museum

9 Rte-183 (3 miles west of Stockbridge) • May–Oct daily 10am–5pm (Aug Thurs till 7pm); Nov–April Mon–Fri 10am–4pm, Sat & Sun 10am–5pm • Charge • ⓦnrm.org

The most comprehensive of several tributes to the artist in New England, the **Norman Rockwell Museum** displays some 574 of his original paintings and drawings, most of which were *Saturday Evening Post* covers. Despite Rockwell's penchant for advertising endorsements, and the idealism that infused much of his work, it's hard not be drawn in by the artist's obsessive attention to detail, and his simple but clever ideas – see *Girl Reading the Post, Four Freedoms* and the witty *Triple Self-Portrait.*

ACCOMMODATION   STOCKBRIDGE

Red Lion Inn 30 Main St ⓦredlioninn.com. This grandmotherly inn, which also offers accommodation in historic cottages all over town, is for many the quintessential New England inn, with a vast range of rooms. Repair to the *Lion's Den*, its atmospheric cellar tavern, to get down with the rest of the town. $$

Lenox and around

Roughly five miles north of Stockbridge on US-7, tourists flock to **LENOX** each year for its summer performing arts festivals (see box, page 81), but there are also a couple of literary attractions hereabouts worth checking out. In 1902, writer **Edith Wharton** (1862–1937) joined a long list of artists summering in the Berkshires when she moved into **The Mount**, 2 Plunkett St, US-7 (May–Oct daily 10am–5pm; Nov–Feb Sat & Sun 10am–5pm; charge; ⓦedithwharton.org), an elegant country house she designed. Guided tours (50min) of the house provide a mine of information.

Author **Herman Melville** moved to **Arrowhead**, 780 Holmes Rd (late May to late Oct daily 9.30am–5pm; tours hourly 10am–4pm; charge; ⓦmobydick.org), near Pittsfield, north of Lenox, in 1850, finishing *Moby Dick* here soon after. Guided tours (45min) of his creaking wooden home – which dates from 1796 – add colour to his life and work (it's the only museum dedicated to Melville in the USA).

PERFORMING ARTS IN LENOX

Lenox is home to some of the Berkshires' most popular festivals: the summer season of **Shakespeare & Company** (70 Kemble St; ⓦshakespeare.org) and **Tanglewood**, the summer home of the Boston Symphony Orchestra (297 W St; advance tickets Sept–May ⓦbso. org); it's cheaper and arguably more enjoyable to sit on the grass [tickets from \$22]. On Rte-20 between Becket and Lee, **Jacob's Pillow** (mid-June to Aug Wed–Sun; ⓦjacobspillow.org) puts on one of the best contemporary dance festivals in the country.

1

Hancock Shaker Village

1843 W Housatonic St • Daily: mid-April to June 10am–4pm; July–Oct 10am–5pm • Charge • ⓦ hancockshakervillage.org

From 1790 until 1960, the **Hancock Shaker Village**, eleven miles northwest of Lenox, was an active **Shaker community**, and today offers an illuminating insight into this remarkable Christian sect. A branch of the Quakers that had fled England to America in 1774, the Shakers were named for the convulsive fits of glee they experienced when worshipping. Hancock retains one of the biggest collections of Shaker furniture in the country and is home to eighteen preserved clapboard buildings. Top off the experience at the Seeds Market Café, with a menu rooted in the herbs and heirloom vegetables grown in the village gardens.

ACCOMMODATION AND EATING

LENOX AND AROUND

Brava 27 Housatonic St ⓦ bravalenox.com. Popular tapas restaurant with a relaxed ambience, an excellent wine list and stellar Spanish fare like crispy calamari and *patatas bravas*. 5̄

Garden Gables Inn 135 Main St ⓦ gardengablesinn. com. Stylish, luxurious B&B set in a farm that dates back to 1780; all rooms come with LCD TVs, DVD players and afternoon sherry; many have working fireplaces. Huge breakfast buffet included. Also boasts a spa and the largest pool in the Berkshires. 5̄5̄5̄

★ **Hampton Terrace** 91 Walker St ⓦ hamptonterrace. com. This elegant 1852 gem offers deluxe rooms with clawfoot tubs, antique furniture and all the extras – the swimming pool is a real bonus in summer. 5̄5̄–5̄5̄5̄

★ **Nudel** 37 Church St ⓦ nudelrestaurant.com. Regional favourite *Nudel* offers three-course tasting menus, with dishes curated around what is local and in season; for example, roasted beets with strawberries and heirloom tomato salad with toasted bread and bacon. Reservations recommended. 5̄5̄–5̄5̄5̄

North Adams and Williamstown

In the northwest corner of the Berkshires, sleepy **NORTH ADAMS** and bucolic **WILLIAMSTOWN** are the unlikely locations of the region's premier art showcases. The former is home to the glorious **Mass MoCA** (Massachusetts Museum of Contemporary Art), 1040 Mass MoCA Way (July & Aug Mon–Wed & Sun 10am–6pm, Thurs–Sat 10am–7pm; Sept–June daily except Tues 11am–5pm; charge; ⓦmassmoca.org), a sprawling collection of modern installations (including **Sol LeWitt**'s mind-bending work), captivating changing exhibits, a wonderfully eclectic array of performers (including plenty of big names), videos and multimedia and upside-down trees in a captivating old textile mill.

In Williamstown, the highlight of **The Clark**, 225 South St (July & Aug daily 10am–5pm; Sept–June closed Mon; June–Oct charge (admission valid for two consecutive days), Oct–April first Sun free; ⓦclarkart.edu), is its 32-strong collection of Renoirs, while the ravishing **Williams College Museum of Art**, at 15 Lawrence Hall Drive (daily 10am–5pm; Thurs till 8pm; Sept–May closed Wed; free; ⓦwcma.williams.edu), specializes in American art from the late eighteenth century onwards, including the world's largest repository of work by brothers **Maurice** and **Charles Prendergast**.

ACCOMMODATION AND EATING

NORTH ADAMS AND WILLIAMSTOWN

The Guest House at Field Farm 554 Sloan Rd, Williamstown ⓦ thetrustees.org/field-farm. Six stylish bedrooms, each with private bath, in a 1948 Bauhaus-inspired country home littered with modern art and surrounded by more than 300 acres of meadows and woodlands. Open May–Dec. 5̄5̄–5̄5̄5̄

Mezze 777 Cold Spring Rd (US-7), Williamstown ⓦ mezzerestaurant.com. Urban contemporary meets rural gentility. The seasonal and locally sourced menu features

Mediterranean, Moroccan and American-influenced dishes such as roast mushrooms with cauliflower puree and crispy garlic and pasta with pork ragu and sausage. 5̄5̄

The Porches Inn 231 River St, North Adams ⓦ porches. com. Just across the street from Mass MoCA, this cosy, modern hotel occupies a row of nineteenth-century houses formerly lived in by mill workers. There's a heated outdoor swimming pool and hot tub, bonfire pit and free breakfast buffet. 5̄5̄–5̄5̄5̄

Rhode Island

A mere 48 miles long by 37 miles wide, **RHODE ISLAND** is the smallest state in the Union, yet it had a disproportionately large influence on national life: in 1652 it enacted the first law against slavery in North America, and just over ten years later it was the first to guarantee religious freedom – in the eighteenth century it also saw the beginning of the **Industrial Revolution** in America. Today, Rhode Island is a prime tourist destination, boasting nearly four dozen National Historic Landmarks and four hundred miles of spectacular coastline.

More than thirty tiny islands make up the state, including Hope, Despair and the bay's largest, Rhode Island (also known by its Native American name "Aquidneck"), which gives the state its name. **Narragansett Bay** has long been a determining factor in Rhode Island's economic development and strategic military importance, as the **Ocean State** developed through sea trade, whaling and smuggling before shifting to manufacturing in the nineteenth century. Today, the state's principal destinations are its two original ports: the colonial college town of **Providence**, and well-heeled **Newport**, home to extravagant mansions that once belonged to America's most prominent families, and still a major yachting centre.

Providence

Spread across seven hills on the Providence and Seekonk rivers, **PROVIDENCE** was Rhode Island's first settlement, founded in 1636 "in commemoration of God's providence" on land granted to Roger Williams by the Narragansett tribe.

The state's **capital** since 1790, today Providence is the third largest city in New England, with a vibrant arts scene, excellent restaurants and lots of students, drawn by the city's prestigious higher education institutions, Ivy League **Brown University** and the **Rhode Island School of Design** (RISD, or "Rizdee"). Just as enticing are the city's historic **neighbourhoods**: west of Downcity, the vibrant Italian community on **Federal Hill** boasts some exceptional restaurants, while east of the river lies **College Hill**, the oldest part of town, with many historic buildings – in fact, the city holds one of the finest collections of colonial and early Federal buildings in the nation.

Downcity and around

The hub of downtown ("**Downcity**") is the transport centre at Kennedy Plaza, surrounded by new, modern buildings, with the notable exception of the 1878 **City Hall** at its western end. Nearby **Westminster Street** is especially good for independent shops and cafés.

Just north of Downcity at the top of Constitution Hill, the **State Capitol** (Mon–Fri 8.30am–4.30pm; free; call ahead for guided tours ⍟sos.ri.gov/publicinfo/tours) dominates the city skyline with a vast dome constructed between 1895 and 1904 by noted architects McKim, Mead & White.

Just across the Providence River from the State Capitol, the **Roger Williams National Memorial** (April–Dec daily 9am–5pm; Jan–March Wed–Sun 9am–5pm; free; ⍟nps. gov/rowi) was the site of the original settlement of Providence in 1636. It's now a four-acre park honouring the life of the founder of Rhode Island – there's not much to see in the park itself, but the small **visitors' centre** at the north end includes replicas of Williams' personal effects.

College Hill and around

Much of Providence's historic legacy can be found across the river from Downcity in the **College Hill** area, an attractive tree-lined district of colonial buildings, museums and **Brown University**. The white clapboard **First Baptist Meeting House** (Tours: Mon–Fri 10am–2pm; charge; ⍟firstbaptistchurchinamerica.org), at the foot of the hill at 75 N Main St, dates from 1638, and testifies to the state's origins as a "lively experiment" in religious freedom.

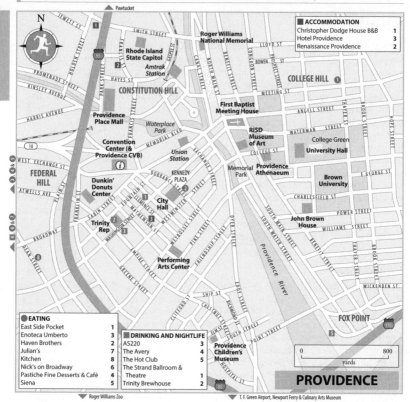

Founded in 1764 (and moved here six years later), the leafy, historic campus of **Brown University** is a rich trove of historic buildings and libraries; free guided tours are offered on weekdays and select Saturdays from the Welcome Center at 75 Waterman St (ⓦbrown.edu).

RISD Museum of Art

224 Benefit St, second entrance at 20 N Main St • Tues–Sun 10am–5pm (Thurs till 9pm) • Charge, free Sun & third Thurs of the month between 5–9pm • ⓦ risdmuseum.org

Providence's second major college is the prestigious **Rhode Island School of Design**, founded in 1877. The school's impressive **Museum of Art** houses over eighty thousand works in 45 galleries, a skilfully melded hotchpotch of five industrial buildings and houses between Benefit and Main streets. The collection covers everything from ancient Egypt to Asian arts and European paintings from just about every period – everything is superbly presented and the galleries are small enough to be easily absorbed.

WATERFIRE

Throughout the summer months, the spectacular event known as **WaterFire** (select Sat evenings May–Oct; free; ⓦ waterfire.org) enthralls visitors and locals alike with one hundred bonfires set at sunset along the centre of the Providence River. Tended by gondoliers and accompanied by suitably inspiring music, the fires burn until just past midnight, while entertainers and food vendors keep the crowds happy.

Federal Hill

Federal Hill, west of Downcity, is Providence's **Little Italy**, greeting visitors with the traditional symbol of welcome, a bronze pine cone, on the entrance arch on Atwells Avenue. Settled by Italian immigrants in the 1910s and 1920s, this area is now one of the friendliest in the city, alive with cafés, delis, bakeries and bars, and with a lively piazza around the Italianate fountain in **DePasquale Square**.

ARRIVAL AND DEPARTURE   PROVIDENCE

By plane T.F. Green Airport (ⓦpvdairport.com) in Warwick, 9 miles south of downtown, is served by most US carriers. RIPTA bus #14 and #20 ($2) run to downtown (Kennedy Plaza). Taxis should be around $40.

By train The train station, 100 Gaspee St, is served by Amtrak services from Boston and New York, and the MBTA commuter rail from Boston. Taxis meet most trains.

Destinations Boston (20 daily; 50min); New Haven (18 daily; 1hr 25min); New York City (18–20 daily; around 3hr).

By bus Greyhound and Peter Pan buses stop downtown at the Kennedy Plaza hub.

Destinations Boston (3 daily; 1hr); New Haven (3 daily; 2hr 45min); New London (3 daily; 1hr 45min); New York City (3–4 daily; 5hr 25min).

GETTING AROUND AND TOURS

By bus Local RIPTA buses are easy to use and convenient (ⓦripta.com).

Historical tours The Rhode Island Historical Society (ⓦrihs.org) leads walking tours through the city.

ACCOMMODATION   SEE MAP PAGE 84

Christopher Dodge House B&B 11 W Park St ⓦprovidence-hotel.com. Small boutique hotel in an Italianate townhouse dating from 1858, boasting 11ft ceilings, marble fireplaces and full breakfasts. Standard rooms are simply but comfortably decked out with plush beds and cable TV; superior rooms are a lot bigger. $$

Hotel Providence 139 Mathewson St ⓦhotelprovidence.com. Newish luxury hotel with eighty plush and colourful rooms themed on classic novels from the likes of Tolstoy and Dumas, and a number of trendy restaurant downstairs. $$–$$$

★ **Renaissance Providence** 5 Avenue of the Arts ⓦmarriott.com. Luxurious downtown hotel on the site of a former Masonic temple, with 272 comfortable, well-appointed rooms, some overlooking the State House. A 5min walk from the train station. $$$

EATING   SEE MAP PAGE 84

Providence boasts excellent **food** options. Thayer Street is lined with inexpensive places popular with students, while nearby Wickenden Street has a more mature clientele. Rhode Island is the proud home of several unique (and sickeningly sweet) beverages, the most famous of which is the state drink, **coffee milk**, made with syrup and served all over Providence; a "**coffee cabinet**" is a milkshake prepared by blending ice cream with milk and said syrup.

★ **East Side Pocket** 278 Thayer St ⓦeastsidepocket. com. Bulging falafel sandwiches and other Middle Eastern "pockets" – filled with everything from creamy hummus to baba ganoush – served hot, fresh and cheap at this popular student hangout. $

Enoteca Umberto 256 Atwells Ave ⓦfacebook.com/enotecaumberto. Dining at this small and warmly lit restaurant is like pulling up a chair at an Italian family table. Co-owner and chef Lia Bellini turns out lovingly prepared pastas, like the classic Pomodoro, tossed with ripe tomatoes, olive oil and mascarpone, and the stellar Ceci, with chickpeas, white wine, garlic and Pecorino Romano. Toast the meal with a glass (or three) of Italian red. $–$$

Haven Brothers Next to City Hall, Fulton St ⓦhavenbrothersmobile.com. This diner-on-wheels has

pitched up here nightly since 1888, serving classic hot dogs, burgers and fries. $

Julian's 318 Broadway ⓦjuliansprovidence.com. Innovative contemporary restaurant, serving everything from curried pork rolls to vegan black bean burgers to crispy smoked tofu salad. $–$$

Kitchen 94 Carpenter St ☎401 272 1117. For breakfast devotees: only fourteen seats, and usually an hour wait to get in, but you're rewarded with fluffy croissant French toast, *huevos rancheros* and slamming bacon. Cash only. $

★ **Nick's on Broadway** 500 Broadway ⓦnicksonbroadway.com. Though it's a fair hike from anything else (it's in the West End), brunch lovers flock here for the best-in-town breakfast specials and brioche French toast. $

Pastiche Fine Desserts & Café 92 Spruce St ⓦpastichefinedesserts.com. This blue clapboard cottage on Federal Hill offers fabulous home-baked lemon custard tarts, mascarpone torte, banana creams and more. $

Siena 238 Atwells Ave ⓦsienari.com. The current trendsetter in Federal Hill, with a sparkling Tuscan menu featuring wood-fired pizzas, superb pastas and luscious wood-grilled meats. $$

1

DRINKING AND NIGHTLIFE

SEE MAP PAGE 84

The city's nightlife bustles around Empire and Washington streets, south of Kennedy Plaza in Downcity, and along Thayer Street near Brown University during term-time.

AS220 115 Empire St ⓦ as220.org. This one-of-a-kind café/bar/gallery – hip, eclectic and celebrating the joy of creativity – features local art, photography, performances and all manner of classes, from dance to printmaking. Check the website to find out about its other galleries and events. $\overline{\underline{\$\$}}$

★ **The Avery** 18 Luongo Memorial Sq ⓦ averyprovidence.com. When the night calls for creative cocktails in sultry, speakeasy-style digs, come to The Avery. The drinks menu changes with the season, the music is unique and hopping and the lights are perennially dim, maximizing the cosy, intimate factor. $\overline{\underline{\$\$}}$

The Hot Club 575 S Water St ⓦ hotclubprov.com. This Providence institution is more of a bar than a club, where you can sip drinks and enjoy free popcorn – or heartier fare like juicy fish nuggets – on an outdoor terrace right on the river. $\overline{\underline{\$}}$

The Strand Ballroom & Theatre 79 Washington St ⓦ thestrandri.com. Formerly Lupo's Heartbreak Hotel – which was *the* spot in town to see nationally recognized bands – The Strand is continuing the legacy with big names in rock, pop, blues, funk, country, metal and more. $\overline{\underline{\$\$}}$–$\overline{\underline{\$\$\$}}$

Trinity Brewhouse 186 Fountain St ⓦ trinitybrewhouse.com. The interior of this hip brewhouse-meets-sports-bar feels a bit like the dining hall of Harry Potter's Hogwarts – all oversized chandeliers, wood-panelled walls and cathedral windows. Everything on tap has been brewed in-house; try the Rhode Island IPA. $\overline{\underline{\$\$}}$

Newport

With its gorgeous location on Aquidneck Island, fleets of polished yachts, rose-coloured sunsets and long-standing association with America's fine and fabulous, **NEWPORT** is straight out of a fairy tale. The Kennedys were married here (Jackie was a local girl); and though F. Scott Fitzgerald set his novel **The Great Gatsby** in Long Island, it's no surprise that the iconic 1974 movie version was filmed in Newport. Indeed, many of the town's opulent *fin-de-siècle* mansions – former summer homes of the likes of the Astors and Vanderbilts – are still owned by America's current crop of mega-wealthy.

Stroll beyond the extravagant facades, though, and you'll find much more. The streets are laden with history, and sights commemorate everything from the town's pioneering role in religious freedom in America to the landing of French forces during the Revolutionary War. Newport's prime seaside location also means that the views are often, if not always, free – a short drive and you're greeted by unrivalled shores, with rugged seascapes and long swaths of sand.

The Newport mansions

Daily: April to mid-Nov usually 10am–6pm but check online as hours fluctuate according to property; Marble House, The Elms & The Breakers also mid-Nov to Jan daily 10am–5pm • Charge; combined tickets available (you can easily walk between these properties but parking is also available at all of them) • ⓦ newportmansions.org

When sociologist Thorstein Veblen visited Newport at the turn of the twentieth century, he was so horrified by the extravagance that he coined the phrase "conspicuous consumption". From the 1880s, this had been the summer playground of the New York elite, with wealthy families competing to outdo each other with lavish **mansions** and annual parties. The Gilded Age lasted just a few decades; beginning with the introduction of US income tax in 1913, by the early 1940s most of the mansions had

---

NEWPORT'S FESTIVALS

There's always something afoot in Newport, particularly at the end of July for the **Newport Folk Festival** (where Bob Dylan got his start in 1963; ⓦ newportfolk.org) and in August during the high-profile **Jazz Festival** (ⓦ newportjazzfest.org). **Bridgefest** (ⓦ newportbridgefest.com) also brings forth live music, so named because it "bridges" the days between the Folk and Jazz festivals. The **Newport Music Festival** (ⓦ newportmusic.org) in July boasts classical music performed at the mansions, while the clam chowder cookoff in June is one of the region's biggest events (ⓦ newportwaterfrontevents.com).

closed for good; the **Preservation Society of Newport County** maintains the bulk of the dozen or so houses open for public viewing today.

The mansions each boast their own version of Gilded Age excess: **Marble House**, built in 1892 for William Vanderbilt with its golden ballroom and adjacent Chinese teahouse; **Rosecliff**, with a colourful rose garden and heart-shaped staircase; the ornate French **The Elms**, known for its gardens; and Cornelius Vanderbilt II's **The Breakers**, an Italian Renaissance-style palace overlooking the ocean and the grandest of the lot. Besides those, a number of earlier, smaller houses, including the quirky Gothic Revival cottage **Kingscote**, built in 1841, may well make for a more interesting excursion. Note that many houses can only be seen on hourly tours; unless you're a mansion nut, viewing one or two should suffice to get a glimpse of the opulence.

One way to see the mansions on the cheap is to peer in the back gardens from the **Cliff Walk**, which begins on Memorial Boulevard where it meets First (Easton) Beach. This spectacular three-and-a-half-mile oceanside path alternates from pretty stretches lined by jasmine and wild roses to rugged rocky passes.

ARRIVAL AND GETTING AROUND   NEWPORT

By bus Peter Pan buses and RIPTA bus #60 from Providence arrive at the visitor centre downtown. From here, RIPTA bus #67 runs every 15–20min (Mon–Sat 8am–8pm, Sun 9.40am–8pm) downtown along Bellevue Ave, past most of the mansions, ending beyond Rough Point at the end of the Cliff Walk.

By bike Rent bikes at Ten Speed Spokes, 18 Elm St (Mon–Fri 10am–6pm, Sat 10am–5pm, Sun noon–5pm; ⓦ tenspeedspokes.com).

INFORMATION AND TOURS

Visitor centre 23 America's Cup Ave (daily 9am–5pm; ⓦ discovernewport.org).

Walking tours Newport Historical Society (ⓦ newporthistorytours.org) runs a range of themed walking tours through downtown.

Cruises Easily the most relaxing way to see Newport is on a cruise; try Classic Cruises of Newport (ⓦ cruisenewport. com), which offers trips from Bannister's Wharf on the beautiful 72ft schooner *Madeleine* (5 daily in summer; 1hr 30min) and motor yacht *Rum Runner II* (5 daily in summer; 1hr 15min).

ACCOMMODATION AND EATING

★ **Belle's Cafe** Newport Shipyard, 1 Washington St ⓦ newportshipyard.com. At this well-kept secret, tucked away from the downtown bustle, you can grab two delicious lobster rolls, plus excellent breakfasts – try the crab cake benedict in the company of the world's finest yachts. \$–\$\$

Black Pearl Bannister's Wharf ⓦ blackpearlnewport. com. Harbourside institution famous for its clam chowder; opt for more formal options in the *Commodore's Room* (*escargots bourguignon*) and less formal ones in the *Tavern* (*escargots* with garlic butter). \$\$–\$\$\$

Flo's Clam Shack 4 Wave Ave ⓦ flosclamshacks.com. Hugely popular joint across from First Beach. With extremely cheap and good bowls of clam chowder and platters of a dozen clam cakes, it's worth the wait. Cash only. \$

★ **Forty 1° North** 351 Thames St, ⓦ 41north.com. This boutique waterfront hotel is a sun-flooded blend of classy and casual, with spacious rooms, mosaic-tiled bathrooms, rainfall showers and cosy fireplaces. Or, splurge on one of four lovely cottages, each with a full kitchen. The Red Cottage is a charm, with wood floors, a breezy courtyard and loft-style bedroom. The Grill at Forty 1° North offers waterside dining of grilled seafood and meats. \$\$\$\$,

cottages from \$\$\$\$

Hilltop Inn 2 Kay St, at Bellevue Ave ⓦ hilltopnewport. com. Newport's most popular B&B occupies a gorgeous house completed in 1910. The five rooms all have comfy Victorian interiors, LCD TVs with generous bathrooms and quality breakfasts. Enjoy the afternoon tea (daily 3–5pm), and home-made cakes and port left out in the evenings. \$\$\$

★ **Ivy Lodge** 12 Clay St ⓦ ivylodge.com. Boasting a stunning 33ft gothic entry hall with wraparound balconies, this B&B beauty has eight rooms filled with antique reproduction furniture and modern amenities like cable TV, DVR and whirlpool tubs. Prices plummet in the off-season. \$\$\$

Mamma Luisa 673 Thames St ⓦ mammaluisa.com. The best Italian restaurant in Newport, with fabulous home-made pastas and refreshing fruit sorbets. \$\$

Marshall Slocum Guest House 29 Kay St ⓦ marshallslocuminn.com. Eleven comfortable period-style rooms in a historic 1855 B&B near Bellevue Ave, with gardens and gourmet breakfasts. \$\$

Rose Island Lighthouse Rose Island, Narragansett Bay

1

Ⓦ roseislandlighthouse.org. Worth it for the sheer novelty of staying in a lighthouse (a museum during the day), and for the magical sunset views. It's a bit like camping, with an outdoor shower, a bring-your-own food policy and limited water. Leave your car in Newport (the hotel arranges a car permit) and you'll be taken over by ferry. $–$$

Salvation Café 140 Broadway Ⓦ salvationcafe.com. Hip spot off the main drag, with exotic concoctions such as salmon with lemon-coconut rice and Mongolian barbecue ribs with snow peas. $$

Scarpetta 1 Goat Island Ⓦ scarpettarestaurants.com. The splashy Scarpetta brings Hamptons style and flair to Newport. The classy restaurant forms part of the waterfront Gurneys Newport, which opened in 2017 on Goat Island, and is the sister resort to Gurneys Montauk in Long Island, New York. Gurneys can get pricey in high season, so if you're not ready to splurge on a room, dine at Scarpetta, which gives you the chance to experience the resort over dinner, while taking in the gorgeous view of sparkling waters, bobbing sailboats and the elegant arc of the Newport bridge. The Italian cuisine includes fresh seafood and grilled meats, from branzino with snap peas to lobster with asparagus to duck and foie gras ravioli. $$$

William Gyles Guesthouse 16 Howard St Ⓦ newporthostel.com. Newport's only hostel is welcoming and comfortable, with basic breakfast, shared kitchen and a small garden. Lower rates in the cooler months. Open May–Nov. Dorms $

Connecticut

Just ninety miles long by 55 miles wide, **CONNECTICUT** is New England's southernmost state and the most influenced by New York City; thousands of commuters make the trip each day, and many of the opulent mansions are owned by Wall Street bankers. As a result, tourism here is of a sophisticated sort, with art galleries, vineyards, historical houses, museums and increasingly eclectic cuisine on offer, while the state's lesser-known natural offerings along the densely populated coast make for pleasant exploring.

The coast is studded with enticing small towns, from the colonial charms of **Mystic** and **Stonington** to hip **New London** and intellectual **New Haven**, home of Yale University. Further inland, the state capital at **Hartford** is a real surprise, with a gradually regenerating downtown and a trio of attractions.

Mystic

Thanks to Julia Roberts, **MYSTIC** is best-known throughout the USA for its pizza joint, but this elegant New England town offers far more than that – a host of independent stores and galleries, the intriguing maritime re-creations of **Mystic Seaport** and the beluga whales at **Mystic Aquarium**. Most of the attractions lie in the **historic downtown** area, a major shipbuilding centre in the nineteenth century, while **Old Mystic** comprises a couple of quaint streets a few miles north. The two are divided by I-95 (exit 90) and **Olde Mistick Village**, a slightly kitsch shopping mall.

Mystic Aquarium & Institute for Exploration

55 Coogan Blvd, I-95 exit 90 • Daily: April to early Oct 9am–5.50pm; mid-Oct to Nov & March 9am–4.50pm; Dec–Feb 10am–4.50pm • Charge • Ⓦ mysticaquarium.org

The outstanding **Mystic Aquarium & Institute for Exploration** is home to more than four thousand marine specimens, including penguins, sea lions, sharks, stingrays, piranhas and the only **beluga whales** in New England – specially designed tanks allow close-up encounters with these three graceful snow-white creatures (albeit through reinforced glass).

Mystic Seaport

75 Greenmanville Ave • April–Oct daily 9am–5pm; Nov daily 10am–4pm; Dec & mid-Feb to March Thurs–Sun 10am–4pm • Charge • Ⓦ mysticseaport.org

The **Museum of America & the Sea**, or just **Mystic Seaport**, north of downtown, is one of the nation's largest and most enjoyable maritime museums. Founded in 1929 on a nineteen-acre wedge of riverfront once occupied by shipyards, the site is roughly divided into three parts: the **Preservation Shipyard** is primarily dedicated to the restoration of the 1841 *Charles W. Morgan*, while further along, more than sixty buildings housing old-style workshops and stores reflect life in a seafaring **village** c.1876. The final section contains a series of more formal **exhibit halls**, including the absorbing **Voyages** gallery, with multimedia displays covering the whole span of American maritime history.

ARRIVAL AND INFORMATION | MYSTIC

By bus Greyhound stops in New London, 10 miles west of Mystic.

By train Amtrak services from New York and Boston pull in at 2 Roosevelt Ave off US-1 downtown (no ticket office; buy at platform kiosks or on the train).

Visitor centres Mystic's main information office lies in Olde Mistick Village, off I-95 (Mon–Sat 10am–5pm, Sun 11am–4pm; ⓦ ctvisit.com), and can help with finding hotels. There's a smaller welcome centre (Mon–Fri 9am–4.30pm, Sat & Sun 10am–4pm; ⓦ mysticchamber.org) at the train station.

ACCOMMODATION AND EATING

Bravo Bravo 19 E Main St ⓦ bravobravoct.com. This Italian seafood specialist is the best place for a gourmet splurge in Mystic. Feast on lobster ravioli, linguine with clams or seafood stew. $\overline{\$\$\$}$

Mystic Pizza 56 W Main St ⓦ mysticpizza.com. The tourists outside this otherwise ordinary family-run pizza place are here because of the eponymous 1988 Julia Roberts movie, largely filmed in the area – business boomed in the 1990s as a result, and though things have calmed down since, plenty of pilgrims still come to taste a "slice of heaven"; huge, tasty pizzas. $\overline{\$}$–$\overline{\$\$}$

S&P Oyster Co 1 Holmes St ⓦ sp-oyster.com. Fine seafood on the waterfront overlooking the drawbridge – the best place to enjoy Mystic in the summer. Start with the halibut ceviche, and then dive into the seafood paella, heaped with monkfish, shrimp, mussels and Spanish chorizo. $\overline{\$\$}$–$\overline{\$\$\$}$

★ **Steamboat Inn** 73 Steamboat Wharf ⓦ steamboatinnmystic.com. A luxurious downtown option, whose eleven elegant rooms overlook the water and are furnished in a modern, country-inn style with sherry and sweets at night and lots of wood-burning fireplaces. $\overline{\$\$\$}$

Whaler's Inn 20 E Main St ⓦ whalersinnmystic.com. Right in the heart of downtown Mystic, near the drawbridge over the river, this is the most central choice. The well-run hotel comprises five historic buildings – *Hoxie House* rooms have the best river views. Parking included. $\overline{\$}$–$\overline{\$\$}$

Stonington

Tucked away on the coast near the state's eastern border, **STONINGTON** is a gorgeous old fishing village, originally settled in 1649. Its main road, **Water Street**, is dotted with restaurants and shops, while parallel **Main Street** contains some dazzling examples of colonial and Federal clapboard architecture. At 7 Water St, the **Old Lighthouse Museum** (May–Oct daily except Wed 10am–5pm; charge, includes admission to Captain Nathaniel B. Palmer House; ⓦ stoningtonhistory.org) recounts town life through the centuries, with exhibits on seal-hunting, a collection of local salt-glazed ceramics from the short-lived Stonington potteries and trinkets from Asia brought back by the town's notable seafarers. Museum admission includes access to the Italianate **Captain Nathaniel B. Palmer House**, 40 Palmer St (May–Oct daily 1–5pm; charge, includes admission to Old Lighthouse Museum; ☎ 860 535 8445), at the north end of town, celebrating Stonington's premier seafarer (credited with one of the earliest sightings of Antarctica in 1820).

ACCOMMODATION AND EATING | STONINGTON

Inn at Stonington 60 Water St ⓦ theinnatstonington.com. In the heart of Stonington's historic centre, this charming hotel features eighteen rooms with views of the harbour or village, with fireplaces, jacuzzis and polished stone tiles. $\overline{\$\$\$}$

★ **Noah's Restaurant** 113 Water St ⓦ noahsfinefood.com. This place is known for its superb home-style cooking, with an eclectic menu featuring everything from jambalaya to something conjured up from that day's local catch. $\overline{\$\$}$

Orchard Street Inn 41 Orchard St ⓦ orchardstreetinn.com. Five elegant rooms, some with garden patio, in a quiet clapboard cottage. There are free bikes to explore the local area. $\overline{\$\$\$}$

1 New London

A booming **whaling port** in the nineteenth century, **NEW LONDON** is a lively, multicultural working city, with two absorbing attractions on its outskirts. The town relied heavily on military-base revenue in the twentieth century, but struggled in the 1990s due to spending cuts. Though parts of town remain edgy, New London is reviving today, thanks largely to the presence of Connecticut College, the US Coast Guard Academy and pharmaceutical giant Pfizer's R&D headquarters in nearby Groton.

Monte Cristo Cottage

325 Pequot Ave • June–Aug Wed–Sun 11am–4pm • Charge • ⓦ theoneill.org

Two miles south of downtown, the **Monte Cristo Cottage** faithfully preserves the memory of **Eugene O'Neill** (1888–1953), one of America's most acclaimed playwrights and winner of the Nobel Prize for Literature in 1936. His summer house is full of period fittings and furnishings (some original), and enthusiastic guides fill in the biographical details.

US Coast Guard Academy

Academy 31 Mohegan Ave, I-95 exit 83 • Tours Mon & Fri; self-guided tours daily 9am–4.30pm; cadet drill fall and spring Fri 4pm • Free, ID required • ⓦ uscga.edu

The **US Coast Guard Academy**, just off I-95 (1.5 miles north of downtown), spreads out on a leafy 103-acre, red-brick campus built in the 1930s and overlooking the Thames. Visitors are welcome to explore the grounds and the **US Coast Guard Museum**, charting two centuries of Coast Guard history and housing the figurehead from the USS *Eagle*, a 295ft barque launched in 1936.

The **National Coast Guard Museum** is currently being planned on the banks of the Thames River. The proposed museum will include a concert pavilion to showcase live music and bands, including the esteemed United States Coast Guard Band. No official opening date has yet been announced.

ARRIVAL AND INFORMATION   NEW LONDON

By bus Greyhound buses stop downtown at 45 Water St, connecting New London with Boston via Providence, and New York via New Haven.

By train Trains serve New London's Union Station, at 27 Water St, right in the heart of downtown and conveniently close to the ferry docks.

By ferry The New London Ferry Dock, 2 Ferry St, hosts ferries to Orient Point on Long Island via the Cross Sound Ferry (hourly; 1hr 20min; ⓦ longislandferry.com) and one to Block Island, RI (Block Island Express; June–Sept up to 4/day; 1hr 15min; ⓦ goblockisland.com).

EATING

Fred's Shanty 272 Pequot Ave ⓦ freds-shanty.com. This classic food shack has been knocking out tasty hot dogs, fries, shakes, burgers, lobster salad rolls and more since 1972. Overlooks the Thames River, south of downtown. 💲

Lazy Leopard Thai Café 45 Bank St ☎ 860 333 1329. Very close to the train station, this friendly place serves excellent takes on Thai classics like green curry, coconut soup and iced tea in addition to a rainbow of sushi. 💲💲

Hartford

The capital of Connecticut, **HARTFORD**, is fast becoming one of the most alluring destinations in New England. The legacy of America's greatest writer is evocatively preserved at the **Mark Twain House and Museum**, while the **Wadsworth Atheneum** owns an astonishing collection of art. The town was a **manufacturing** hub in the eighteenth century, and its architectural highlights include the gold-domed **State Capitol** at 210 Capitol Ave (1hr tours hourly Mon–Fri 9.15am–1.15pm; July & Aug additional tour at 2.15pm; free; ⓦ cga.ct.gov/capitoltours), an 1878 concoction of styles. By contrast, down by the river the cutting-edge **Connecticut Science Center** (July & Aug daily

10am–5pm; Sept–June closed Mon; charge; ⓦctsciencecenter.org) is a magnet for families, with mind-boggling (and wildly entertaining) interactive exhibits.

The city remains a bit rough outside the centre. To be on the safe side, use common-sense precautions and stick to the main sights.

Wadsworth Atheneum Museum of Art

600 Main St • Wed–Fri 11am–5pm, Sat & Sun 10am–5pm • Charge, free Wed–Sun 4–5pm and second Sat of the month 10am–1pm • ⓦ thewadsworth.org

Hartford's pride and joy is the Greek Revival **Wadsworth Atheneum Museum of Art**, founded by Daniel Wadsworth in 1842 and the nation's oldest continuously operating public art museum. In 2015, the museum unveiled the fruits of its extraordinary $33 million, five-year renovation. The palatial **Morgan Great Hall** (1915) is the showpiece, painted a striking deep blue and hung to the rafters with Baroque and modern works. Elsewhere, the museum's world-class collection, spanning more than five thousand years, includes a precious ensemble of 160 **Hudson River School** paintings and a significant contemporary collection.

Mark Twain House and Museum

351 Farmington Ave • Daily 9.30am–5.30pm • Charge • ⓦ marktwainhouse.org • CT Transit buses #60, #62, #64, #66 from downtown Hartford

A mile west of downtown, the hilltop community known as Nook Farm was home in the 1870s to next-door neighbours Mark Twain and Harriet Beecher Stowe. The bizarrely ornate **Mark Twain House and Museum** was where the giant of American literature penned many of his classic works between 1874 and 1891. Tours offer tantalizing insights into the author's life, and also draw attention to the lavish and somewhat eccentric way the house was furnished – black-and-orange brickwork, whimsical carvings and the only domestic Tiffany interior open to the public. Twain's legendary wit and innovative writing style are highlighted by exhibits of his work and the engrossing Ken Burns biographical documentary shown in the **museum**.

Harriet Beecher Stowe Center

77 Forest St • April–Dec Mon–Sat 9.30am–5pm, Sun noon–5pm; Jan–March closed Tues • Charge • ⓦ harrietbeecherstowecenter.org

In 1852, **Harriet Beecher Stowe** made history with *Uncle Tom's Cabin*, her groundbreaking and best-selling anti-slavery novel. As a woman of the nineteenth century Stowe had no right to vote, yet she was able to turn public opinion decisively against slavery and became hugely influential. The **Harriet Beecher Stowe Center** serves as a poignant memorial to the author, and includes the white Victorian Gothic home she bought in 1873.

ARRIVAL AND INFORMATION   HARTFORD

By plane Bradley International Airport (ⓦbradleyairport. com), 12 miles north of the city, is served by the hourly CT Transit Bradley Flyer (ⓦcttransit.com) to Union Station and Old State House in downtown Hartford. Taxis are also available outside (around $45 to downtown).

By bus Long-distance buses pull into the Union Station terminal.

Destinations Boston (12 daily; 1hr 50min–2hr 40min); Brattleboro, VT (1 daily; 2hr 20min); New Haven (6 daily;

1hr); New York City (26 daily; 2hr 30min–3hr); Providence, RI (2 daily; 2hr 15min).

By train Union Station is at 1 Union Place, just off I-84, exit 48/49, on the western edge of downtown Hartford.

Destinations New Haven (6 daily; 47–58min); New York City (2–3 daily; around 3hr); Springfield, MA (6 daily; 40–50min).

Visitor centre 100 Pearl St (Mon–Fri 9am–5pm; ⓦletsgoarts. org). There's also information at the Old State House.

EATING

First & Last Tavern 939 Maple Ave ⓦhartford. firstandlasttavern.com. Local favourite, no-frills Italian diner since 1936, with great pasta (try the exquisite clam sauce) and brick-oven pizzas – mediums (15-inch). $–$$

★ **Mozzicato De Pasquale's Bakery & Pastry Shop** 329 Franklin Ave ⓦmozzicatobakery.com. Historic old-time Italian café combining the DePasquale Bakery founded in 1908 with the pastry shop opened by Italian immigrant

1

Gino Mozzicato in 1973. Serves delicious coffee and pastries – try the whipped cream cakes, Italian cookies and ethereal gelato. ⑤

★ **Rein's Deli** 435 Hartford Turnpike, 11 miles north in Vernon (exit 65 off I-84) ⓦ reinsdeli.com. Since 1973, road-weary souls have made the pilgrimage to this New York-style deli for its bulging pastrami sandwiches and

addictive home-made pickles. ⑤

Salute 100 Trumbull St ⓦ salutehartford.com. Top-notch contemporary Italian cuisine enhanced by super-attentive, friendly service. Try the penne à la vodka or sweet potato ravioli, but save space for the cheesecake. Stop by the lounge for draft beers and wines during weekday happy hour. ⑤⑤

New Haven

One of Connecticut's founding colonies, **NEW HAVEN** is best known for the idyllic Ivy League campus of **Yale University**, quality **pizza** joints and two world-class **art galleries**. It also offers some of the best restaurants, most exciting nightspots and most diverting cultural festivals in all of New England. Founded in 1638 by a group of wealthy Puritans from London, New Haven became the seat of Yale University in 1716, the third oldest college in the nation. Today, its leafy campus and magnificent Gothic architecture continue to exert a veritable historic presence. Tensions between the city and the university once made New Haven an uneasy place, though an active symbiosis has thrived since the early 2000s. Residents are encouraged to take advantage of the university's cultural and public offerings, and more than half of the student body volunteers in some sort of local outreach programme. The city is undergoing significant **development** in the downtown area, with vacant spaces around George Street slowly being transformed into new residential, cultural and commercial spaces.

The Green

Downtown, centred on the **Green**, retains a historic atmosphere. Laid out in 1638, the Green was the site of the city's original settlement and also functioned as a meeting area and burial ground. In its centre, the crypt of the 1814 **Center Church** (April–Oct Thurs & Sat 11am–1pm; free; ⓦ newhavencenterchurch.org) holds tombs dating back to 1687. Surrounding the Green are a number of stately government buildings and the student-filled **Chapel Street district**, a lively area filled with bookshops, independent stores, cafés and bars.

Yale University campus

Yale Visitor Information Center, 149 Elm St • Tours Mon–Fri 10.30am & 2pm, Sat & Sun 1.30pm • Free • ⓦ visitorcenter.yale.edu/tours

Founded in 1701, **Yale University** is one of the world's great seats of learning, with some eleven thousand students and one of the largest libraries in the USA. You can visit most of the major buildings (just north of the Green) on self-guided tours, but to get inside one of the twelve colleges and learn about contemporary life at Yale, take a **guided tour** from the **visitor centre** (the oldest house in New Haven, built in 1767), conducted by students. Tour highlights include the cobbled courtyards of **Old Campus**, 216ft **Harkness Tower** and cathedral-like **Sterling Memorial Library**.

Yale Center for British Art

1080 Chapel St • Tues–Sat 10am–5pm, Sun noon–5pm • Free • ⓦ britishart.yale.edu

The Louis Kahn-designed **Yale Center for British Art** contains an exceptional collection of British paintings and sculpture, donated to Yale by Paul Mellon in 1966. The highlights reside in the fourth-floor galleries of pre-1850 work, with special sections on **Turner**, **Hogarth** and **Constable**.

Yale University Art Gallery

1111 Chapel St • Tues–Fri 10am–5pm, Sat & Sun 11am–5pm; guided tours Sat & Sun 1.30pm • Free • ⓦ artgallery.yale.edu

The beautifully presented work on display at the **Yale University Art Gallery** has to be one of the best culture-vulture bargains in New England. The collection now has more than 185,000 objects dating from ancient Egyptian times to the present. Highlights include the exquisite **Italian Renaissance** collection, with pieces from Sienese School masters such as **Duccio**, and vivid Dutch portraits by **Frans Hals** and **Rubens**.

Yale Peabody Museum of Natural History

170 Whitney Ave • Tues–Sat 10am–5pm, Sun noon–5pm • Charge • ⓦ peabody.yale.edu

Yale's **Peabody Museum of Natural History** is easily recognizable by the huge bronze statue of a *Torosaurus latus* out front, a good indication of what's inside – a gasp-inducing collection of complete **dinosaur fossils**. The museum offers plenty more, however; skeletons of giant mastodons and sabre-tooth cats, early human fossils and rare Native American artefacts, including Red Cloud's feathered headdress.

ARRIVAL AND INFORMATION
NEW HAVEN

By bus Union Station, six blocks southeast of the Yale downtown campus, is home to Peter Pan and Greyhound services.
Destinations Boston (3–4 daily; 4hr); Hartford (6 daily; 1hr); New York (9 daily; 1hr 50min).
By train Union Station serves Amtrak trains and Metro-North (ⓦmta.info/mnr), which serve all the stations between here and New York City at 30min intervals (up to

10min intervals during rush hours). If you arrive at night, grab a taxi to your hotel; Bradley Taxi (ⓞ 860 992 2112) has a good reputation.
Destinations Boston (17 daily; 2hr 30min); New London (11 daily; 50min); New York (20 daily; 1hr 35min).
Visitor centre Just off the Green at 1000 Chapel St (Mon–Wed 10am–9pm, Thurs–Sat 10am–10pm, Sun noon–5pm; ⓦinfonewhaven.com).

ACCOMMODATION

Book well in advance if you intend to visit around Yale graduation in June, before the beginning of the term in September, and during Parents' Weekend in October. Cheaper **motels** are available along the I-91 corridor.
★ **The Blake Hotel** 9 High St ⓦtheblakenewhaven. com. A welcome addition to the New Haven hotel landscape, this industrial-chic boutique property opened in 2019, and is named after Alice Blake, the first female graduate of Yale Law School. The studio-style rooms, complete with kitchenette with Williams Sonoma kitchenware, have rustic flair, including hardwood floors, snow-white walls and linens and upholstered headboards. The on-site Hamilton Park restaurant, helmed by chef Matt Lambert, features New England cuisine. Sip craft cocktails at the sexy rooftop

bar High George, while nibbling from the raw bar. $\overline{S}\overline{S}$
Courtyard New Haven at Yale 30 Whalley Ave ⓦmarriott.com. Conveniently located just west of Yale campus, with 207 plush, modern rooms; some good weekend deals. $\overline{S}\overline{S}$
New Haven Hotel 229 George St ⓦnewhavenhotel. com. Stylish hotel offering modern rooms equipped with flatscreen TVs. There's also a handy 24hr laundry and gym. $\overline{S}\overline{S}$
★ **The Study at Yale** 1157 Chapel St ⓦstudyatyale. com. This elegant boutique hotel features sizeable rooms with flatscreen TVs, large workspaces and marble-floored bathrooms. Its oversized windows have postcard-perfect views of the Yale campus, and there's great coffee and reading material in the lobby. $\overline{S}\overline{S}$–$\overline{S}\overline{S}\overline{S}$

EATING

New Haven offers an eclectic range of restaurants, many located around the Green and on Chapel and College streets. Savour this university town's intellectual atmosphere at one of many fine downtown cafés, and don't leave without trying the pizza, available at the family-run Italian restaurants in Wooster Square. In warm weather months, enjoy a moveable feast – dozens of food carts (Thai, Italian, Greek, baked goods) set up shop on Sachem Street.
Atticus Bookstore Café 1082 Chapel St ⓦatticusbookstorecafe.com. Artisan breads, sandwiches, scones and great breakfast plates including bacon, gruyère cheese, two eggs over easy and arugula heaped on a brioche bun, all served in a relaxed bookshop. $\overline{S}$
Frank Pepe's Pizzeria 157 Wooster St ⓦpepespizzeria. com. A Wooster St institution since 1925, drawing crowds

with its coal-fired pizzas. Order the white clam pizza for the full experience. $\overline{S}$
Louis' Lunch 261–263 Crown St ⓦlouislunch.com. This small, dark, ancient burger landmark allegedly served America's first hamburger, c.1900. It's still served on slices of toasted flat bread, with strictly no ketchup – cheese, tomato and onion are the only acceptable garnishes. Cash only. Hours vary, but generally $\overline{S}$
Sally's Apizza 237 Wooster St ⓦsallysapizza.com. *Sally's* is the connoisseur's pizza choice (it only serves pizza, soda and beer), with fresh, zesty sauces and perfectly baked coal-fired pizzas. The downside: you sometimes wait more than an hour to get your food (get in line before 5pm). $\overline{S}$
Union League Café 1032 Chapel St ⓦunionleaguecafe. com. Superb but pricey French brasserie specializing in

1

fresh, seasonal produce. Dishes might include appetizers of New England sea scallops with pine nuts, and mains of ginger-crusted duck with rhubarb. $\overline{\$\$}$

NIGHTLIFE AND ENTERTAINMENT

Bar 254 Crown St ⓦbarnightclub.com. A simple name for a not-so-simple spot that's a combination pizzeria, brewery, bar and stylish nightclub. $\overline{\$}$

Cafe Nine 250 State St ⓦcafenine.com. Intimate club – with the apt moniker of "The Musician's Living Room." Live music every night, from punk to jazz to R&B. $\overline{\$}$

Owl Shop 268 College St ⓦowlshopcigars.com. Smoky, old-school cigar bar (it dates to 1934) enhanced by good scotch (plus excellent coffee) and frequent jazz. $\overline{\$\$}$

Shubert Performing Arts Center 247 College St ⓦshubert.com. Founded in 1914, this gorgeous historic theatre has staged many world premieres, including *The King and I, Oklahoma!* and *The Sound of Music*, and it still hosts top-quality musicals and plays, from Jersey Boys to Cats. $\overline{\$\$}$–$\overline{\$\$\$}$

★ **Three Sheets** 372 Elm St ⓦthreesheetsnh.com. This self-named "gastrodive" is exactly that – a friendly, divey bar with a stellar beer list, and elevated pub food, like pickled fries – crispy fries brined in pickling juice, beet salad laced with balsamic and topped with chunky gorgonzola, and loads of tasty vegetarian options, including the E, L & T (eggplant bacon, lettuce, avocado sriracha). $\overline{\$\$}$

Toad's Place 300 York St ⓦtoadsplace.com. Mid-sized live music venue where Bruce Springsteen and the Stones used to "pop in" to play impromptu gigs. Hosts everything from hip-hop to cover bands. $\overline{\$}$

Vermont

With its white churches and red barns, covered bridges and clapboard houses, snowy woods and maple syrup, **VERMONT** comes closer than any other New England state to fulfilling the quintessential image of small-town Yankee America. Much of the state is smothered by verdant, mountainous forests; indeed, the name Vermont supposedly comes from the French *vert mont*, or green mountain.

This was the last area of New England to be settled, early in the eighteenth century. The leader of the New Hampshire settlers, the now-legendary **Ethan Allen**, formed his **Green Mountain Boys** in 1770, and during the Revolutionary War, this all-but-autonomous force helped to win the decisive Battle of Bennington. In 1777, Vermont declared itself an independent republic, with the first constitution in the world explicitly forbidding slavery and granting universal (male) suffrage; in 1791 it became the first state admitted to the Union after the original thirteen colonies. A more recent example of Vermont's progressive attitude occurred in 2000, when former governor Howard Dean signed the **civil union** bill into law, making the state the first in the USA to sanction marital rights for same-sex couples. Today, Vermont remains liberal when it comes to politics: the state continually attracts a mix of hippies, environmentalists and professionals escaping the rat race, most of them aspiring to an eco-friendly philosophy best epitomized by **Ben & Jerry's** additive-free, locally produced ice cream.

With the occasional exception, such as the extraordinary assortment of Americana at the **Shelburne Museum** near **Burlington** (a lively city worth visiting in any case), there are few specific sights. Tourism here is more activity-oriented, and though the state's rural charms can be enjoyed year-round, most visitors come during two well-defined seasons: to see the spectacular **fall foliage** in the first two weeks of October, and to **ski** in the depths of winter, when resorts such as **Killington** and **Stowe** spring to life.

The Green Mountains

North of western Massachusetts, the Berkshires roll into the much higher **Green Mountains**, Vermont's forested backbone. Most visitors begin their explorations of the area at **Brattleboro**, a lively college town with plenty of enticing stores and bars, or **Bennington**, forty miles on the other side of the hills and home to a smattering of historic attractions. From either town routes lead north through a hinterland of traditional Vermont villages – **Grafton**, **Chester** and **Weston** – to the ski resort at **Killington**.

1

THE LONG TRAIL

Running along the ridge of Vermont's Green Mountains, 272 miles from the Massachusetts border to Québec, the **Long Trail** is one of America's premier **hiking routes**. Those planning on hiking its entire length should count on it taking between 25 and 30 days. The most conventional way of accomplishing this feat is to hike from shelter to shelter, maintained during summer and usually no more than a gentle day's hike apart. A moderate fee is charged at sites with caretakers, and availability is on a first-come, first-served basis; if the shelter itself is full, you'll have to camp, so unless you plan to arrive early you'll need to carry a tent. All shelters are on the primitive side (no electricity or running water). Contact the Green Mountain Club (⊚greenmountainclub.org) for more information.

Bennington

Little has happened in **BENNINGTON** to match the excitement of the days when Ethan Allen's Green Mountain Boys were based here more than two hundred years ago. A 306ft hilltop obelisk (May to Oct daily 9am–5pm; charge) commemorates the 1777 **Battle of Bennington**, in which the Boys were a crucial factor in defeating the British under General Burgoyne (though the battle itself was fought just across the border in New York). Nearby, acclaimed New England poet **Robert Frost** (see page 104) was buried in the cemetery of Old First Church on Main St in 1963. You should also check out the **Bennington Museum**, 75 Main St (June–Oct daily 10am–5pm; Feb–May & Nov–Dec closed Wed; charge; ⊚benningtonmuseum.org), which contains a memorable array of Americana and the largest collection of paintings by folk artist Grandma Moses.

ACCOMMODATION, EATING AND DRINKING   BENNINGTON

★ **Blue Benn Diner** 314 North St (US-7) ⊚bluebenn. com. This authentic, 1940s-era diner draws a diverse crowd of hard-boiled locals and artsy students. In addition to the usual comfort foods, vegetarian dishes also feature on the menu. ⑤
★ **Harwood Hill Motel** 864 Harwood Hill Rd ⊚harwoodhillmotel.com. If you don't mind staying out

of town, this friendly motel is a superb deal, with spacious, immaculate rooms tucked into the base of the mountains. ⑤ **Madison Brewing Co** 428 Main St ⊚madisonbrewingco.com. Fun, stylish brewpub with hearty burgers and six varieties of in-house beer. Live blues most nights. ⑤

Brattleboro

Home to yoga studios, vintage record shops and bookstores catering to the town's youthful population, **BRATTLEBORO** is essentially a red-brick college town with little in the way of conventional sights – instead, it boasts a cosmopolitan art and live music scene, as well as tubing, kayaking and river skating and **ice-fishing** in winter. Just outside the centre at 400 Linden St, visit the excellent local fromagerie and wine shop at **Grafton Cheese** (daily 10am–6pm; free; ⊚graftonvillagecheese.com).

ACCOMMODATION, EATING AND DRINKING   BRATTLEBORO

Chelsea Royal Diner 487 Marlboro Rd, W Brattleboro (exit 2, I-91) ⊚chelsearoyaldiner.com. Great local diner, offering breakfast plates, plus meaty lasagne, roast turkey and stuffing and pizzas. Home of the "original Cajun skillet". ⑤
★ **Inn on Putney Road B&B** 192 Putney Rd ⊚booking.com. Superb B&B in a grand French Baronial-

style house dating from 1929, with plush, contemporary-style rooms. Grab a pint by the fire in the cosy tavern, stroll the gardens or relax with a book in the gazebo. ⑤⑤
Mocha Joe's 82 Main St ⊚mochajoes.com. Good espresso in a stylish basement with exposed beams and slate floors – they roast their own beans. Free wi-fi. ⑤⑤

Grafton and Chester

Heading north from Brattleboro, routes 30 and 35 offer a less-travelled alternative into central Vermont. Few places come closer to the iconic image of rural New England than **GRAFTON**, a truly gorgeous ensemble of brilliant white clapboard buildings,

1

shady trees and a bubbling brook in the centre. Further north, sleepy **CHESTER** blends prototypical Vermont clapboard houses with more ornate, Victorian architecture, laid out charmingly where Rte-11 runs along a narrow green.

ACCOMMODATION AND EATING
GRAFTON AND CHESTER

★**Grafton Inn** 92 Main St, Grafton ⓦgraftoninnvermont.com. Around since 1801, this luxurious inn and restaurant has accommodated everyone from Rudyard Kipling to Teddy Roosevelt. The old carriage house is now a cosy pub, *Phelps Barn* (Sun–Tues 5–8pm,

Wed–Sat 5–9pm). $\overline{\$\$}$

Inn Victoria 321 Main St, Chester ⓦinnvictoria.com. Built in 1851, this elegant B&B goes to town on the Victorian theme with its eight ornate and comfortable rooms (albeit with flatscreen TVs and DVD players). $\overline{\$\$}$

Weston

One of the prettiest villages along scenic Rte-100 (running north along the Green Mountains from Wilmington, almost halfway between Brattleboro and Bennington) is **WESTON**, which spreads out beside a little river and centres on an idyllic green. Most of the action revolves around the labyrinthine **Vermont Country Store** (daily 8.30am–6pm; ⓦvermontcountrystore.com), and the smaller but more authentic **Weston Village Store**, established in 1891 across the road at 660 Main St (daily 9am–6pm; ☏802 824 3184, ⓦwestonvillagestore.com). Both sell a range of vaguely rural and domestic articles, such as locally produced maple syrup and cheeses.

ACCOMMODATION AND EATING
WESTON

Bryant House 657 Main St ☏802 824 6287. A magnificent soda fountain dominates the 1885 mahogany bar of this restaurant. The menu includes classic New England fare such as chicken pie and "johnnycakes", made with cornbread and topped with molasses, as well as burgers and sandwiches. $\overline{\$}$–$\overline{\$\$}$

Colonial House Inn & Motel 287 Rte-100 ⓦcohoinn. com. Gorgeous old house dating back to 1790, with

relatively cheap motel rooms in newer wings, and a tasty and filling breakfast. $\overline{\$}$

Inn at Weston 630 Main St ⓦinnweston.com. This inviting, centrally located place offers the best accommodation in town, with a main building dating back to 1848 and cheaper rooms in the Coleman House annexe; check out the greenhouse, with around one thousand orchids, or relax on the deck or in the gazebo. $\overline{\$\$}$

Calvin Coolidge State Historic Site

3780 Rte-100A, Plymouth Notch • Late May to mid-Oct daily 10am–5pm • Charge • ⓦhistoricsites.vermont.gov

Future president **Calvin Coolidge** was born in **Plymouth Notch** in 1872 (and buried in the local cemetery in 1933), and most of the village is now preserved as the immaculate **Calvin Coolidge State Historic Site**. Coolidge never lost ties to Plymouth Notch, conducting a "Summer White House" here during his presidency (1923–29). All of the buildings in which Coolidge's life played out have been kept more or less the way they were; the humble timber Birthplace (1845), the more comfortable Homestead (1876) where he grew up (preserved as it was when Coolidge was sworn in as president here in 1923) and his father's general store (1855).

Killington

Rte-100 eventually winds its way to **KILLINGTON**, a sprawling resort nine miles north of Plymouth Notch/Calvin Coolidge State Historic Site that, since 1958, has grown from sleepy wilderness to become the most popular ski destination in the state. Other than a small collection of stores and motels on US-4, you'll find most of the action along **Killington Road**, which starts just before the northern intersection of US-4 and Rte-100. **Killington Resort** (4763 Killington Rd; ⓦkillington.com) itself sits at the top of the road, which terminates at the *K-1 Lodge*; in **summer** the focus is on **hiking** and **mountain biking**, with 45 miles of trails (adventure-filled day passes include tubing, ropes courses, labyrinths and more; bike rentals also available). You can also take the **K-1 Express Gondola** (July, Aug & Oct daily 10am–5pm; Sept Sat & Sun 10am–5pm) from the *K-1 Lodge* to the summit of **Killington Peak** (4241ft) and hike down.

★ **Birch Ridge Inn** 37 Butler Rd ⓦbirchridge.com. This extra-cosy B&B offers classic, old-fashioned Vermont hospitality in a modern alpine ski lodge, with rooms in various styles and home-baked breads and muffins. $\overline{\underline{\$\$}}$

Inn at Long Trail 709 US-4, Sherburne Pass ⓦinnatlongtrail.com. After several nights spent in primitive shelters, hikers on the Long Trail will appreciate the comfort of this family-run B&B with tree-trunk beams and a stone fireplace. $\overline{\underline{\$}}$–$\overline{\underline{\$\$}}$

Sun-up Bakery 2250 Killington Rd ⓦsunupbakery.com. Across the street from the *Wobbly Barn*, this is another Killington favourite, great for pesto egg sandwiches with provolone in the morning or a rosemary chicken wrap come lunch. $\overline{\underline{\$}}$

★ **Wobbly Barn Steakhouse** 2229 Killington Rd ⓦwobblybarn.com. Some sort of entertainment every weekend, but the draw since 1963 has really been the beef and prime rib (broiled, mesquite-grilled and barbecued). Reservations recommended. $\overline{\underline{\$\$}}$

Woodstock and around

Since its settlement in the 1760s, beautiful **WOODSTOCK**, a few miles west of the Connecticut River up US-4, has been one of Vermont's more refined centres (not to be confused with Woodstock, New York, namesake of the 1969 music festival). Its distinguished houses cluster around an oval green, now largely taken over by art galleries and cafés.

Marsh-Billings-Rockefeller National Historical Park

54 Elm St, 1 mile north of Woodstock • Late May to Oct daily 10am–5pm; tours run every 30min–1hr • Charge • ⓦnps.gov/mabi

Hard to imagine today, but thanks to intensive logging, the leafy hills of Vermont were virtually stripped bare by the 1860s. The **Marsh-Billings-Rockefeller National Historical Park** encompasses the nineteenth-century mansion of three generations of groundbreaking conservationists who managed to reverse this trend. Illuminating one-hour ranger **tours** (the only way to visit) provide plenty of context. You can also explore 553 acres of forest around the site, which contain a twenty-mile network of **hiking trails** across Mount Tom (1359ft). Park your car and reserve a tour at the Billings Farm and Museum across the road.

Billings Farm and Museum

5302 River Rd (off Rte-12), 1 mile north of Woodstock • April–Oct daily 10am–5pm; Nov–Feb Sat & Sun 10am–4pm • Charge • ⓦbillingsfarm.org

Across the street from the Marsh-Billings-Rockefeller National Historical Park lies the **Billings Farm and Museum**, the working part of the former Billings and Rockefeller property, established in 1871. Exhibits in the barn cover various aspects of farm life, as well as the history of the site. In the grounds are various sheds and displays, but the real crowd-pleaser is **milking time** in the cowshed (daily 3.15–5pm), and especially for kids, the chance to pet horses and Jersey calves.

Apple Hill Inn 10 Hartwood Way in Taftsville, 4 miles east of Woodstock ⓦapplebutterinnvt.com. Cosy B&B in a lovely country house overlooking forests and mountains, with comfortable beds, personable proprietors and huge breakfasts that kick off with tasty home-made granola. $\overline{\underline{\$\$}}$

Braeside Motel 908 East Woodstock Rd (US-4) ⓦbraesidemotel.com. Clean and simple family-owned motel a mile east of the village, with spacious rooms with flatscreen TVs. $\overline{\underline{\$}}$–$\overline{\underline{\$\$}}$

Mon Vert Café 67 Central St ⓦmonvertcafe.com. Right in the heart of things, this stellar café has great salads and sandwiches like the smoked salmon club, topped with velvety local salmon, bacon and garlic aioli on a baguette. There's an excellent breakfast menu as well. $\overline{\underline{\$}}$–$\overline{\underline{\$\$}}$

Mountain Creamery 33 Central St ⓦmountaincreameryvt.com. Filling country breakfasts – try the fat omelettes – and lunch served daily, as well as some fine home-made ice cream downstairs. $\overline{\underline{\$}}$

★ **Silvia** 42 Mill Hill Rd ⓦsilviawoodstockny.com. Fifteen years after closing, the beloved Woodstock bar Joyous Lake – where music stars and locals mingled – now has a new lease of life as Silvia, opened in 2018. Run by two sisters – Berry and Doris Choi – Silvia celebrates the regional bounty with farm-to-fork menu that includes grilled squash with sorrel-anchovy pesto, bibimbap (a nod to the sisters' Korean heritage) with mushrooms and zucchini and pork chop with mashed root vegetables. The bright and airy restaurant has a wonderfully communal feel, with an open

1

kitchen, spacious dining room and a lovely deck for alfresco dining on gorgeous summer days. $\overline{\underline{\$\$}}$

★ **Woodstock Inn and Resort** 14 The Green ⓦ woodstockinn.com. One of the area's fanciest places to stay, with sumptuous rooms, manicured grounds dotted with Adirondack chairs, an eighteen-hole golf course and four gourmet restaurants. It's also got a winter sports facility, a fitness centre and a luxurious spa with a Scandinavian sauna. $\overline{\underline{\$\$}}$–$\overline{\underline{\$\$\$}}$

Quechee

Six miles east of Woodstock, **QUECHEE** is off the main US-4 highway, a combination of quaint Vermont village and expensive new condos. The main highlight here lies on US-4 itself, **Quechee State Park**, which preserves the splendours of the **Quechee Gorge**. A delicate bridge spans the 165ft chasm of the Ottauquechee River, and hiking trails lead down from the **visitor centre** (daily May–Oct 9am–5pm; Nov–April 10am–4pm; ☎ 802 295 2990).

The river spins the turbines of the **Simon Pearce Glass Mill** (daily 10am–9pm; ⓦ simonpearce.com), housed in a former wool mill along Main Street back in Quechee. Here, you can watch glass bowls and plates being blown, and then eat from them at the superb on-site **restaurant**.

ACCOMMODATION AND EATING

QUECHEE

★ **The Mill at Simon Pearce Glass** 1760 Main St ⓦ simonpearce.com. Enjoy inventive New American-type cuisine with lovely views of the Ottauquechee River waterfall and covered bridge. Try the horseradish-crusted cod with herb mashed potatoes and ginger-glazed rack of lamb. $\overline{\underline{\$\$}}$

Quality Inn at Quechee Gorge 5817 Woodstock Rd, (US-4) ⓦ qualityinnquechee.com. Standard motel accommodation with well-maintained rooms, indoor heated pool and continental breakfast included. $\overline{\underline{\$}}$

Montpelier

Some 55 miles north of Quechee on I-89, **MONTPELIER** is the smallest state capital in the nation, with fewer than ten thousand inhabitants. Surrounded by leafy gardens, the golden-domed **Vermont State House** at 115 State St (free guided tours Nov–June Mon–Fri 9am–3pm; July–Oct Mon–Fri 10am–3.30pm Sat 11am–2.30pm; ⓦ vtstatehousefriends.org) is well worth a peek for its marble-floored and mural-lined hallways – the House and Senate chambers are among the oldest legislative venues in the country that have preserved their original interiors.

INFORMATION

MONTPELIER

Visitor centre 134 State St (Mon–Fri 6am–5pm, Sat & Sun 9am–5pm; ⓦ vermontvacation.com). Offers plenty of information on local and statewide attractions.

ACCOMMODATION AND EATING

Capitol Grounds 27 State St ⓦ capitolgrounds.com. Chill out at this Montpelier staple that pours its own brand of brew (802Coffee) plus aromatic teas, kombucha, pastries, soups and inventive sandwiches like the sriracha hummus with tomatoes and pepper jack. $\overline{\underline{\$}}$

Capitol Plaza Hotel 100 State St ⓦ capitolplaza.com. The best hotel in downtown Montpelier offers comfortable and spacious digs across from the Art Deco Capitol Theatre, though you are paying a premium for the location. $\overline{\underline{\$\$}}$

Three Penny Taproom 108 Main St ⓦ threepennytaproom.com. Renowned, fun craft-beer bar with more than twenty microbrews on tap (many hailing from Vermont or at least New England) and great burgers, buttermilk-fried wings and hefty sausage sandwiches. $\overline{\underline{\$}}$

Wilaiwan's Kitchen 34 State St ⓦ wilaiwanskitchen. com. Come lunchtime, queues snake out the door at this little Thai superstar with an ever-shifting, tiny menu (only three dishes served per week). Cash only. $\overline{\underline{\$}}$

Ben & Jerry's Ice Cream Factory

1281 Waterbury–Stowe Rd • Tours every 30min daily: July to mid-Aug 9am–9pm; mid-Aug to late Oct & June 9am–7pm; late Oct to May 10am–6pm; store and "scoop shop" close 1hr later • Charge, under-12s free • ⓦ benjerry.com

1

Few people paid much attention to **WATERBURY** before 1985, when Ben Cohen and Jerry Greenfield (whose ice-cream-making history began in 1978, in a renovated Burlington gas station) decided to locate their new manufacturing facility in the tiny town. Today **Ben & Jerry's Ice Cream Factory** is nestled one mile north of I-89 in the village of Waterbury Center. Tours of the production factory, where (weekdays only) machines turn cream, sugar and other natural ingredients into more than fifty flavours, are followed by a free mini-scoop of the stuff – you can buy more at the gift shop and ice-cream counter outside.

Stowe

At the foot of Vermont's highest mountain, **Mount Mansfield** (4393ft), there is still a beautiful nineteenth-century village at the heart of **STOWE**, with its white-spired meeting house and town green. Though it has been a popular summer destination since before the Civil War, what really put the town on the map was the arrival of the **Von Trapp family** in 1941, whose story inspired *The Sound of Music*. While most of historic Stowe village lies along Main Street, Mountain Road is Stowe's primary thoroughfare, stretching from the main village up to the **Stowe Mountain Resort** (daily 8am–4pm; ⓦstowe.com), and on through the mountain gap known as **Smugglers' Notch**.

Mount Mansfield

Mountain Rd • ⓦstowe.com

Ascending to the peak of **Mount Mansfield**, the highest point in Vermont, is a challenge no matter how you do it, but you'll be rewarded by dizzying views that go all the way to Canada. Weather permitting, the easiest approach is to drive up the **Toll Road**, a winding 4.5-mile ascent of mostly dirt track that begins seven miles up from Stowe village on Mountain Road (late May to mid-Oct daily 9am–4pm). The road ends at a tiny **visitor centre** (3850ft); from here it's a short scramble to the ridge that runs along the mountain top, and around 1.5 miles to the peak, known as "the Chin" (4393ft). Alternatively, you can take the **Gondola SkyRide** (late-June to mid-Oct daily 10am–4.15pm; ⓦgostowe. com), which affords jaw-dropping views and ends at **Cliff House** (3660ft).

GETTING AROUND AND INFORMATION   STOWE

Bike rental In summer, when the crowds thin out considerably, Stowe's cross-country skiing trails double as mountain bike routes. AJ's Ski & Sports, 350 Mountain Rd, rents bikes (daily 9am–6pm; ⓦstowesports.com).

Visitor centre 51 S Main St, at Depot Rd (June–Aug Mon–Sat 9am–8pm, Sun 9am–5pm; Sept–May hours vary; ⓦgostowe.com).

ACCOMMODATION

★ **Green Mountain Inn** 1 Main St ⓦgreenmountaininn. com. Gorgeous hotel built in 1833, centrally located and amply outfitted – options range from opulent suites with jacuzzi tubs and fireplaces to plush rooms. Offers two good restaurants, free health club use, free tea and cookies (daily 4–5pm), winter wine and cheese parties (Dec–March Wed 5.30–6.30pm) and a heated pool. $$

The Lodge at Spruce Peak 7412 Mountain Rd ⓦsprucepeak.com. The pride of Stowe Mountain Resort stands right next to the Spruce Peak ski area, offering real luxury; floor-to-ceiling windows make the most of

the scenery, while rooms boast designer furnishings and contemporary art, as well as stone-frame fireplaces and marble-tiled bathrooms. $$–$$$

Trapp Family Lodge 42 Trapp Hill Rd ⓦtrappfamily. com. Austrian-themed ski resort (as fancy as it is expensive) on the site of the original Trapp family house, also the first cross-country ski centre in America. Rates include cross-country ski passes and access to skiing and hiking trails. The Austrian-accented dining options include the Bierhall and Kaffeehaus. $$$

EATING AND ENTERTAINMENT

Kaffeehaus 42 Trapp Hill Rd ⓦtrappfamily.com. The Trapp family bakery serves up Austrian *wurst,* large

1

pretzels with Bavarian beer cheese and all sorts of tempting pastries. $

Matterhorn 4969 Mountain Rd ⓦ matterhornbar.com. The region's best bands have been coming here for years – you can enjoy live music in the nightclub most weekends, or listen from the downstairs wood-panelled dining room (specializing in, oddly, pizzas and sushi). $$

McCarthy's 2043 Mountain Rd ⓦ mccarthysrestaurantstowe.com. Irish-themed joint, but especially noted for its huge, all-American breakfasts: Mansfield Valley eggs, Vermont maple bacon, corned beef hash and thick pancakes. It's been a local favourite since 1974 – expect long queues at the weekend. $$

Burlington and around

Lakeside **BURLINGTON**, Vermont's largest city, with a population near forty thousand, is one of the most enjoyable destinations in New England. Renowned for its liveability and green development, it's home to a hip, eclectic community that fuses urbanism with rural Vermont values. The city faces 150-mile-long **Lake Champlain**, which forms the natural boundary between Vermont and New York State. Burlington's founders included Revolutionary War hero Ethan Allen and his family; Ethan's brother Ira founded the University of Vermont. Home to five colleges and universities, the area has blossomed as a youthful and outward-looking college town. Its downtown is easily strolled by foot, notably around the **Church Street Marketplace**.

The waterfront

In the summertime, locals and visitors alike stroll leisurely along the pedestrian boardwalks that line Burlington's **waterfront**, taking in gorgeous views of the Adirondack Mountains (in wintertime, they may be strolling *on* Lake Champlain, which often freezes over in February). The highly interactive **ECHO Lake Aquarium and Science Center** (1 College St; daily 10am–5pm; charge; ⓦ echovermont. org), situated at the water's edge, is an excellent place to bring young children. Burlington's annual waterfront **Winter Festival** (first week in Feb) boasts fabulous ice sculptures, carved on the premises. If you're looking to get onto Lake Champlain, opt for the convivial *Spirit of Ethan Allen III* (May–Oct; 1hr 30min narrated cruises; ⓦ soea.com), which sets out from the Burlington Boathouse at 1 College St. You can also embark on sunset cruises (mid-June to Aug daily 6.30pm–9pm; spring and fall Fri–Sat only) and a variety of other lunch and dance cruises.

Shelburne Museum

6000 Shelburne Rd (US-7), Shelburne (7 miles south of Burlington) • May–Dec daily 10am–5pm; Jan–April Wed–Sun 10am–5pm • Charge, tickets valid for two successive days • ⓦ shelburnemuseum.org

It takes a whole day, if not more, to take in the fabulous 45-acre collection of unalloyed Americana gathered at **Shelburne Museum**, seven miles south of Burlington. More than thirty buildings dot the beautifully landscaped grounds, from the 80ft-diameter **McClure Round Barn** and horseshoe-shaped **Circus Building** to the enormous, 892-ton steam paddlewheeler **Ticonderoga**.

Shelburne Farms

1611 Harbor Rd, Shelburne (7 miles south of Burlington) • Daily: mid-May to mid-Oct 9am–5.30pm; mid-Oct to mid-May 10am–4pm • Charge • ⓦ shelburnefarms.org

Next to the Shelburne Museum, **Shelburne Farms** is a working farm reborn as a nonprofit environmental education centre; activities include cow milking, egg collection and rabbit petting. The hilly landscape is peppered with three massive buildings: the main house, a coach barn and a U-shaped farm barn. You can get some exercise by walking the 4.5-mile Farm Trail, which circles the property, or the half-mile Lone Tree Hill trail and numerous side paths diverging from the roadways.

ARRIVAL AND DEPARTURE

By plane Burlington International Airport (ⓦbtv.aero) is a few miles east of downtown along US-2 (bus #12 to downtown runs every 30min 6.30am–10pm).

By bus Greyhound buses drop off at the airport.
Destinations Boston (4 daily; 4hr 25min–5hr 25min); Montpelier (4 daily; 45min); Montréal (4 daily; 2hr 30min).

By train Amtrak's *Vermonter* trains arrive at 29 Railroad Ave, Essex Junction, an inconvenient 5 miles northeast of town. Note that the station only opens twice a day (for the two trains) and there is no ticket office.
Destinations Brattleboro (1 daily; 3hr 7min); Montpelier (1–2 daily; 38min); Springfield, MA (5hr 13min); Waterbury (1 daily; 25min); Windsor (1 daily; 2hr 5min).

BURLINGTON AND AROUND

GETTING AROUND AND INFORMATION

By bus The local CCTA bus (ⓦcctaride.org) connects points all over the downtown area, and travels to the nearby towns of Winooski, Essex and Shelburne. You can get route maps and schedules at the main downtown terminal on the corner of Cherry and Church streets. CCTA also operates the very convenient (free) College Street Shuttle between the University of Vermont and the waterfront, with stops at the Fleming Museum and the Church Street Marketplace (every 15–30min: Mon–Fri 6.30am–7pm; late May to June & Sept to mid-Oct also Sat & Sun 9am–9pm; no services July & Aug).

Chamber of Commerce 60 Main St (mid-May to Aug Mon–Fri 8am–5pm, Sat & Sun 9am–5pm; Sept to mid-May Mon–Fri 8am–5pm; ⓦvermont.gov).

ACCOMMODATION

Courtyard Burlington Harbor 25 Cherry St ⓦmarriott. com. A great downtown option, with a fabulous location near the waterfront and newish, luxurious rooms and amenities; buffet breakfast, indoor pool and LCD TVs included. Parking charged extra. $\overline{5}\overline{5}\overline{5}$

Hotel Vermont 41 Cherry St ⓦhotelvt.com. This boutique hotel has stylishly renovated rooms, friendly staff and thoughtful perks like a complimentary coffee bar and snack pantry on every floor. Parking charged extra. $\overline{5}\overline{5}$

The Made Inn 204 S Willard St ⓦmadeinnvermont. com. This isn't your typical B&B. Quirky, hip, playful and pet-friendly, the art-filled Made Inn offers four unique rooms with comfy beds, robes and a chalkboard wall. It's a historic building, so detached, keyed bathrooms are just down the hall. The included breakfast is an organic spread of fresh fruit, French toast and, of course, Vermont maple syrup. In the mood for a mimosa? They have that too. $\overline{5}\overline{5}$–$\overline{5}\overline{5}\overline{5}$

★ **Willard Street Inn** 349 S Willard St ⓦwillardstreetinn.com. The large rooms at this distinctive 1881 Queen Anne are brilliantly restored (but not frilly). You'll get lots of home-baked goodies, excellent breakfasts served in a glass sunroom and a lush, relaxing English garden. $\overline{5}\overline{5}$

EATING AND DRINKING

American Flatbread 115 St Paul St ⓦamericanflatbread.com. Wildly popular pizza place, especially at weekends, for its organic wheat dough and all-natural toppings, including local cheeses and sausage. $$

Farmhouse Tap & Grill 160 Bank St ⓦfarmhousetg. com. Built on the heap of a former *McDonald's*, with a beer garden that has a huge list of brews and a restaurant with gourmet burgers and locally sourced pub grub, including grilled bratwurst. Fun tip: check out the old *McD's* tiles on the dining room floor. $\overline{5}\overline{5}$

★ **Hen of the Wood** 55 Cherry St ⓦhenofthewood. com. The revered *Hen* serves imaginative small plates in a spacious dining room with a striking wood-panelled, triangulated ceiling. Though the menu changes daily, the mouthwatering "mushroom toast" topped with bacon and a poached egg is here to stay. Reservations recommended. $\overline{5}\overline{5}$

Leunig's Bistro 115 Church St ⓦleunigsbistro.com. Sleek, modern bistro serving contemporary French cuisine, including poached octopus with white beans; the lunch plates include good-value deals. Outdoor dining when the weather permits. $\overline{5}\overline{5}$

Muddy Waters 184 Main St ⓦfacebook.com/muddywatersvt. A popular coffeehouse whose crazy interior is lined with used furniture, thrift-store rejects, plants and rough-hewn panelled walls. Extremely potent caffeinated beverages. $\overline{5}$

★ **Myer's Bagel Bakery** 377 Pine St ⓦmyersbagels. com. Get a taste of Montréal-style bagels at this local early-morning favourite; the Montréal Spice bagel is an addictive treat (the "spice" is steak seasoning). Don't be put off by the out-of-the-way location. Excellent sandwiches too. $

★ **Penny Cluse Café** 169 Cherry St ⓦpennycluse.com. All-day breakfast nook famed for its gingerbread pancakes and biscuits doused in herb gravy. Lunchtime offerings include fish tacos with avocado salsa. Expect queues at the weekend. $\overline{5}$

Trattoria Delia 152 St Paul St ⓦtrattoriadelia.com. Traditional regional Italian fare that goes beyond the usual pasta dishes – try the grilled rabbit served over soft polenta – and a tempting wine list, at reasonable prices. A great date spot. $\overline{5}\overline{5}$

1

New Hampshire

"Live Free or Die" is the official motto of **NEW HAMPSHIRE**, summing up a deeply held belief in rugged individualism and independence that goes back to colonial times. The state boasts densely forested mountains, whitewater rivers and challenging ski resorts, making it the premier state in the region for outdoor activities.

New Hampshire's short Atlantic coastline is a stretch of mellow, sun-drenched beaches capped by **Portsmouth**, a well-preserved colonial town with a crop of excellent restaurants and stylish inns. Inland, there are more than 1300 lakes; the largest, **Lake Winnipesaukee**, is ringed with both tourist resorts and quiet villages. The magnificent **White Mountains** spread across northern New Hampshire, culminating in the highest peak in New England, formidable **Mount Washington**.

Portsmouth

New Hampshire's most urbane city, **PORTSMOUTH**, just off I-95 at the mouth of the Piscataqua River, blends small-town accessibility with a dash of sophistication. It has always been an important port – it was state capital until 1808 – but retains the feel of a New England village, with the spire of **North Church** in the central **Market Square**, dating from 1854, remaining the tallest structure in town. Having endured the cycles of prosperity and hardship typical of many New England cities, Portsmouth has found its most recent triumphs in the cultural arena, attracting artists, musicians, writers and, notably, gourmet chefs. In addition to a wealth of tantalizing restaurants, Portsmouth's unusual abundance of well-preserved colonial buildings makes for an absorbing couple of days.

Moffatt-Ladd House

154 Market St • June to late Oct Mon–Sat 11am–5pm, Sun 1–5pm • Charge • ⓦ moffattladd.org

Of the grand old mansions in Portsmouth, the **Moffatt-Ladd House** is one of the most impressive. Completed in 1763, the building is particularly notable for its Great Hall, which occupies more than a quarter of the first floor. Using inventories left by Captain John Moffatt, who designed the home, historians have transformed the **Yellow Chamber** (also on the second floor) into one of the best-documented eighteenth-century American rooms.

John Paul Jones House

43 Middle St • May–Oct daily 11am–5pm • Charge • ⓦ portsmouthhistory.org

Home to the Portsmouth Historical Society's museum, the 1758 Georgian **John Paul Jones House** was where the US's first great naval commander boarded in 1777 while his ships were outfitted in the Langdon shipyards. Inside the boxy yellow structure you can view some of his naval memorabilia and lavish period-furnished rooms. Upstairs there's an incredibly detailed exhibit on the **1905 Portsmouth Peace Treaty** between Russia and Japan.

Strawbery Banke Museum

14 Hancock St • May–Oct daily 10am–5pm • Charge • ⓦ strawberybanke.org

Portsmouth was officially founded by English Settlers (led by Captain Walter Neal) in 1630, but was known as **Strawbery Banke** until 1653 for the abundance of wild strawberries in the area. The **Strawbery Banke Museum** is a collection of 37 meticulously restored and maintained historic wooden buildings, including the **Shapley Drisco House**: half of the house is outfitted as from the 1790s, the other half, from the 1950s. The 1766 **Pitt Tavern** holds the most historic significance, having acted as a meeting place for patriots and loyalists during the Revolution, while one of the most intriguing exhibits occupies the **Shapiro House** (1795), twentieth-century home of a Russian-Jewish immigrant family. The stained-wood **Sherburne House** is a rare survivor from 1695 – its interior focuses on seventeenth-century architecture. The museum also hosts a rich variety of events throughout the year, including the Vintage & Vine Wine Festival in September.

ARRIVAL, INFORMATION AND TOURS | PORTSMOUTH

By bus C&J (ⓦridecj.com) has frequent daily services from Boston/Logan Airport and New York that terminate at its Portsmouth Transportation Center, 185 Grafton Drive (ⓘ603 430 1100), on the outskirts of town at exit 3A I-95. Greyhound buses arrive at 55 Hanover St, a short walk from Market Square.

Chamber of Commerce 500 Market St (Mon–Fri 8.30am–5pm; ⓦportsmouthchamber.org), a 15min walk from Market Square (parking on site). It also operates an information kiosk in Market Square (May–Oct daily 10am–5pm). See also ⓦgoportsmouthnh.com.

Tours Portsmouth Harbor Cruises at Ceres Street Dock offers several trips and has a full bar on every boat (ⓦportsmouthharbor.com). The Gundalow Company offers fantastic sails on its reproduction "gundalow" – a form of cargo carrier popular in the eighteenth and nineteenth centuries (ⓦgundalow.org).

ACCOMMODATION

★ **Ale House Inn** 121 Bow St ⓦalehouseinn.com. Portsmouth's only waterfront inn, above the town's theatre, is a truly luxurious treat – a contemporary boutique hotel with each room equipped with a flatscreen TV. The cosy rooms occupy a remodelled brick brewery warehouse dating from 1880. $\overline{\underline{\$\$}}$

Port Inn 505 US-1 Bypass, at the traffic circle ⓦportinnportsmouth.com. These good-value, stylish and clean rooms, all with renovated bathrooms and some with kitchenettes, are among the cheapest in Portsmouth. $\overline{\underline{\$\$}}$

EATING, DRINKING AND NIGHTLIFE

3S Artspace 319 Vaughan St ⓦ3arts.org. This funky hybrid space celebrates the arts in Portsmouth, with gallery shows, live music, film and eclectic events like the Loading Dock Concert Series, featuring indie acts from around the region. Round out the visit with dinner at Barrio, a colourful taco restaurant with Day of the Dead murals, and build-your-own-tacos with such inventive ingredients as Coca-Cola-marinated steak, smoked cheddar and pineapple salsa. $\overline{\underline{\$\$}}$

The Friendly Toast 113 Congress St ⓦthefriendlytoast. com. Kitschy thrift-store decor with an interesting selection of breakfasts, sandwiches and omelettes, a huge menu of mixed drinks, shakes, beers and coffees and an equally eclectic crowd. $\overline{\underline{\$}}$

★ **Jumpin' Jay's Fish Café** 150 Congress St ⓦjumpinjays.com. Hands down the best seafood in Portsmouth (and probably the state), with an amazing raw bar, dishes such as lobster mac and cheese and fish tacos and a "fresh catches" menu, which might offer Florida *mahi-mahi* and Atlantic scallops. $\overline{\underline{\$\$}}$

Music Hall 28 Chestnut St ⓦthemusichall.org. Portsmouth's largest performance space hosts well-known, nationally touring folk, rock, jazz and blues bands, classical concerts, plus dance, theatre and other performances every day of the year. The Beaux Arts building dates from 1878. $\overline{\underline{\$\$}}$

Portsmouth Brewery 56 Market St ⓦportsmouthbrewery.com. More like a restaurant than a pub, with most of the interior taken up by wait-staffed tables – cosy up to the bar if you just want to sample their range of exceptional beers. Come by for happy hour (weekdays 4–6pm) – beers are cheap, and the pub menu (nachos, crab dip) is half-price. $\overline{\underline{\$}}$

Press Room 77 Daniel St ⓦpressroomnh.com. Popular for its nightly live jazz, blues, folk and bluegrass performances. Also serves decent microbrews, inexpensive salads, burgers and pizza in a casual pub-style setting. $\overline{\underline{\$}}$

Ristorante Massimo 59 Penhallow St ⓦristorantemassimo.com. Intimate, smart Italian restaurant, with fresh pasta and plenty of seafood main courses, such as scallops with stewed leeks and butternut squash. Service is exceptional. Reservations essential. $\overline{\underline{\$\$}}$

Row 34 Portsmouth 5 Portswalk Pl ⓦrow34.com. Boston favourite Row 34 has extended into Portsmouth, serving a menu that's rooted in something exquisitely simple: New England seafood. The raw bar is one of the best in town, as are the lobster rolls. Equally a draw is the space – airy, high-ceilinged and sleek, with earthy touches. $\overline{\underline{\$\$}}$

The Merrimack Valley

The financial and political heartland of New Hampshire is the **Merrimack Valley**, home to the state capital, **Concord** (pronounced "conquered"), with its elegant, gold-domed **State House** (107 N Main St; Mon–Fri 8am–4.15pm; free; ⓦnh.gov), and with a few worthy detours off I-93, the main highway through the region.

Canterbury Shaker Village

288 Shaker Rd, Canterbury (I-93 exit 18) • Mid-May to Oct daily 10am–5pm • Charge, ticket valid for two consecutive days • ⓦshakers.org

About twenty minutes north of Concord, **Canterbury Shaker Village** is New England's premier museum of Shaker life. In 1792, this tranquil village became the sixth Shaker

1

community in the USA and, at its zenith in the mid-nineteenth century, there were some three hundred people living on the grounds; the last Shaker living in Canterbury died in 1992 aged 96. You can take several engrossing one-hour **tours** of the site, which introduce the Shaker ideals, day-to-day life and architecture (there are 25 perfectly restored buildings in the village). Shaker Saturdays is a kid-friendly program on one Saturday a month (check website for dates) that features a scavenger hunt and more.

Robert Frost Farm

122 Rockingham Rd (exit 4 from I-93), Derry • May, June & Sept to mid-Oct Wed–Sun 10am–4pm; July & Aug daily 10am–4pm • Gardens and barn free, farmhouse charge • ⓦ robertfrostfarm.org

South of Concord, on the outskirts of Derry, the **Robert Frost Farm** is the most illuminating New England memorial to the great poet, and the only one he himself wished to preserve (Frost lived here with his young family between 1900 and 1909). Fans should visit for the optional **free guided tours** as much as the house itself, entertaining hour-long introductions to Frost's life, character and poetry.

The Lakes Region

Of the literally hundreds of lakes occupying the state's central corridor, the biggest by far is **Lake Winnipesaukee**, which forms the centre of the holiday-oriented **Lakes Region**. Long segments of its three-hundred-mile shoreline, especially in the east, consist of thick forests sweeping down to waters dotted with little islands, disturbed only by pleasure craft. The most sophisticated of the towns along the shoreline is **Wolfeboro**; the most fun has to be **Weirs Beach**. To get on the water consider a trip on **M/S Mount Washington**, a 230ft monster of a boat that departs from the dock in the centre of Weirs Beach several times a day to sail to Wolfeboro (mid-May to Oct; ⓦ cruisenh.com).

Wolfeboro

Because Governor Wentworth of New Hampshire built his summer home nearby in 1768, tiny **WOLFEBORO** claims to be "the oldest summer resort in America". Sandwiched between lakes Winnipesaukee and Wentworth, it's certainly the most attractive town in the region – access to the **waterfront**, with wide, fine views, is one of the best reasons to stay. The **Wright Museum of World War II**, 77 Center St (May–Oct Mon–Sat 10am–4pm, Sun noon–4pm; charge; ⓦ wrightmuseum.org), is chock-a-block with relics and nostalgic ephemera.

Weirs Beach

The short boardwalk at **WEIRS BEACH**, the very essence of seaside tackiness (even if it is fifty miles inland), is the social centre of the Lakes Region in the summer. Its little wooden jetty throngs with vacationers, the amusement arcades jingle with cash and there's even a neat little crescent of sandy beach, suitable for family swimming. A quieter diversion here is the **Winnipesaukee Railroad** (June to late Oct; ⓦ hoborr.com), which operates scenic trips along the lakeshore between Weirs Beach and Meredith, four miles north.

ACCOMMODATION AND EATING   **THE LAKES REGION**

WOLFEBORO

★ **Bailey's Bubble** 5 Railroad Ave ⓦ baileysbubble. com. Luscious ice cream in the centre of town, with a vast array of treats, from banana splits to cookie sundaes. Try flavours like "Maine Black Bear" (raspberry, chocolate chips and truffles) or "Moose Tracks" (vanilla, fudge and peanut

butter cups). $̄

Mise en Place 96 Lehner St ⓦ miseenplacenh.com. Fantastic high-end French restaurant with rotating dishes such as mussels in tomato broth and tuna tartare, served on the patio or in the cosy dining room. $$–$$$

Wolfeboro Inn 90 N Main St ⓦ wolfeboroinn.com. Built

in 1812, this historic inn is on the waterfront with its own beach and some of the best restaurants in town. It has 44 elegant rooms, some dating back to the inn's foundation – some have private balconies overlooking the lake. $\overline{\underline{\$\$}}$

WEIRS BEACH
Cozy Inn, Lakeview House & Cottages 12 Maple St ⓦ cozyinn-nh.com. Multisite property comprising the

charming 1880s inn with basic but comfy rooms, the hilltop 1860 house with larger rooms and sixteen rustic cottages – shared-bath rooms go for very cheap in summer. $\overline{\underline{\$}}$–$\overline{\underline{\$\$}}$
Half Moon Motel & Cottages 28 Tower St ⓦ weirsbeach.com/halfmoon/motel. This old motel might look like an army barracks, but the renovated rooms have fridges and microwaves. The views of the lake are jaw-dropping. $\overline{\underline{\$}}$–$\overline{\underline{\$\$}}$

The White Mountains

Thanks to their accessibility from both Montréal and Boston, the enchanting **WHITE MOUNTAINS** have become a year-round tourist destination. It's a commercialized region, with quite a lot of development flanking the main highways, but the great granite massifs retain much of their majesty. **Mount Washington**, at 6288ft the highest peak in the entire Northeast, claims some of the most severe weather in the world. Much of the region is protected within the **White Mountains National Forest**, established in 1918 and covering almost 1250 square miles today.

Piercing the range are a few high passes, called "**notches**", and the roads through these gaps, such as the **Kancamagus Highway** between **Lincoln** and **Conway**, make for enjoyably scenic routes. However, you won't really have made the most of the White Mountains unless you also set off on foot, bike or skis across the long expanses of thick evergreen forest that encircles them.

Franconia Notch

Ten miles beyond **Lincoln**, I-93 passes through **Franconia Notch State Park**, a slender valley crammed between two great walls of stone. From the **Flume Visitor Center** (May to late Oct daily 9am–5pm; ☏ 603 745 8391), you can walk along a two-mile boardwalk-cum-nature trail to the Pemigewasset River as it rages through the narrow, rock-filled Flume gorge (charge). Alternatively, take a cable-car ride up the sheer granite face of **Cannon Mountain** (late May to mid-Oct daily 9am–5pm; ⓦ cannonmt.com) – and ascend to stunning views. On a clear day, you can see the peaks of four states – New Hampshire, Maine, Vermont, New York – and Canada. Also, various, well-marked trails lead up to the panoramic views for free.

HIKING, SKIING AND CYCLING IN THE WHITE MOUNTAINS

Hiking in the White Mountains is coordinated by the **Appalachian Mountain Club** or "AMC" (ⓦ outdoors.org), whose chain of information centres, hostels and huts along the Appalachian Trail, traversing the region from northeast to southwest, is detailed below. Call ☏ 603 466 2721 for trail and weather information before you attempt any serious expedition.

Downhill and cross-country **skiers** can choose from several resorts that double up as summertime activity centres. The Waterville Valley Resort (☏ 603 236 8311, ⓦ waterville.com) and Loon Mountain (☏ 603 745 8111, ⓦ loonmtn.com), both just east of I-93, are good for downhill, while Jackson (☏ 603 383 9355, ⓦ jacksonxc.org), about fifteen miles north of Conway on Rte-16, has some of the finest cross-country skiing trails in the northeast. General information on the skiing centres is available from Ski NH (☏ 603 745 9396, ⓦ skinh.com).

In the summer, the cross-country skiing trails can make for strenuous but exhilarating **biking** (you can take lifts up the slopes and ride back down). Both Waterville and Loon have bikes for rent on site; Loon also runs a zip-line.

1

Frost Place

Ridge Rd, off Bickford Hill Rd, Franconia • May–June Thurs–Sun 1–5pm; July & Aug daily except Tues 1–5pm; Sept & Oct daily except Tues 10am–5pm • Charge • Ⓦ frostplace.org

One mile south of the friendly village of **FRANCONIA**, **Frost Place** is another former home of poet Robert Frost (see page 104), memorable largely for the inspiring panorama of mountains in its backdrop. Frost lived here from 1915 to 1920, and the house is now a "Center for Poetry and the Arts", with a poet-in-residence, readings, workshops and a small display of Frost memorabilia, such as signed first editions and photographs.

Mount Washington

From the awe-inspiring peak of 6288ft-high **Mount Washington** you can, on a clear day, see all the way to the Atlantic and into Canada. But the real interest in making the ascent lies in the extraordinary severity of the weather here, which results from the summit's position right in the path of the principal storm tracks and air-mass routes affecting the northeastern USA. Winds exceed hurricane strength on more than a hundred days of the year, and have even reached 231mph. You can ascend the mountain via a number of **hiking trails**, but most visitors opt for the easier option of driving via **Mount Washington Auto Road**, or taking the train along the **Mount Washington Cog Railway**.

Mount Washington Auto Road

Great Glen Trails Outdoor Center (Rte-16, 3 miles north of Pinkham Notch) • Early May to late Oct – weather permitting – 7.30am–6pm in peak season; call to check • Charge • Ⓦ mtwashingtonautoroad.com

The drive up **Mount Washington Auto Road** isn't quite as spine-tingling as you may expect, although the hairpin bends and lack of guard-rails certainly keep you alert. The toll includes a "This car climbed Mt. Washington" bumper sticker and a short audio-tour CD. Driving takes thirty or forty minutes under normal conditions.

Specially adapted **minibuses**, still known as "stages" in honour of the twelve-person horse-drawn carriages that first used the road, give narrated tours (daily 8.30am–5pm; charge; 2hr return) as they carry groups of tourists up the mountain.

Mount Washington Cog Railway

3168 Base Station Rd, Marshfield Station • Trains run late April to Dec; check website for dates and times • Charge • Ⓦ thecog.com

A three-hour return trip on the **Mount Washington Cog Railway** (with a scant 20min at the summit) is a truly momentous experience, inching up the steep wooden trestles while avoiding descending showers of coal smut (there is also a clean, biodiesel service), though anyone who's not a train aficionado might find it not really worth the money.

The summit

Assuming the weather cooperates (and be prepared to be disappointed), the views from the summit of Mount Washington are gasp-inducing, but look closer and you'll see the remarkable spectacle of buildings actually held down with great chains. The utilitarian **Sherman Adams Summit Building** (daily: mid-May to Aug 8am–6pm; Sept 8am–5pm; Oct 8am–4.30pm; free; Ⓦ nhstateparks.org) serves as the headquarters of Mount Washington State Park and contains a cafeteria, restrooms and a gift shop, as well as the **Mount Washington Weather Observatory**. The observatory's various findings, exhibits illuminating the crazy winter weather, simulated snowcat drives and gorgeous panoramic imagery is on display at the **Extreme Mount Washington museum** downstairs (mid-May to mid-Oct daily 9am–6pm; free for Auto Road or Cog Railway users, otherwise charge; Ⓦ mountwashington.org). You can also climb the few remaining feet to the actual (and humble-looking) summit point, or visit nearby **Tip Top House**; erected in 1853, this is the only original building to survive the devastating fire of 1908. Its saloon-like interior has been preserved, frozen in time (usually open late May to mid-Oct daily 10am–4pm; free).

North Conway

Surrounded on all sides by shopping malls, factory outlets and fast-food chains, **NORTH CONWAY** is a major resort town and can be fairly depressing, with the strip south towards Conway particularly over-developed. Fortunately, there is some relief in the centre, a village core that manages to maintain a hint of rustic backcountry appeal – you'll also find plenty of **budget accommodation** and **places to eat** here.

The Kancamagus Highway

The **Kancamagus Highway** (Hwy-112), connecting North Conway and Lincoln, is the least busy road through the mountains, and makes for a very pleasant 34-mile drive. Several campgrounds are situated in the woods to either side, and various walking trails are signposted. The half-mile hike to **Sabbaday Falls**, off to the south roughly halfway along the highway, leads up a narrow rocky cleft in the forest to a succession of idyllic waterfalls. If you plan on a picnic, though, take note: there is no food or gas available along the highway.

GETTING AROUND AND INFORMATION

By bus You'll need a car to make the most of the White Mountains, but the AMC runs a hiker shuttle bus service (June to early Sept daily; early Sept to mid-Oct Sat & Sun) with stops at many of the trailheads and AMC lodges throughout the Mount Washington region (visit ⓦoutdoors.org for information, reservations strongly

recommended; discount for AMC members).
Visitor centre In Lincoln on Rte-112, just off I-93 at exit 32 (daily: July–Sept 8.30am–6pm; Oct–June 8.30am–5.30pm; ⓦvisitwhitemountains.com); has a small exhibit on the region, gives lodging advice and sells compulsory parking passes and maps.

ACCOMMODATION

Thanks to the influx of young hikers and skiers to the White Mountains, there's a relative abundance of budget accommodation in the area. Keep in mind, too, that rates vary dramatically between seasons, and even from weekday to weekend. **Campers** can pitch their tents anywhere below the tree line and away from the roads in the White Mountains National Forest, provided they show consideration for the environment. There are also numerous official campgrounds, particularly along the Kancamagus Highway.

AMC LODGES

Highland Center Lodge at Crawford Notch Rte-302, Bretton Woods ⓦoutdoors.org. Great choice year-round: lodging in two- or four-person dorms or private double rooms. Hearty alpine breakfasts and family-style dinners are included, as are activities including guided hikes and game nights. Dorms $\overline{\underline{S}}$–$\overline{\underline{SS}}$, doubles $\overline{\underline{SS}}$
Joe Dodge Lodge Pinkham Notch, 361 Rte-16 ⓦ

ⓦoutdoors.org. Popular with walkers aiming to get a full day's hike in around Pinkham Notch – unless you camp, this is the only choice for miles around. All rooms are simple, and dressed throughout with pine wood finish: double rooms or bunks with a shared bathroom; two meals included. No TVs, but there is wi-fi access. Dorms $\overline{\underline{S}}$, doubles $\overline{\underline{S}}$

MOTELS, HOTELS AND B&BS
Omni Mount Washington Resort 310 Mt Washington Hotel Rd, Bretton Woods ⓦomnihotels.com. One of the grandest hotels in the state, with lavish rooms to match. Amenities abound, including a beautiful spa with views over the mountains, a pool and a wide variety of dining. $\overline{\underline{SSS}}$
School House Inn 2152 White Mountain Hwy, North Conway ⓦschoolhousenh.com. Probably the cheapest place in town, all with cable TV and free morning coffee. $\overline{\underline{S}}$
★ **Sugar Hill Inn** 116 Rte-117, Sugar Hill ⓦsugarhillinn.com. This posh secluded inn, set in a

---

AMC LODGES

The Appalachian Mountain Club (ⓦoutdoors.org) operates eight delightfully remote **mountain huts** in New Hampshire along a 56-mile stretch of the **Appalachian Trail**, each about a day's hike apart. Generally offering full service in season (June to mid-Oct, exceptions noted below), including mixed bunkrooms (blankets but no sheets), toilets, cold water and two hot meals per day, they are a fairly popular choice – reservations are required (call ☎603 466 2727). Carter Notch, Lonesome Lake and Zealand Falls huts are open out of season (without heat, running water or food).

1

converted eighteenth-century farmhouse, is ideal for romantic getaways, with antique-filled rooms, fireplaces and mountain views. Gourmet breakfasts (included) show off local produce; there's also a guest-only tavern menu and exquisite fine dining. $$

Thayer's Inn 111 Main St, Littleton ⓦ thayersinn.com. A creaky but comfortable local landmark established in 1843, having hosted the likes of Richard Nixon and Ulysses S. Grant. Rooms are dressed in Victorian style (with floral,

period wallpaper) and there's breakfast included. The suites have kitchenettes with a toaster and a microwave. $–$$

The Wentworth 1 Carter Notch Rd ⓦ thewentworth. com. For the full New England mountain-getaway experience, there's no place better than this handsome, historical country inn. There's elegant rooms as well as suites, some with gas fire places and outdoor hot tubs; a soothing spa; an 18-hole golf course; and more. $$$–$$$$

EATING AND DRINKING

Chef's Bistro 2724 Main St, North Conway ⓦ chefsbistronh.com. This cosy café has great sandwiches, pasta salads and smoothies for lunch, with more substantial dinners such as seared tuna with lemongrass rice and pork chop with parmesan and mushroom risotto. $$–$$$

Littleton Diner 145 Main St, Littleton ⓦ littletondiner. com. Open since 1930, this landmark diner has heaps of character. Best known for its delicious buckwheat pancakes and local maple syrup, the kitchen also cranks out New England comfort food (think roast turkey with cranberry sauce), sandwiches and pie. Cash only. $

★ **Polly's Pancake Parlor** 672 Rte-117 (I-93 exit 38), Sugar Hill ⓦ pollyspancakeparlor.com. *Polly's* might be in the middle of nowhere, but it's a scenic nowhere and well worth the trip if you love pancakes. Add blueberries, choc chips, coconut or walnuts. $

Schilling Beer Co. Littleton Grist Mill, 18 Mill St, Littleton ⓦ schillingbeer.com. Popular microbrewery in a red wooden building beside the old mill, with a tasting room where you can sample the IPAs, German lagers and continental ales while enjoying a delicious wood-fired pizza. $$

Maine

Celebrated as "the way life should be", **MAINE** more than lives up to its unofficial motto. Filled with lobster shacks, dense forests, scenic lakes and seaside enclaves, the state offers ample opportunities for exploring, or for just lounging in Adirondack chairs and watching the leaves change colour – there's a little something for everyone here. As large as the other five New England states combined, Maine has barely the year-round population of Rhode Island. In theory, therefore, there's plenty of room for all the visitors who flood the state in summer; in practice, though, most people head straight for the extravagantly corrugated coast.

At the southern end of the coastline, the beach towns of **Ogunquit** and **Old Orchard Beach** quickly lead up to Maine's most cosmopolitan city, **Portland**. The **Mid-Coast**, between Brunswick and Bucksport, is characterized by its craggy shores, windswept peninsulas and sheltered inlets, though the towns of **Boothbay Harbor** and **Camden** are certainly busy enough. Beyond the idyllic Blue Hill Peninsula, **Down East** Maine is home to **Acadia National Park**, the state's most popular outdoor escape, in addition to the bustling summer retreat of **Bar Harbor**. Farther north, you'll find foggy weather and exhilarating scenery, capped by the candy-striped lighthouse at **Quoddy Head**, the easternmost point in the United States.

Inland, you'll really begin to appreciate the size and space of the state, where vast tracts of mountainous forest are dotted with lakes and barely pierced by roads. This region is ideal territory for hiking and canoeing, particularly in **Baxter State Park**, site of the northern terminus of the Appalachian Trail.

Maine's climate is famously harsh. In **winter**, the state is covered in snow, and often ice, while even in what is officially **summer** temperatures don't really start to rise until June or even July. This is Maine's most popular season, its start heralded by sweet corn and the reopening of lobster shacks, and its end marked by the wild blueberry harvest. Brilliant **fall colours** begin to spread from the north in late September and the cool weather is great for apple-picking, leaf gaping or simply curling up with a blanket and a book.

The Maine coast

Although the water is chilly, Maine's **beaches** are unequivocally beautiful, and there are plenty of rocky coastal footpaths and harbour villages to explore. The liveliest destinations are **Portland** and arty **Rockland**; there's a wide choice of smaller seaside towns, such as **Bath** and **Blue Hill**, if you're looking for a more peaceful base. **Beaches** are more common (and the sea warmer) further south, for example at **Ogunquit**.

The best way to see the coast itself is by **boat**: ferries and excursions operate from even the smallest harbours, with major routes including the ferries to Canada from Portland and Bar Harbor, shorter trips to **Monhegan** island via Port Clyde, Boothbay Harbor and New Harbor and **Vinalhaven** via Rockland.

Ogunquit and around

The three-mile spit that shields gay-friendly **OGUNQUIT** from the open ocean is one of Maine's finest **beaches** (charge for parking), a long stretch of sugary sand and calm surf that is ideal for leisurely strolls.

Ogunquit Museum of American Art

543 Shore Rd • May–Oct daily 10am–5pm • Charge • ⓦ ogunquitmuseum.org

The compact **Ogunquit Museum of American Art** is endowed with a strong collection of nineteenth- and twentieth-century American art, such as seascapes by Marsden Hartley and Rockwell Kent. Displays are enhanced by the building's spectacular ocean views. In the garden, grinning animal sculptures mingle with serene marble women.

Perkins Cove and Marginal Way

Perkins Cove, a pleasant knot of restaurants and shops a few miles south of downtown, is best reached by walking along **Marginal Way**, a winding path that traces the crescent shoreline from Ogunquit Beach. The 1.5-mile trail offers unspoilt views of the Atlantic coast, particularly stunning in fall.

ACCOMMODATION AND EATING   OGUNQUIT AND AROUND

It's worth paying a bit more to **stay** near the centre of town, as Ogunquit traffic can snarl (you'll also save on hefty beach parking fees).

★ **Bread and Roses Bakery** 246 Main St ⓦ breadandrosesbakery.com. A community hub with tempting displays of eclairs, "mousse bombs", whoopie pies, fruit tarts and cupcakes. $̄

Footbridge Lobster 108 Perkins Cove Rd ⓦ footbridge-lobster.com. Located right in Perkins Cove, this famed stand is the place to go for an outstanding lobster roll. The fisherman-owner catches all his own crustaceans. $̄–$̄$̄

Gazebo Inn 527 Main St ⓦ gazeboinnogt.com. Within walking distance of Footbridge Beach, this Ogunquit favourite has fifteen modern rooms – including four suites in a renovated barn – that seem to overflow with amenities: rain showers, heated floors, fireplaces and posh linens. There is also a pool, hot tub, library with internet stations and massage room. Full breakfast included. Rates much lower outside of summer. $̄$̄–$̄$̄$̄

Wells-Ogunquit Resort Motel 203 Post Rd, 1.5 miles north in Moody ⓦ wells-ogunquit.com. Impeccably kept modern motel rooms have cable TV and refrigerators, and there's a pool and barbecue setups. Breakfast showcases great-grandma's recipe for sugar-baked beans. May–Oct only. $̄$̄

Kennebunkport

There's a reason former presidents **George Herbert Walker Bush** (known locally as "41") and **George "W" Bush** summer in genteel **Kennebunkport** – it's beautiful, historic and full of great places to eat.

The best beach in these parts is **Goose Rocks**, about three miles north of **Dock Square** (the town centre) on King's Highway (off Dyke Rd via Rte-9). It's a premium stretch of expansive sand, though you will need a permit to park ($15 daily, $50 weekly; call the Kennebunkport police ⓿ 207 967 2454). Neighbouring **Kennebunk** is home to a trio of attractive beaches; permits for these (from $16 daily, $52 weekly) can be purchased at kiosks on-site.

1

The Colony Hotel 140 Ocean Ave, Kennebunkport ⓦ thecolonyhotel.com. This meandering old resort dates from 1914, with 125 rooms spread between three buildings and two houses. Rooms are delightfully old-fashioned – those in the main property don't have TVs or a/c – with stunning ocean views and access to the hotel's heated saltwater pool, eighteen-hole putting green and private slip of beach. Pet-friendly. Open mid-May to Oct. $\overline{\underline{\$\$\$}}$

Franciscan Guest House 26 Beach Ave, Kennebunk ⓦ franciscanguesthouse.com. In the gardened grounds of a monastery (of all things), the *Franciscan* has rates that simply cannot be beat. Guestrooms, located in what were once school classrooms, are basic, with no daily maid service. Still, the property is pleasant, with a saltwater pool, full breakfasts and a fun return crowd. The Franciscan Guest House Auditorium also hosts a wonderful series of concerts and events, from chamber music to silent films accompanied

by a string quartet – check website for dates. $\overline{\underline{\$\$}}$

The Inn at English Meadows 141 Port Rd, Kennebunk ⓦ englishmeadowsinn.com. Housed in an elegant grey-painted wooden building, dating from the mid-19th century and built in the Greek Revival style, this B&B is taste personified. Vera Wang beds are adorned with fine linens, the bathrooms boast luxurious Malin+Goetz toiletries, and innkeeper Elizabeth ensures you get every day off to the best possible start with her freshly prepared breakfasts of scones, granola, and cooked dishes. $\overline{\underline{\$\$\$}}$

Nonantum Resort 95 Ocean Ave ⓦ nonantumresort. com. Rising over the Kennebunk River, this waterfront resort offers an inviting, all-in-one stay – comfortable rooms (with included buffet breakfast), family-friendly activities, multiple dining options – from seafood to pub grub – and all manner of outdoor fun, including kayaking, sailing tours and more. $\overline{\underline{\$\$}}$–$\overline{\underline{\$\$\$}}$

EATING AND DRINKING

★ Bandaloop 2 Dock Square, Kennebunkport ⓦ bandaloeprestaurant.com. Colourful, eclectic, tucked-away locals' favourite serving inventive fare like halibut with sweetcorn and saffron rice. The emphasis is on organic produce, and vegetarians will be well pleased. Reservations recommended. $\overline{\underline{\$\$}}$

Clam Shack 2 Western Ave, just before the Kennebunkport Bridge, Kennebunk ⓦ theclamshack. net. The mighty, mini *Clam Shack* – established in 1968 –

lives up to the hype with fried clams endorsed by Barbara Bush and celebrity chef Rachael Ray, whoopie pies favoured by Martha Stewart and takeaway fried fish and lobster rolls. $\overline{\underline{\$\$}}$

The Ramp 77 Pier Rd (at Pier 77 Restaurant), Cape Porpoise ⓦ pier77restaurant.com. Head below deck to this lively little bar with ocean views and a decor that evokes the belly of a ship. Great pub food too. $\overline{\underline{\$\$}}$

Portland

The largest city in Maine, **PORTLAND** was founded in 1632 in a superb position on the Casco Bay Peninsula, and quickly prospered, building ships and exporting great inland pines for use as masts. A long line of wooden **wharves** stretched along the seafront, with the merchants' houses on the hillside above.

From its earliest days, Portland was a cosmopolitan city. When the **railroads** came in the 1840s, the Canada Trunk Line had its terminus right on Portland's quayside, bringing the produce of Canada and the Great Plains one hundred miles closer to Europe than it would have been at any other major US port. **Custom House Wharf** remains much as it must have looked when novelist Anthony Trollope passed through in 1861 and said, "I doubt whether I ever saw a town with more evident signs of prosperity".

As with much of New England, the good times didn't last through the mid-twentieth century. Grand Trunk Station was torn down in 1966, and downtown Portland appeared to be in terminal decline – until, that is, a group of committed residents undertook the energetic redevelopment of the area now known as the **Old Port**. Their success has revitalized the city, keeping it at the heart of Maine life – though you shouldn't expect a hive of energy. Portland is quite simply a pleasant, sophisticated and very attractive town, where you can experience the benefits of a large city at a lesser cost and without the hassle of crowds.

Portland Museum of Art

7 Congress Square • Mon–Wed, Sat & Sun 11am–6pm, Thurs–Fri 11am–8pm • Charge, Fri free 4–8pm • ⓦ portlandmuseum.org

1

WINSLOW HOMER'S STUDIO

In 2006, the Portland Museum of Art acquired **Winslow Homer's** studio in Prouts Neck – a coastal summer colony in Scarborough, twelve miles south of Portland. Lauded as one of America's greatest nineteenth-century painters, Homer (1836–1910) kicked off his art career at 21 working as an illustrator for *Harper's Weekly* magazine. He moved into Prouts Neck in 1884, where he completed many of the majestic seascapes that are the hallmarks of his work, such as *Weatherbeaten* and *The Gulf Stream*. Opened in 2012 after extensive renovations, the refurbished studio gives visitors an intimate peek into the life of a master painter. Those who make the trip will also enjoy the view of the pounding Atlantic from the studio's porch – gallery-worthy in its own right. For more information on tours of the studio (2hr 30min), contact PMA.

Portland's single best destination, the **Portland Museum of Art** was designed in 1983 by I.M. Pei and Partners. Modernist works, scenes of Maine and stirring seascapes are prevalent, exemplified by Winslow Homer's colossal *Weatherbeaten*, the museum's centrepiece. An earthy alternative to the maritime pieces is *Woodsmen in the Woods of Maine* by Waldo Peirce. Rich and dark, it was commissioned by the Westbrook Post Office in 1937 and is displayed here with the clouded-glass mailroom door still intact.

Wadsworth-Longfellow House/Maine Historical Society

485–489 Congress St • Guided tours on the hour May–Oct Mon–Sat 10am–5pm, Sun noon–5pm; last tour leaves at 4pm • Charge • ⓦ mainehistory.org

The **Wadsworth-Longfellow House/Maine Historical Society** was Portland's first brick house when built in 1785 by Revolutionary War hero Peleg Wadsworth. More famously, it was the boyhood home of Wadsworth's grandson, the poet Henry Wadsworth Longfellow. Next door, the **Historical Society Museum** has changing displays of state history and art.

The Old Port and waterfront

The restored **Old Port** near the quayside, between Exchange and Pearl streets, can be quite entertaining, with all sorts of red-brick antiquarian shops, bookstores, boutique clothing spots (especially on Exchange Street) and other diversions. Several companies operate **boat trips** from the nearby wharves.

If you follow Portland's waterfront to the end of the peninsula, you'll come to the **Eastern Promenade**, a remarkably peaceful two-mile harbour trail that culminates in a small beach, below the headland.

ARRIVAL AND DEPARTURE   PORTLAND

By car Both I-95 and Rte-1 skirt the peninsula of Portland, within a few miles of the city centre, while I-295 goes through it.

By plane Portland International Jetport (ⓦ portlandjetport. org) abuts I-95, and is connected with downtown by the city bus (#5; limited Sun service; ⓦ gpmetro.org).

By bus Concord Coach Lines (ⓦ concordcoachlines.com), also at the Transportation Center, is the principal bus operator along the coast, with frequent services from Boston and

Bangor. Greyhound runs to Montréal, New Hampshire and Vermont, as well as destinations within Maine; the station is at 950 Congress St, on the eastern edge of downtown.

By train Amtrak's *Downeaster* arrives five times daily at the Portland Transportation Center (100 Thompson's Point Rd, 3 miles from downtown) from Boston's North Station.

Destinations Boston (5–6 daily; 2hr); Dover, NH (5 daily; 1hr); Exeter, NH (5 daily; 1hr 20min).

GETTING AROUND, INFORMATION AND TOURS

By bike CycleMania, at 59 Federal St (ⓦ cyclemania1.com), rents bicycles for $30/day, which you can ride around the city's hundreds of acres of undeveloped land.

Visitor centre 14 Ocean Gateway Pier, via Commercial St (April–June Mon–Sat 9.30am–4.30pm; July–Oct Mon–Fri

9am–5pm, Sat & Sun 9am–4pm; Nov–March Mon–Fri 9am–3pm, Sat 10am–3pm; ⓦ visitportland.com); also staffs an information office at the Jetport (ⓘ 207 775 5809).

Land and sea tours The amphibious World War II vehicles of Maine Duck Tours, 177 Commercial St (May–Oct; 1hr;

1

BOAT TRIPS FROM PORTLAND

Several companies operate **boat trips** from the wharves near the Old Port: the Portland Schooner Co. (daily in summer; 2hr trip; ⓦ portlandschooner.com) has two vintage schooners that sail around the harbour and to the Casco Bay islands and lighthouses from the Maine State Pier, adjacent to Casco Bay Lines on Commercial Street. With Lucky Catch Cruises, at 170 Commercial St, ⓦ luckycatch.com) shellfish fans don a pair of overalls and head out to catch their very own lobster. Casco Bay Lines runs a twice-daily mailboat all year, and additional cruises in summer, to eight of the innumerable **Calendar Islands** in Casco Bay, from its terminal at 56 Commercial St at Franklin (ⓦ cascobaylines.com). **Long, Chebeague** and **Peaks islands** have accommodation or camping facilities.

reservations recommended; ⓦ maineducktours.com), cavort through the Old Port and then plunk into Casco Bay. Portland Discovery, 170 Commercial St (May–Oct; 90min;

ⓦ portlanddiscovery.com), runs entertaining tours that include the Portland Harbour and lighthouses.

ACCOMMODATION

Blind Tiger 163 Danforth St ⓦ blindtigerportland.com. Previously known as *The Danforth*, this 1823 Federal-style mansion overflows with architectural delights: opaque windows in the billiard room (a holdover from Prohibition days), an herb garden on the second floor and a rooftop cupola with harbour views. Many of the nine rooms have working fireplaces, and all feature richly patterned textiles, posh soaps and original art. $\overline{\underline{S}}\overline{\underline{S}}\overline{\underline{S}}$

The Chadwick 140 Chadwick St ⓦ thechadwick.com. Tucked away in Portland's West End, this 1891 Victorian has four guestrooms that are a tasteful marriage of antiques and modern design. You'll find gourmet breakfasts, a garden with a hammock for two and a welcoming host. $\overline{\underline{S}}\overline{\underline{S}}\overline{\underline{S}}$–$\overline{\underline{S}}\overline{\underline{S}}\overline{\underline{S}}\overline{\underline{S}}$

Inn at St John 939 Congress St ⓦ innatstjohn.com. Just outside downtown, in a slightly dodgy area near the Greyhound station, this creaky yet charming 1897 Victorian offers reasonably priced, comfortable rooms, some with shared baths. Breakfast included, no elevator. Shared bath $\overline{\underline{S}}\overline{\underline{S}}$, en-suite $\overline{\underline{S}}\overline{\underline{S}}$–$\overline{\underline{S}}\overline{\underline{S}}\overline{\underline{S}}$

Inn on Carleton 46 Carleton St ⓦ innoncarleton.com. Nineteenth-century Victorian with six stylish high-ceilinged rooms done up in a soothing colour palette and furnished with four-poster beds and fireplaces. Located in the West End, a few minutes' walk from downtown. The heavenly breakfasts can be taken in the English garden. $\overline{\underline{S}}\overline{\underline{S}}\overline{\underline{S}}$

Marriott Residence Inn 145 Fore St ⓦ marriott.com. A slinky hotel garnering rave reviews for its smart waterfront location and suites stocked with fridge, microwave and dishwasher. On-site laundry facilities, a pool, jacuzzi, fitness centre and free continental breakfast are among the many perks. $\overline{\underline{S}}\overline{\underline{S}}\overline{\underline{S}}$

Press Hotel 119 Exchange St ⓦ thepresshotel.com. Set in a former newspaper office and printing press dating from 1923, this contemporary boutique hotel is filled with local art, while the comfortable rooms have flatscreen TVs and well-appointed bathrooms. Free bike use for guests. Their top-notch Union restaurant serves locavore cuisine. $\overline{\underline{S}}\overline{\underline{S}}\overline{\underline{S}}$

EATING, DRINKING AND NIGHTLIFE

Portland is famed for its outstanding restaurants, and most of its bars serve good food as well. The bountiful Farmers' Market, in Monument Square (May–Nov Wed 7am–1pm; ⓦ portlandmainefarmersmarket.org) offers the perfect opportunity to sample local produce. The city also has a wealth of superlative gelato and ice-cream shops. Portland's bar scene is rowdier than you might expect, with fun seekers packing the pubs every weekend. Portland Parks and Recreation (ⓦ portlandmaine.gov) sponsors free outdoor noon and evening jazz and blues concerts during the summer.

★ **Central Provisions** 414 Fore St ⓦ central-provisions.com. Set in a historic brick building, you'll find a rotating menu and inventive small plates such as fried cauliflower with feta and Halibut with Romesco and

mushrooms. Get there early to put your name down – wait times can be extreme in summer (upwards of an hour), and reservations are not taken. $\overline{\underline{S}}\overline{\underline{S}}$

Duckfat 43 Middle St ⓦ duckfat.com. Unassuming sandwich shop where local spuds are cut and fried in duck fat, salted and served with a choice of home-made dipping sauces. Singing with flavour, these humble *pommes frites* give this outwardly modest restaurant best-in-town status. $\overline{\underline{S}}$

Eventide Oyster Co. 86 Middle St ⓦ eventideoysterco. com. Sleek oyster *boîte* with just a few tables and a handful of stools hugging the marble bar. In addition to raw shellfish, you'll find excellent lobster rolls, drizzled with brown butter. The "clam bake" – steamed clams, mussels, lobster, potatoes, pork and a hard-boiled egg – is a superb New England feast. $\overline{\underline{S}}\overline{\underline{S}}$

★ **Fore Street** 288 Fore St ⓦ forestreet.biz. This elegant restaurant highlights the best of seasonal Maine cuisine, from local seafood to just-picked berries and organic greens. Try the Maine mussels in garlic-almond butter, grilled pork and homemade ice cream in such flavours as maple ginger and sweetcorn. $$–$$$

Holy Donut 7 Exchange St ⓦ theholydonut.com. Some people come to Portland just for the doughnuts here. Popular flavours include dark chocolate with sea salt, maple-bacon, pomegranate and fresh lemon, but really, you can't go wrong with anything you choose. They're all tender and fluffy, but denser than your yeasty variety – the key ingredient is mashed Maine potatoes. Great vegan and gluten-free options, too. Arrive early for the best assortment. $$

Lobster Shack at Two Lights 225 Two Lights Rd, 9 miles south in Cape Elizabeth ⓦ lobstershacktwolights.com. Perhaps the best seafood-eating scenery in all of Maine: lighthouse to the left, unruly ocean to the right, and a lobster roll overflowing on the plate in front of you. $

★ **The Maine Brew Bus** 111 Commercial St ⓦ themainebrewbus.com. Hop on the lime-green bus and head out on a tour of a great array of local breweries. There are plenty of samples included in the price, and the guides are smart, fun and friendly. $$

★ **Miyake** 468 Fore St ⓦ miyakerestaurants.com. This Portland favourite serves sushi with a French flair; the menu garners quite a buzz for its four-course tasting menu, which may include sea urchins and marinated salmon. The chef-

owner harvests his own clams and has a farm with pigs, chickens and veggies. $$–$$$

★ **Novare Res Bier Café** 4 Canal Plaza, Suite 1 (enter through alleyway on lower Exchange St, by KeyBank sign) ⓦ novareresbiercafe.com. A little tricky to find, this very cool Old Port beer spot has more than 500 brews with 25 on tap, outdoor and indoor picnic tables and tasty charcuterie and cheese plates. $$

Portland Hunt and Alpine Club 75 Market St ⓦ huntandalpineclub.com. Ease into the night at this handsome bar, which features a vibrant array of craft cocktails with sassy names, like the Green Eyes (gin, lime, chartreuse, egg white) and the Bonecrusher (mezcal, lime, agave, red pepper). The Scandinavian-style small plates are equally inspired, from gravlax with horseradish cream to open-faced sandwiches to Swedish meatballs. $–$$

SPACE Gallery 538 Congress St ⓦ space538.org. Artsy space that displays contemporary artworks and always has something interesting going on, whether it's films, music, art shows or local bands. Sometimes a cover.

Standard Baking Co. 75 Commercial St ⓦ standardbakingco.com. Preeminent French-inspired bakery serving devilishly good croissants, sticky buns, olive bread, macaroons, madeleines, butter cookies and more. $

Street and Co. 33 Wharf St ⓦ streetandcompany.net. Special-occasion seafood spot where the cuts are grilled, blackened or broiled to perfection and served in a cosy dining room with exposed beams and plank floors. A few good non-fish items as well. Reservations recommended. $$

Freeport

Much of the current prosperity of **FREEPORT**, fifteen miles north of Portland, rests on the invention by Leon L. Bean, in 1912, of a funky-looking rubber-soled fishing boot. That original boot is still selling (there's now an enormous replica at the entrance), and **L.L. Bean** has grown into a multinational clothing conglomerate, with a mammoth store on Main Street that literally never closes. Originally, this was so pre-dawn hunting expeditions could stock up; all the relevant equipment is available for rent or sale, and the store runs regular workshops to teach backcountry activities and survival skills. In practice, though, the late-night hours seem more geared toward high school students, who attempt to fall asleep in the tents without being noticed by store personnel. L.L. Bean is now more of a fashion emporium and Freeport has expanded to include a mile-long stretch of top-name **factory outlets**. To get away from the shops, head a mile south of Freeport to the sea. The very green promontory visible just across the water as you drive is **Wolfe's Neck Woods State Park**. In summer, for a small charge, you can follow hiking and nature trails along the unspoiled fringes of the headland (daily 9am–sunset; ☎ 207 865 4465).

ARRIVAL AND DEPARTURE   FREEPORT

By train Amtrak's *Downeaster* arrives twice daily from Boston's North Station at 36 Depot St, in the heart of downtown.

Destinations Boston (2 daily; 3hr 10min); Exeter, NH (2 daily; 2hr); Dover, NH (2 daily; 1hr 30min).

ACCOMMODATION AND EATING

Applewood Inn 8 Holbrook St ⓦ applewoodusa.com.   Welcoming, pet-friendly B&B with artful decor in a great

1

location just behind L.L. Bean (next door to Mr. Bean's former house, no less). Some rooms are fancier and have jacuzzis, and there is one lovely suite that sleeps eight. The charming hosts moonlight as hot-dog vendors. $\overline{\underline{\$\$}}$, suite $\overline{\underline{\$\$\$}}$

Broad Arrow Tavern Harraseeket Inn, 162 Main St ⓦharaseeketinn.com. Gourmet pizzas, pulled-pork sandwiches and a great lunch buffet served in a lodge-style dining room with an open kitchen and a roaring fire. $\overline{\underline{\$}}$–$\overline{\underline{\$\$}}$

Harraseeket Inn 162 Main St ⓦharaseeketinn.com. After a day spent chasing down outlet sales, retreat to this renowned clapboard inn with some eighty rooms, two good restaurants and an indoor pool. Genteel quarters are spruced up with posh linens, canopy beds and antiques;

deluxe rooms include fireplaces and jacuzzi tubs. $\overline{\underline{\$\$\$}}$

Maine Idyll Motor Court 1411 Rte-1 ⓦmaineidyll. com. Basic but romantic cottage quarters in a woodsy area a few miles north of town, with blueberry muffins in the morning. Family owned- and -maintained since the 1930s. Open May–Oct. $\overline{\underline{\$\$}}$

Tuscan Brick Oven Bistro 140 Main St ⓦtuscanbrickovenbistro.com. Hearty Tuscan fare· is the order of the day at this down-home Italian bistro, with dishes like capellini alla Toscana (roasted artichokes, peppers and tomatoes tossed in white wine) and delicious pizzas, topped with rustic ingredients like crimini and portobello mushrooms and walnut pesto. $\overline{\underline{\$\$}}$

Bath

The charming small town of **BATH**, seventeen miles northeast of Freeport, has an exceptionally long history of **shipbuilding**: the first vessel to be constructed and launched here was the *Virginia* in 1607, by Sir George Popham's short-lived colony. **Bath Iron Works**, founded in 1833, continues to produce ships – during World War II, more destroyers were built here than in all Japan. At the superb **Maine Maritime Museum**, 243 Washington St (daily 9.30am–5pm; charge; ⓦmainemaritimemuseum. org), you can take a tram (trolley) tour of the Iron Works (reservations recommended; end-May to end-Oct; charge), explore several visiting historic vessels or browse the museum's intriguing collection of ship-related paintings, photographs and artefacts.

ACCOMMODATION AND EATING   BATH

Beale Street Barbeque and Grill 215 Water St ⓦmainebbq.com. Hickory-smoked Memphis barbecue in an airy, modern dining room. Try the delectable honey jerk ribs with green onions and sour cream. $\overline{\underline{\$}}$

The Cabin 552 Washington St ⓦcabinpizza.com. Old-school favourite near the Maritime Museum where you can enjoy some of Maine's best pizza in dark, wooden booths. Cash only. $\overline{\underline{\$}}$

★ **Coveside B&B** 6 Gotts Cove Lane, 13 miles south in Georgetown ⓦcovesidebandb.com. This idyllic hideaway, tucked between a boat-filled cove and a beautiful garden, has seven stylish rooms, friendly hosts,

kayaking opportunities and phenomenal breakfasts. Open late May to Oct. $\overline{\underline{\$\$}}$

Five Islands Lobster Co. 1447 Five Islands Rd (off Rte-127), 14 miles south in Georgetown ⓦfiveislandslobster.com. One of the most picturesque settings in Maine to eat lobster or great fried clams: the picnic tables have spectacular views of sailboats, forested islands and a lighthouse. $\overline{\underline{\$\$}}$–$\overline{\underline{\$\$\$}}$

Inn at Bath 969 Washington St ⓦinnatbath.com. An 1840 Greek Revival house with friendly service and tastefully decorated rooms, some with wood-burning fireplaces and jacuzzis. $\overline{\underline{\$\$}}$

Boothbay Harbor

BOOTHBAY HARBOR, at the southern tip of Hwy-27, twelve miles south from Rte-1, is a crowded, yet undeniably pretty, waterfront resort town. The dock lays on **boat trips** of all kinds, including Balmy Days Cruises (ⓦbalmydayscruises.com), which offers all-day trips to Monhegan Island as well as harbour tours. One of the state's most beloved attractions, the **Coastal Maine Botanical Gardens** (call for directions; April–Oct daily 9am–5pm, July & August till 6pm; charge; ⓦmainegardens.org) is honeycombed by well-tended trails and twelve winsome gardens.

ACCOMMODATION AND EATING   BOOTHBAY HARBOR

Boathouse Bistro 12 The By-Way (Pier 1) ⓦtheboathousebistro.com. Fun, rooftop tapas bar with excellent lobster thermidor (market price), seafood risotto,

a great array of vegetarian options, like coconut and curry tofu, and an eclectic wine list. $\overline{\underline{\$\$}}$

Cabbage Island Clam Bakes Pier 6, at the Fisherman's

1

Wharf Inn ⓦcabbageislandclambakes.com. Lobster nirvana: head out on a harbour cruise (complete with full bar), then disembark at 5.5-acre Cabbage Island for an authentic clambake of steamed shellfish, chowder, corn on the cob and blueberry cake. $$$

The Inns at Greenleaf Lane 65 Commercial St ⓦgreenleafinn.com. Right in the centre of town, this affable B&B has an international crowd, a sociable breakfast hour, a book and movie library, a fitness centre and eight appealing guest rooms with a traditional look. The owners also have the adjacent *Admiral's Inn*. $$$

Ports of Italy 47 Commercial St ⓦportsofitaly.com. Authentic northern Italian food – such as home-made gnocchi in parmesan cream sauce – served in a candlelit dining room. There's also a polished mahogany bar, just right for swilling one of the perfect Cabernets. Reservations recommended. $$

★**Topside Inn** 60 McKown St ⓦtopsideinn.com. Perched on top of a steep hill, this former sea captain's home boasts Boothbay's most spectacular vantage point. The chic rooms are the best in town and breakfast is served in a sunny dining room. Open May to mid-Oct. $$$

Rockland

ROCKLAND, where Rte-1 reaches Penobscot Bay, has historically been Maine's largest lobster distributor and has the state's busiest working harbour. The town has become a hip enclave, with a strong arts and cultural scene, boasting some remarkable museums and a happening Art Deco theatre. Rockland's cultural centrepiece is the outstanding **Farnsworth Art Museum**, 16 Museum St (10am–5pm: June–Oct daily; Nov, Dec, April & May Tues–Sun; Jan–March Wed–Sun; charge; ⓦfarnsworthmuseum.org), with a collection that spans two centuries of American art. Much of the work here, spread over several buildings, is Maine-related; the **Wyeth Center**, a beautiful gallery in a converted old church, holds two floors' worth of works by Jamie and N.C. Wyeth.

ACCOMMODATION   ROCKLAND

★**LimeRock Inn** 96 Limerock St ⓦlimerockinn.com. Elegant rooms with striped wallpaper and antique cherry furniture in a turreted Queen Anne mansion. Excellent breakfasts. $$

Ripples Inn at the Harbor 16 Pleasant St

ⓦripplesinnattheharbor.com. Endearing little Victorian with five cheerful rooms and nice design details such as antique washstands, wainscoting and hand-painted walls. Run by a gem of a proprietor. Daily breakfast and tea. $$

EATING AND ENTERTAINMENT

The Causeway 5 3rd St, 9 miles south in Spruce Head ⓦthecauseway.square.site. Crab cakes, octopus, and king oyster mushrooms are among the fresh produce foraged from coast and country and put to delicious effect in this laid-back restaurant close to the ocean. $$

Home Kitchen Café 650 Main St ⓦhomekitchencafe. com. Breakfast-all-day joint with wittily named menu items – the "Pig's Boogie" omelette (or "homelet" in a nod to the restaurant name) is made with bacon and red peppers. The Hippy Scramble features tofu mixed with green onion and garlic. Don't miss the justly famous cinnamon buns. $

★**In Good Company** 415 Main St

ⓦingoodcompanymaine.com. Superb New American spot located in an eclectic, cosy storefront (formerly a bank) right downtown. Staff are very friendly, and the food is phenomenal – try the blue cheese tenderloin with mashed potatoes, and red snapper with sweet potato hummus. $$

Primo 2 S Main St ⓦprimorestaurant.com. In a rambling Victorian house, *Primo* is one of Maine's top-rated restaurants, with a menu dictated by what's fresh outside – nearly all of its veggies and animals are raised on-site. This is, indeed, a "full-circle kitchen" as they describe themselves. There's fine dining downstairs, but the second-floor lounge, which has a copper bar and velvet banquettes, is livelier.

ROCKLAND FESTIVALS

In the first weekend of August, up to 100,000 visitors descend on Rockland's Harbor Park for the annual **Maine Lobster Festival** (ⓦmainelobsterfestival.com) – some 20,000 pounds of lobster is consumed over the course of the five-day celebration, which also sees the coronation of the "Maine Sea Goddess". The **North Atlantic Blues Festival** (mid-July; ⓦnorthatlanticbluesfestival.com) is another popular event, a two-day jamboree held on the waterfront and boasting top-billed performers.

1

Reservations required for downstairs. $\overline{\$}\overline{\$}$
Strand Theatre 345 Main St ⊛ rocklandstrand.com.
One of Rockland's star attractions is this grand, 1920s

Art Deco venue. Shows run the gamut from theatre
performances and comedy acts to live bands and arthouse
films. $\overline{\$}\overline{\$}$

Monhegan Island

Deliberately low-key **Monhegan Island**, eleven miles from the mainland, has long attracted a hardy mix of artists and fishermen. It also pulls its fair share of tourists, but for good reason: it's the most worthwhile jaunt away from the mainland along the entirety of the Maine coast.

On this rocky outcrop, **lobsters** are the main business, though the stunning cliffs and isolated coves have also drawn artists, including Edward Hopper and Rockwell Kent. The small village huddles around the tiny harbour, protected by Manana and Smutty Nose islands. Other than a few old hotels and some good restaurants, there's not much urbanity. Seventeen miles of **hiking trails** twist through the wilderness and past a magnificent 1824 lighthouse.

ARRIVAL AND DEPARTURE   MONHEGAN ISLAND

By boat You can access Monhegan from Port Clyde (18 miles south of Rockland), Boothbay Harbor, New Harbor and Muscongus. From Port Clyde, it takes about 1hr via Monhegan Boat Lines (May–Oct daily; Nov–April Mon, Wed & Fri; three sailings a day in summer, fewer at other times; ⊛ monheganboat.com). Reservations recommended. Sailing time from other ports: Boothbay Harbor (90min), New Harbor (70min), Muscongus (6hr).

ACCOMMODATION

Island Inn ⊛ islandinnmonhegan.com. This sea-salted 1816 summer inn is quintessentially Maine. Its 28 updated rooms (and four suites) have painted floors, oak furniture and bright white beds, but the best amenity is the view. Enjoy a hearty complimentary breakfast. Open late May to mid-Oct. Shared bath $\overline{\$}\overline{\$}$, en suite $\overline{\$}\overline{\$}\overline{\$}$

Trailing Yew ⊛ trailingyew.com. Eclectic, old-fashioned but well-regarded abode, with 33 rooms (some singles) spread among several buildings; some rooms do not have heat or electricity, but rather fireplace and oil lamps. Breakfast included. Open May–Oct. $\overline{\$}\overline{\$}$

Camden and Rockport

The adjacent communities of **CAMDEN** and **ROCKPORT** split into two separate towns in 1891, in a dispute over who should pay for a new bridge over the Goose River between them. Rockport is now a quiet working port, among the prettiest on the Maine coast, home to lobster boats, pleasure cruisers and little else; Camden, another beauty, has clearly won the competition for visitors. One essential regional stop is **Camden Hills State Park**, two miles north of Camden (charge; ☎ 207 236 3109), where you can hike or drive up to a tower that affords one of the best views of the Maine coastline; on a clear day it's possible to see as far as Acadia National Park.

Don't underestimate the magnetism of the Belted Galloway cows at **Aldermere Farm**, at 70 Russell Ave in Rockport (⊛ aldermere.org). These endearing "Oreo cows" (so named for their black-white-black stripe pattern) have been amusing passers-by for ages. The farm offers year-round educational programming, but most people just pop by for a glimpse of the belties.

ACCOMMODATION   CAMDEN AND ROCKPORT

The Belmont 6 Belmont Ave, Camden ⊛ thebelmontinn.com. Decorated with conservative elegance, this 1891 Victorian sits on a quiet residential street just beyond the commercial district. Rooms are gussied up in soothing tones of white and forest green, and there's a wraparound porch. Breakfast (included) is an event. $\overline{\$}\overline{\$}$
Ducktrap Motel 12 Whitney Rd, Lincolnville ⊛ ducktrapmotel.com. Cute, basic, affordable roadside motel just north of Camden. It also has an ocean-view cottage and two larger, family-sized rooms. Open mid-April

to Oct. Doubles $\overline{\underline{5}}$, cottage $\overline{\underline{55}}$

The Hawthorn 9 High St, Camden ⓦ camdenhawthorn.com. Well situated by the harbour and with nice views of Mount Battie, this Camden favourite has lush gardens, traditional decor, a veranda and a lovely, helpful proprietor. The inn's Victorian shape leads to fun design details, such as a guestroom inside a turret. $\overline{\underline{5}}-\overline{\underline{55}}$

EATING AND DRINKING

Boynton-McKay 30 Main St, Camden ⓦ boyntonmckay.com. Order a tall stack of pancakes, eggs over-easy or brisket hash with sautéed greens at this one-time apothecary that retains its original fixtures and is famed for breakfasts. $\overline{\underline{5}}$

★ **Long Grain** 31 Elm St, Camden ⓦ longgraincamden.com. Remarkable Asian cuisine – a sampling of Thai, Vietnamese and Korean fare – that's very well priced. While the ambience is laidback, the kitchen skill level is serious – the chef was a James Beard semi-finalist. Don't skip dessert. $\overline{\underline{5}}-\overline{\underline{55}}$

Mount Desert Island

Considering that two million visitors come to **MOUNT DESERT ISLAND** each year, and that it boasts not only a genuine fjord but also the highest headland on the entire Atlantic coast north of Rio de Janeiro, it is an astonishingly small place, measuring just fifteen miles by twelve. The most accessible of the innumerable rugged granite islands along the Maine coast, it has been linked to the mainland by bridge since 1836, and has great facilities. "MDI" is a breathtakingly beautiful place – a glorious melding of ocean-battered cliffs, cool, hushed forests, stocky lupin flowers and sherbet-coloured sunrises.

The social centre, **Bar Harbor**, has accommodation and restaurants to suit all wallets, while you'll find lower-key communities, such as **Southwest Harbor**, all over the island. **Acadia National Park**, which covers much of the region, offers active travellers plenty of outdoor opportunities.

Bar Harbor

The town of **BAR HARBOR** began life as an exclusive resort, summer home to the Vanderbilts and the Astors; the great fire of October 1947 that destroyed their opulent "cottages" changed the direction of the town's growth. It's now firmly geared towards tourists, though it's by no means downmarket.

Abbe Museum

26 Mount Desert St • May–Oct daily 10am–5pm; Nov, Dec & Feb to late May Thurs–Sat 10am–4pm • Charge, admission includes Sieur de Monts location, off the Park Loop Rd • ⓦ abbemuseum.org

The native Wabanaki heritage – and current happenings – are maintained by the **Abbe Museum**, which has gorgeously constructed exhibit spaces full of light and pale wood panelling. Although the opening displays on Wabanaki culture are well put together, the Abbe's knockout piece is the "Circle of the Four Directions", a contemplative, circular space built of cedar panels that span upward into an arced skylight.

OUT TO SEA

In high season, more than twenty different **sea trips** set off each day from Bar Harbor, for purposes ranging from deep-sea fishing to cocktail cruises. Among the most popular are the **whale-watching**, puffin and seal trips run by Bar Harbor Whale Watch Company, 1 West St (3hr; charge; ⓦ barharborwhales.com). If you're travelling with children, don't miss **Diver Ed's** Dive-In Theater (leaving from the *College of Atlantic*, 105 Eden St; charge; ⓦ divered.com); Ed documents his madcap undersea adventures with a live, on-boat broadcast, then surfaces with a wealth of creatures. Lulu Lobster Boat Rides (2hr; charge; ⓦ lululobsterboat.com) offers authentic **lobstering** trips with Captain John, who raises traps, spots seals and charms passengers with nautical folklore.

1

Acadia National Park

Open all year • Charge for vehicle or individual (cyclist, hiker, pedestrian); valid for seven days • **Hulls Cove visitor centre** Just off Rte-3 at the entrance to Park Loop Rd • April–Oct daily 8.30am–4.30pm • ⓦ nps.gov/acad • **Park headquarters** (for out-of-season info) 20 McFarland Hill Drive • Nov & Dec daily 8am–4.30pm; Jan & Feb Mon–Fri 8am–4.30pm

Stretched out over most of Mount Desert Island, **ACADIA NATIONAL PARK** is the most visited natural place in Maine. It's visually stunning, with all you could want in terms of mountains and lakes for secluded rambling, and **wildlife** such as seals, beavers and bald eagles. The two main geographical features are the narrow fjord of **Somes Sound**, which almost splits the island in two, and lovely **Cadillac Mountain**, 1530ft high, which offers tremendous ocean views. The summit can be reached either by a moderately strenuous climb or by a very leisurely drive up a low-gradient road.

The one and only sizeable beach, five miles south of Bar Harbor, is a looker: called simply **Sand Beach**, it's a gorgeous strand bounded by twin headlands, with restrooms, a parking lot and a few short hiking trails. The water, unfortunately, is usually arctic.

ARRIVAL AND DEPARTURE

MOUNT DESERT ISLAND

By plane Flights into Bar Harbor are relatively infrequent and expensive – Bar Harbor/Hancock County Airport (ⓦ bhbairport.com), on Rte-3 in Trenton, has a limited service run by Cape Air and PenAir. It's more feasible to fly to Bangor International Airport (ⓦ flybangor.com), 45 miles away, and get the shuttle bus to Bar Harbor (ⓦ barharborshuttle.net).

By bus West's Coastal Connections Buses ⓦ westbusservice. com) travel between Bangor and the border town of Calais via Ellsworth.

By car Mount Desert is easy enough to get to from Rte-1 via Rte-3, although in summer roads on the island itself get congested.

GETTING AROUND AND INFORMATION

By shuttle bus Public transport is minimal outside of Bar Harbor, though once you get there, take advantage of the free Island Explorer shuttle buses (ⓦ exploreacadia. com), with eight routes that loop back to Bar Harbor.

By bike Three companies rent bikes for good rates: Bar Harbor Bicycle Shop, 141 Cottage St on the edge of town (ⓦ barharborbike.com); Coastal Kayak & Acadia Bike, across from the post office at 48 Cottage St (ⓦ acadiabike.com);

and Southwest Cycle, at 370 Main St in Southwest Harbor (ⓦ southwestcycle.com). All provide excellent maps and are good at suggesting routes. Carry water, as there are very few refreshments stops inside the park.

Visitor centres Bar Harbor's main tourist information office is at 1201 Bar Harbor Rd in Trenton just before you cross the bridge to Mount Desert Island (ⓦ barharborinfo. com).

ACCOMMODATION

Many places in Bar Harbor are open May to October only, and rates increase drastically in July and August. Lots book up early, too, so call ahead to check for availability.

BAR HARBOR

Bass Cottage Inn 14 The Field ⓦ basscottage.com. On a quiet private side street steps from downtown, this luxe B&B has lovely trimmings: whirlpool tubs, fireplaces, an evening wine hour and decadent breakfasts. $$$
Seacroft Inn 18 Albert Meadow ⓦ seacroftinn.com. No-frills B&B with welcoming hosts, quilted bedspreads and affordable rooms, with a fridge and microwave, one with a bath down the hall. Great central location, walkable to everything in town, and a continental breakfast in the morning. Open mid-May to Oct. $–$$
★ **Ullikana** 16 The Field ⓦ ullikana.com. Artfully decorated rooms that pop with colour and character. The location is tops, and the sumptuous breakfasts are served

on a terrace overlooking the water. Open late May to Oct. $$–$$$

SOUTHWEST AND NORTHEAST HARBOR

The Claremont 22 Claremont Rd, Southwest Harbor ⓦ theclaremonthotel.com. One of Maine's most beautiful properties, this classic old-fashioned hotel has tennis, croquet, boating and an excellent shorefront. On Friday nights, fine dining is accompanied by live piano music. The Claremont also hosts free Thursday evening lectures, covering everything from Maine history to arts, and Saturday evening concerts with a wonderful array of music, including jazz and classical. Open late May to mid-Oct. $$$
★ **Harbourside Inn** 48 Harborside Rd, Northeast Harbor ⓦ harboursideinn.com. Nineteenth-century woodland inn with patterned wallpaper, clawfoot tubs and working fireplaces. The inn is right on the edge of azalea gardens and hiking trails, and there's an organic breakfast.

INLAND AND WESTERN MAINE

The vast expanses of the **Maine interior**, stretching up into the cold far north, consist mostly of evergreen forests of pine, spruce and fir, interspersed with the white birches and maples responsible for the spectacular fall colours. Distances here are large. Once you get away from the two biggest cities – **Augusta** and **Bangor** – it's roughly two hundred miles by road to the northern border at **Fort Kent**, while to drive between the two most likely inland bases, **Greenville** and **Rangeley**, takes three hours or more. Driving (there's no public transport) through this mountainous scenery can be a great pleasure – it smells like Christmas trees as you go – but be aware that beyond Millinocket some roads are access routes belonging to the lumber companies: gravel-surfaced and vulnerable to bad weather. This is great territory in which to **hike** – the **Appalachian Trail** culminates its two-thousand-mile course up from Georgia at the top of Mount Katahdin – or raft on the **Allagash Wilderness Waterway**.

No TVs, but lots of tranquillity. Family-owned and operated. Open June to mid-Sept. $\overline{\underline{\$}}$–$\overline{\underline{\$\$}}$

CAMPING IN ACADIA NATIONAL PARK

Blackwoods Near Seal Harbor ⓦ recreation.gov. Administered by the National Park Service, this tranquil, all-season campground takes reservations up to a year in advance. $\overline{\underline{\$}}$

Seawall Off Rte-102A, near Bass Harbor ⓦ nps.gov/acad. Lovely forested campsites, where reservations highly recommended. Open late May to Sept. $\overline{\underline{\$}}$

EATING AND NIGHTLIFE

BAR HARBOR

2 Cats 130 Cottage St ⓦ twocatsbarharbor.com. The town's best breakfast place. All the baked goods are made in-house, the herbs are home-grown, and the coffee – which comes in enormous mugs – is Fairtrade. Plus, you can now BYOB – bring the bubbly or vodka, and they'll pour the orange juice or Bloody Mary mix. Nice outdoor patio, but expect to queue for it. $

Lompoc Café 36 Rodick St ⓦ lompoccafe.com. Eclectic, affordable menu in a woodsy outdoor dining room with bocce ball. Order the "bang bang" sandwich (fried chicken, spicy slaw, hot sauce and honey), the mussels in Dijon sauce or the hearty fish chowder with Maine hake and bacon, and wash it down with a regional beer. Live music every weekend. $\overline{\underline{\$\$}}$

Mount Desert Island Ice Cream 7 Firefly Lane ⓦ mdiic.com. Not your average scoop – foodies wax poetic about the varieties here: sweet and salty peanut butter, toasted coconut and blueberry basil sorbet head a long list of exceptional and ever-changing flavours. There's another location at 325 Main St and one in Portland. $\overline{\underline{\$}}$

Reel Pizza Cinerama 33 Kennebec Place, on the Village Green ⓦ reelpizza.net. Eat pizza, drink beer and watch arty or blockbuster films on the big screen – it's fun when your order comes up on the bingo board. $\overline{\underline{\$}}$

Side Street Café 49 Rodick St ⓦ sidestreetbarharbor. com. The beating heart of Bar Harbor, *Side Street Café* pairs pitchers of tangy margaritas with tempting comfort foods such as lobster stew, mussels with chorizo and the seafood mac and cheese, heaped with scallops, shrimp and lobster. Expect a wait at peak times, reservations recommended. $\overline{\underline{\$\$}}$

SOUTHWEST HARBOR

Beal's Lobster Pier 182 Clark Point Rd ⓦ bealslobster. com. Fresh seafood on a rickety wooden pier. You can pick out your own lobster from a tank, or choose from a small menu of other seafood choices. $\overline{\underline{\$\$}}$

ACADIA NATIONAL PARK

Jordan Pond Park Loop Rd ⓦ acadiajordanpondhouse. com. Light meals, ice cream and popovers (puffy egg muffins served with butter and strawberry jam) in the heart of the park, between Bar Harbor and Northeast Harbor. Try the Prosecco & Popovers, or afternoon tea (3–5pm, reservations recommended), an Acadia tradition, is served in the lakeside garden. $\overline{\underline{\$\$}}$

Downeast Maine: the coast to Canada

Few travellers venture into the hundred miles of Maine lying east beyond Acadia National Park, mainly because it is almost entirely unpopulated, windswept and remote. In summer, though, the weather is marked by mesmerizing fogs, and the coastal drive is

1

exhilarating – it runs next to the Bay of Fundy, home to the highest tides in the nation. **Downeast Maine** is also characterized by its wild **blueberry** crops – ninety percent of the nation's harvest comes from this corner of the state.

A short way northeast of Acadia, a loop road leads from Rte-1 to the rocky outcrop of **Schoodic Point**, which offers good birdwatching, great views and a splendid sense of solitude. Each village has one or two B&Bs and well-priced restaurants, such as **Machias**, known for its best-in-state blueberry pie at *Helen's* (see page 120). Close to Canada, you'll find the salt-of-the-earth communities of **Lubec** and **Eastport**, tiny enclaves with marvellous ocean scenery.

EATING   **DOWNEAST MAINE**

Helen's   111   Main   St,   Machias   state, if not the world. Everything on the comfort food-filled
ⓦhelensrestaurantmachias.com.   Make   sure   you   menu is delicious, including the cheesy meatloaf sandwich
don't leave town without trying the blueberry pie at this   and the regional seafood icon, fried clams. ⑤
landmark restaurant – it's considered the finest in the

West Quoddy Head and around

With a distinctive, candy-striped **lighthouse** dramatically signalling its endpoint, **WEST QUODDY HEAD** is the easternmost point of the USA, jutting defiantly into the stormy Atlantic. Just beyond the turnoff for Quoddy Head, tiny **LUBEC** was once home to more than twenty sardine-packing plants – all gone now. Keep your eyes out for a seal as you stroll the main drag. Lubec also hosts the dynamic adult music camp The Summer Keys (ⓦsummerkeys.com).

Campobello Island

Lubec is the gateway to **CAMPOBELLO ISLAND**, in New Brunswick, Canada, where Franklin D. Roosevelt summered from 1909 to 1921, and to which he occasionally returned during his presidency. His barn-red cottage, furnished just as the Roosevelts left it, is now open to the public as the **Roosevelt Campobello International Park** (mid-May to mid-Oct daily 9am–5pm; free; ⓦfdr.net). The rest of the park, located on Canadian soil but held jointly with the United States, is good for a couple of hours' wandering – the coastal trails and the drive out to **Liberty Point** are worth the effort. Remember that you will need a valid passport to cross the border.

The Quoddy Loop

The border between the United States and Canada weaves through the centre of Passamaquoddy Bay; the towns to either side get on so well that they refused to fight against each other in the War of 1812, and promote themselves jointly to tourists as the **Quoddy Loop** (ⓦquoddyloop.com). It's perfectly feasible to take a "two-nation vacation", but each passage through customs and immigration between **Calais** (pronounced "callous") in the States (fifty miles north of Lubec) and **St Stephen** in Canada does take a little while – and be aware, also, that the towns are in different time zones.

Eastport

If you have the driving stamina, **EASTPORT**, some forty miles up the road from the Quoddy Loop, is one of the most spectacular places you'll ever see, with an edge-of-the-earth feel and stunning views of the Canadian shoreline. **Raye's Mustard Mill Museum**, at 83 Washington St (call ahead to confirm hours, but generally Mon–Fri 8.30am–5pm, Sat & Sun 10am–5pm; ⓦrayesmustard.com), is the country's last surviving stone mustard mill and has been producing at least 25 varieties of "liquid gold" for more than a century.

ACCOMMODATION AND EATING

Inn on the Wharf 69 Johnson St, Lubec ⓦ theinnonthewharf.com. Contemporary white rooms with occasional splashes of colour in a renovated sardine factory overlooking the ocean, with an on-site restaurant serving fresh crustaceans. Kayak and whale watching tours available, too. $–$$

The Happy Crab 35 Water St, Eastport ⓦ happy-crab.

WEST QUODDY HEAD AND AROUND

business.site. Feast on ultra-fresh lobster rolls, chowder and clams at this seaside favourite, with the 'Fish Fry Fridays' a particularly good time to visit. $–$$

Peacock House 27 Summer St, Lubec ⓦ peacockhouse. com. A fantastic place to stay: charming proprietors, country-chic guestrooms, quilts and patterned wallpaper in a rambling clapboard house. Open May–Oct. $–$$

Baxter State Park

On a clear day in serenely unspoiled **BAXTER STATE PARK** (charge, ⓦ baxterstateparkauthority.com), the 5268ft peak of **Katahdin** (or "greatest mountain", in the language of the Penobscot tribe) is visible from afar. Forests here – the park is an enormous 200,000 acres – are home to deer, beaver, a few bears, some recently introduced caribou and plenty of **moose**. These endearingly gawky creatures are virtually blind and tend to be seen at early morning or dusk; you may spot them feeding in shallow water. They do, however, cause major havoc on the roads, particularly at night. Aim to be at your destination before the sun sets – each year sees a significant number of moose-related collisions.

INFORMATION AND ACCOMMODATION

Arrival Plan to arrive at the park early in the day, as only a limited number of visitors are permitted access to Katahdin trailheads. The park headquarters is located at 64 Balsam Drive in Millinocket (ⓦ baxterstateparkauthority. com). There is another centre at Togue Pond, the southern

BAXTER STATE PARK

entrance to the park.

Camping There are ten designated campgrounds in Baxter (☎ 207 723 5140), providing an array of options from basic tent sites to cabins equipped with beds, heating stoves, and gas lighting. $

THE MAYFLOWER II

Contexts

History

There is much more to the history of the United States than the history of New England alone. However, as the landing place for the Pilgrim Fathers in the 17th century, this part of America is where the history of the modern nation begins – and what a fascinating story it is.

First peoples

The true pioneers of North America, nomadic hunter-gatherers from Siberia, are thought to have reached what's now **Alaska** around seventeen thousand years ago. Thanks to the last ice age, when sea levels were 300ft lower, a **"land-bridge"** – actually a vast plain, measuring six hundred miles north to south – connected Eurasia to America.

Alaska was at that time separated by glacier fields from what is now Canada, and thus effectively part of Asia rather than North America. Like an air lock, the region has "opened" in different directions at different times; migrants reaching it from the west, unaware that they were leaving Asia, would at first have found their way blocked to the east. Several generations might pass, and the connection back towards Asia be severed, before an eastward passage appeared. When thawing ice did clear a route into North America, it was not along the Pacific coast but via a corridor that led east of the Rockies and out onto the Great Plains.

This migration may well have been spurred by the pursuit of large mammal species, and especially **mammoth**, which had already been harried to extinction throughout almost all of Eurasia. A huge bonanza awaited the hunters when they finally encountered America's own indigenous **"megafauna"**, such as mammoths, mastodons, giant ground sloths and enormous long-horned bison, all of which had evolved with no protection against human predation.

Filling the New World

Within a thousand years, ten million people were living throughout both North and South America. Although that sounds like a phenomenally rapid spread, it would only have required a band of just one hundred individuals to enter the continent, and advance a mere eight miles per year, with an annual population growth of 1.1 percent, to achieve that impact. The mass **extinction** of the American megafauna was so precisely simultaneous that humans must surely have been responsible, eliminating the giant beasts in each locality in one fell swoop, before pressing on in search of the next kill.

At least three distinct waves of **migrants** arrived via Alaska, each of whom settled in, and adapted to, a more marginal environment than its predecessors. The second, five thousand years on from the first, were the **"Nadene"** or Athapascans – the ancestors of the Haida of the Northwest, and the Navajo and Apache of the Southwest – while the third, another two thousand years later, found their niche in the frozen Arctic and became the **Aleuts** and the **Inuits**.

c.60 million BC	15,000 BC	11,000 BC
Two mighty islands collide, creating North America as a single landmass, and throwing up the Rocky Mountains	First nomadic peoples from Asia reach Alaska	Almost all North America's large mammals become extinct, possibly due to over-hunting

Early settlements

The earliest known settlement site in the modern United States, dating back 12,000 years, lay close to what is now New England at Meadowcroft in southwest Pennsylvania. Five centuries later, the Southwest was dominated by the so-called **Clovis** culture, while subsequent subgroups ranged from the Algonquin farmers of what's now New England to peoples such as the Chumash and Macah, who lived by catching fish, otters and even whales along the coasts of the Pacific Northwest.

Nowhere did a civilization emerge to rival the wealth and sophistication of the great cities of ancient Mexico. However, the influence of those far-off cultures did filter north; the cultivation of crops such as beans, squash and maize facilitated the development of large communities, while northern religious cults, some of which performed human sacrifice, owed much to Central American beliefs.

Estimates of the total indigenous population before the arrival of the Europeans vary widely, but an acceptable median figure suggests around fifty million people in the Americas as a whole. Perhaps five million of those were in North America, speaking around four hundred different languages.

Christopher Columbus

Five more centuries passed before the crucial moment of contact with the rest of the world came on October 12, 1492, when **Christopher Columbus**, sailing on behalf of the Spanish, reached the Bahamas. A mere four years later the English navigator John Cabot officially "discovered" Newfoundland, and soon British fishermen were setting up makeshift encampments in what became **New England**, to spend the winter curing their catch.

Over the next few years various expeditions mapped the eastern seaboard. In 1524, the Italian **Giovanni da Verrazano** sailed past Maine, which he characterized as the "Land of Bad People" thanks to the inhospitable and contemptuous behaviour of its natives, and reached the mouth of the Hudson River. The great hope was to find a sea route in the Northeast that would lead to China – the fabled **Northwest Passage**. To the French **Jacques Cartier**, the St Lawrence Seaway seemed a promising avenue, and unsuccessful attempts were made to settle the northern areas of the Great Lakes from the 1530s onwards. Intrepid trappers and traders ventured ever further west.

The growth of the colonies in New England

The 102 **Puritans** remembered as the "**Pilgrim Fathers**" were deposited on Cape Cod by the *Mayflower* in late 1620, and soon moved on to set up their own colony at Plymouth (see page 69). Fifty died that winter, and the whole party might have perished but for their fortuitous encounter with the extraordinary **Squanto**. This Native American had twice been kidnapped and taken to Europe, only to make his way home; he had spent four years working as a merchant in the City of London, and had also lived in Spain. Having recently come home to find his entire tribe exterminated by smallpox, he threw in his lot with the English. With his guidance, they finally managed to reap their first harvest, celebrated with a mighty feast of **Thanksgiving**.

Of greater significance to New England was the founding in 1630 of a new colony, further up the coast at Naumkeag (later Salem), by the Massachusetts Bay Company. Its governor, **John Winthrop**, soon moved to establish a new capital on the Shawmut

c.2500 BC	**1001-02**	**1620**
Agriculture reaches North America from Mexico	Leif Eiriksson sails from Greenland to establish Vinland, in northern Newfoundland	A hundred Puritan colonists reach New England aboard the Mayflower, and settle at Plymouth

peninsula – the city of **Boston**, complete with its own university of Harvard. His vision of a Utopian "City on a Hill" did not extend to sharing Paradise with the Native Americans; he argued that they had not "subdued" the land, which was therefore a "vacuum" for the Puritans to use as they saw fit. While their faith helped individual colonists to endure the early hardships, the colony as a whole failed to maintain a strong religious identity (the Salem witch trials of 1692 did much to discredit the notion that the New World had any moral superiority to the Old), and breakaway groups left to create the rival settlements of Providence and Connecticut.

Between 1620 and 1642, sixty thousand migrants – 1.5 percent of the population – left England for America. Those in pursuit of economic opportunities often joined the longer-established colonies, thereby serving to dilute the religious zeal of the Puritans. Groups hoping to find spiritual freedom were more inclined to start afresh; thus **Maryland** was created as a haven for Catholics in 1632, and fifty years later **Pennsylvania** was founded by the Quakers.

The American Revolution

The American colonies prospered during the **eighteenth century**. Boston, New York and Philadelphia in particular became home to a wealthy, well-educated and highly articulate middle class. Frustration mounted at the inequities of the colonies' relationship with Britain, however. The Americans could only sell their produce to the British, and all transatlantic commerce had to be undertaken in British ships.

Full-scale independence was not an explicit goal until late in the century, but the main factor that made it possible was the economic impact of the pan-European **Seven Years War**. All the European monarchs were left hamstrung by debts, and the British realized that colonialism in America was not as profitable as in those parts of the world where the native populations could be coerced into working for their overseas masters.

An unsuccessful insurrection by the Ottawa in 1763, led by their chief **Pontiac**, led the cash-strapped British to conclude that, while America needed its own standing army, it was reasonable to expect the colonists to pay for it. In 1765, they introduced the **Stamp Act**, requiring duty on all legal transactions and printed matter in the colonies to be paid to the British Crown. Arguing for "no taxation without representation", delegates from nine colonies met in the Stamp Act Congress that October. By then, however, the British prime minister responsible had already been dismissed by King George III, and the Act was repealed in 1766.

However, in 1767, Chancellor Townshend made political capital at home by proclaiming "I dare tax America", as he introduced legislation including the broadly similar Revenue Act. That led Massachusetts merchants, inspired by **Samuel Adams**, to vote to boycott English goods; they were joined by all the other colonies except New Hampshire. Townshend's Acts were repealed in turn by a new prime minister, Lord North, on March 5, 1770. By chance, on that same day a stone-throwing mob surrounded the Customs House in Boston; five people were shot in what became known as the **Boston Massacre**. Even so, most of the colonies resumed trading with Britain, and the crisis was postponed for a few more years.

In May 1773, Lord North's **Tea Act** relieved the debt-ridden East India Company of the need to pay duties on exports to America, while still requiring the Americans to pay

1664	1682	1692
The Dutch settlement of New Amsterdam, captured by the English, becomes New York City	Quaker settlers found Philadelphia. The Sieur de la Salle claims the Mississippi valley for France as Louisiana	Eighteen supposed witches are executed in Salem, Massachusetts

duty on tea. Massachusetts called the colonies to action, and its citizens took the lead on December 16 in the **Boston Tea Party**, when three tea ships were boarded and 342 chests thrown into the sea.

The infuriated British Parliament thereupon began to pass legislation collectively known as both the "Coercive" and the "Intolerable" Acts, which included closing the port of Boston and disbanding the government of Massachusetts. Thomas Jefferson argued that the acts amounted to "a deliberate and systematical plan of reducing us to slavery". To discuss a response, the first **Continental Congress** was held in Philadelphia on May 5, 1774, and attended by representatives of all the colonies except Georgia.

The Revolutionary War

War finally broke out on April 18, 1775, when General Gage, the governor of Massachusetts, dispatched four hundred British soldiers to destroy the arms depot at **Concord**, and prevent weapons from falling into rebel hands. Silversmith **Paul Revere** was dispatched on his legendary ride to warn the rebels, and the British were confronted en route at Lexington by 77 American "Minutemen". The resulting skirmish led to the "shot heard 'round the world".

Congress set about forming an army at Boston, and decided for the sake of unity to appoint a Southern commander, **George Washington**. One by one, as the war raged, the colonies set up their own governments and declared themselves to be states, and the politicians set about defining the society they wished to create. The writings of pamphleteer Thomas Paine – especially *Common Sense* – were, together with the Confederacy of the Iroquois, a great influence on the **Declaration of Independence**. Drafted by Thomas Jefferson, this was adopted by the Continental Congress in Philadelphia on July 4, 1776. Anti-slavery clauses originally included by Jefferson – himself a slave-owner – were omitted to spare the feelings of the Southern states, though the section that denounced the King's dealings with "merciless Indian Savages" was left in.

At first, the Revolutionary War went well for the British. General Howe crossed the Atlantic with twenty thousand men, took New York and New Jersey, and ensconced himself in Philadelphia for the winter of 1777–78. Washington's army was encamped not far away at Valley Forge, freezing cold and all but starving to death. It soon became clear, however, that the longer the Americans could avoid losing an all-out battle, the more likely the British were to over-extend their lines as they advanced through the vast and unfamiliar continent. Thus, General Burgoyne's expedition, which set out from Canada to march on New England, was so harried by rebel guerrillas that he had to surrender at Saratoga in October 1777. Other European powers took delight in coming to the aid of the Americans. Benjamin Franklin led a wildly successful delegation to France to request support, and soon the nascent American fleet was being assisted in its bid to cut British naval communications by both the French and the Spanish. The end came when Cornwallis, who had replaced Howe, was instructed to dig in at Yorktown and wait for the Royal Navy to come to his aid, only for the French to seal off Chesapeake Bay and prevent reinforcement. Cornwallis surrendered to Washington on October 17, 1781.

The ensuing **Treaty of Paris** granted the Americans their independence on generous terms – the British abandoned their Native American allies, including the Iroquois, to

1765	1770	1773
New England responds to British legislation with the cry "no taxation without representation"	In the Boston Massacre, British sentries fire on a mob and kill five colonists	In the Boston Tea Party, two hundred colonists respond to British duties by tipping tea into the sea

THE CONSTITUTION

As signed in 1787 and ratified in 1788, the **Constitution** stipulated the following form of government:

All **legislative** powers were granted to the **Congress of the United States**. The lower of its two distinct houses, the **House of Representatives**, was to be elected every two years, with its members in proportion to the number of each state's "free Persons" plus "three fifths of all other persons" (meaning slaves). The upper house, the **Senate**, would hold two Senators from each state, chosen by state legislatures rather than by direct elections. Each Senator was to serve for six years, with a third of them to be elected every two years.

Executive power was vested in the **President**, who was also Commander in Chief of the Army and Navy. He would be chosen every four years, by as many "**Electors**" from each individual state as it had Senators and Representatives. Each state could decide how to appoint those Electors; almost all chose to have direct popular elections. Nonetheless, the distinction has remained ever since between the number of popular votes, across the whole country, received by a presidential candidate, and the number of state-by-state "electoral votes", which determines the actual result. Originally, whoever came second in the voting automatically became **vice president**.

The President could **veto** acts of Congress, but that veto could be overruled by a two-thirds vote in both houses. The House of Representatives could **impeach** the President for treason, bribery or "other high crimes and misdemeanors", in which instance the Senate could remove him from office with a two-thirds majority.

Judicial power was invested in a **Supreme Court**, and as many "inferior Courts" as Congress should decide.

The Constitution has so far been altered by 27 **Amendments**. Numbers **14** and **15** extended the vote to black males in 1868 and 1870; **17** made Senators subject to election by direct popular vote in 1913; **19** introduced women's suffrage in 1920; **22** restricted the President to two terms in 1951; **24** stopped states using poll taxes to disenfranchise black voters in 1964; and **26** reduced the minimum voting age to 18 in 1971.

the vengeance of the victors – and Washington entered New York as the British left in November 1783. The Spanish were confirmed in possession of Florida.

The victorious US Congress met for the first time in 1789, and the tradition of awarding political power to the nation's most successful generals was instigated by the election of George Washington as the first **president**. He was further honoured when his name was given to the new capital city of **Washington DC**, deliberately sited between the North and the South.

The Civil War

From its inception, the unity of the United States had been based on shaky foundations. Great care had gone into devising a **Constitution** that balanced the need for a strong federal government with the aspirations for autonomy of its component states. That was achieved by giving Congress two separate chambers – the **House of Representatives**, in which each state was represented in proportion to its population, and the **Senate**, in which each state, regardless of size, had two members. Thus,

1775	**1776**	**1777**
The Revolutionary War begins with the "shot heard 'round the world"; George Washington assumes command of the Continental Army	The Declaration of Independence is signed on July 4	General Washington takes up winter quarters at Valley Forge

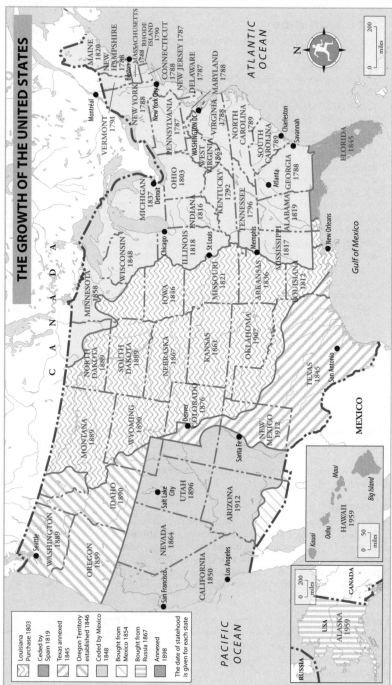

THE GROWTH OF THE UNITED STATES

although in theory the Constitution remained silent on the issue of **slavery**, it allayed the fears of the less populated Southern states that Northern voters might destroy their economy by forcing them to abandon their "peculiar institution".

However, the system only worked so long as there were equal numbers of "Free" and slave-owning states. The only practicable way to keep the balance was to ensure that each time a new state was admitted to the Union, a matching state taking the opposite stance on slavery was also admitted. Thus, the admission of every new state became subject to endless intrigue. The 1820 **Missouri Compromise**, under which Missouri joined as a slave-owning state and Maine as a Free one, was straightforward in comparison to the prevarication and chest-beating that surrounded the admission of Texas, while the Mexican War was widely seen in the North as a naked land grab for new slave states.

Abolitionist sentiment in the North was not all that great before the middle of the nineteenth century. At best, after the importation of slaves from Africa ended in 1808, Northerners vaguely hoped slavery was an anachronism that might simply wither away. As it turned out, Southern plantations were rendered much more profitable by the development of the cotton gin, and the increased demand for manufactured cotton goods triggered by the **Industrial Revolution**. However, the rapid growth of the nation as a whole made it ever more difficult to maintain a political balance between North and South.

The coming of war

The **Civil War** began in April 1861. Over four years, the **Union** of 23 Northern states, holding more than 22 million people and including all of what is now New England, wore down the **Confederacy** of eleven Southern states, with nine million. As for potential combatants, the North initially drew upon 3.5 million white males aged between 18 and 45 – and later recruited blacks as well – whereas the South had more like one million. In the end, around 2.1 million men fought for the Union, and 900,000 for the Confederacy. Of the 620,000 soldiers who died, a disproportionate 258,000 came from the South – one quarter of its white men of military age. Meanwhile, not only did the North continue trading with the rest of the world while maintaining its industrial and agricultural output, it also stifled the Confederacy with a devastating **naval blockade**.

The aftermath of the Civil War can almost be said to have lasted for a hundred years. While the South condemned itself to a century as a backwater, the rest of the re-United States embarked on a period of expansionism and prosperity – nowhere more so than New England.

Industry and immigration

The late nineteenth century saw massive **immigration** to North America, with influxes from Europe to the East Coast paralleled by those from Asia to the West. The fastest growth of all was in the nation's greatest **cities**, especially New York, Chicago and Boston. Their industrial and commercial strength enabled them to attract and absorb migrants not only from throughout Europe but also from the Old South – particularly former slaves, who could now at least vote with their feet.

The nineteenth century had also seen the development of a distinctive American voice in **literature**, which rendered increasingly superfluous the efforts of passing English

1781	**1787**	**1789**
Surrounded by land and sea, British commander Lord Cornwallis surrenders at Yorktown	The Constitution is signed in Philadelphia	George Washington is inaugurated as the first president of the United States

visitors to "explain" the United States. From the 1830s onwards, writers explored new ways to describe their new world, with results as varied as the introspective essays and nature writing of Henry Thoreau and the morbid visions of Edgar Allan Poe – both New Englanders.

New England led the way for the development of infrastructure in the 19th-century United States, funded in part by the financier J.P. Morgan, himself a New England man who had grown up in Hartford, Connecticut. The New Haven railroad commenced operations in 1872 and would continue to play a prominent role in the region until 1968.

The twentieth century

The railroads continued to dominate the economic life of New England in the first decades of the twentieth century, until their monopoly was upended, here as elsewhere, by the emergence of the motorcar.

Though President Wilson kept the USA out of the **Great War** for several years, American intervention was, when it came, decisive. With the Russian Revolution illustrating the dangers of anarchy, the USA also took charge of supervising the peace. However, even as Wilson presided over the negotiations that produced the Treaty of Versailles in 1919, isolationist sentiment at home prevented the USA from joining his pet scheme to preserve future world peace, the League of Nations.

Back home, the 18th Amendment forbade the sale and distribution of alcohol, while the 19th finally gave all American women the vote. Quite how **Prohibition** ever became the law of the land remains a mystery; certainly, in the buzzing metropolises of the Roaring Twenties, it enjoyed little conspicuous support. There was no noticeable elevation in the moral tone of the country, and Chicago in particular became renowned for the street wars between bootlegging gangsters such as Al Capone and his rivals.

The two Republican presidents who followed Wilson did little more than sit back and watch the Roaring Twenties unfold. Until his premature death, **Warren Harding** enjoyed considerable public affection, but he's now remembered as probably the worst US president of all, thanks to the cronyism and corruption of his associates. It's hard to say quite whether **Calvin Coolidge** did anything at all; his laissez-faire attitude extended to working a typical four-hour day, and announcing shortly after his inauguration that "four-fifths of our troubles would disappear if we would sit down and keep still".

The Depression and the New Deal

By the middle of the 1920s, the USA was an industrial powerhouse, responsible for more than half the world's output of manufactured goods. Having led the way into a new era of prosperity, however, it suddenly dragged the rest of the world down into economic collapse. The consequences of the **Great Depression** were out of all proportion to any one specific cause. Possible factors include American over-investment in the floundering economy of postwar Europe, combined with high tariffs on imports that effectively precluded European recovery. Conservative commentators at the time chose to interpret the calamitous **Wall Street Crash** of October 1929 as a symptom of impending depression rather than a contributory cause, but the quasi-superstitious faith in the stock market that preceded it showed all the characteristics of classic

1803	**1929**	**1932**
President Thomas Jefferson buys Louisiana west of the Mississippi for $15 million	The Wall Street Crash plunges the USA into economic turmoil	Franklin D. Roosevelt pledges "a new deal for the American people"

speculative booms. On "Black Tuesday" alone, enough stocks were sold to produce a total loss of ten thousand million dollars – more than twice the total amount of money in circulation in the USA. Within the next three years, industrial production was cut by half, the national income dropped by 38 percent, and, above all, unemployment rose from 1.5 million to 13 million.

National self-confidence, however shaky its foundations, has always played a crucial role in US history, and President Hoover was not the man to restore it. Matters only began to improve in 1932, when the patrician **Franklin Delano Roosevelt** accepted the Democratic nomination for president with the words "I pledge myself to a new deal for America", and went on to win a landslide victory. At the time of his inauguration, early in 1933, the banking system had all but closed down; it took Roosevelt the now-proverbial "Hundred Days" of vigorous legislation to turn around the mood of the country.

Taking advantage of the new medium of radio, Roosevelt used "Fireside Chats" to cajole America out of crisis; among his earliest observations was that it was a good time for a beer, and that the experiment of Prohibition was therefore over. The **New Deal** took many forms, but was marked throughout by a massive growth in the power of the federal government. Among its accomplishments were the National Recovery Administration, which created two million jobs; the Social Security Act, of which Roosevelt declared "no damn politician can ever scrap my social security program"; the Public Works Administration, which built dams and highways the length and breadth of the country; the Tennessee Valley Authority, which by generating electricity under public ownership for the common good was probably the closest the USA has ever come to institutionalized socialism; and measures to legitimize the role of the unions and revitalize the "Dust Bowl" farmers out on the plains.

Roosevelt originally saw himself as a populist who could draw support from every sector of society. By 1936, however, business leaders – and the Supreme Court – were making their opinion clear that he had done more than enough already to kick-start the economy. From then on, as he secured an unprecedented four consecutive terms as president, he was firmly cast as the champion of the little man.

After the work-creation programmes of the New Deal had put America back on its feet, the deadly pressure to achieve victory in **World War II** spurred industrial production and know-how to new heights. Once again the USA stayed out of the war at first, until it was finally forced in when the Japanese launched a pre-emptive strike on Hawaii's Pearl Harbor in 1941. In both the Pacific and in Europe, American manpower and economic muscle eventually carried all before it. By dying early in 1945, having laid the foundations for the postwar carve-up with Stalin and Churchill at Yalta, Roosevelt was spared the fateful decision, made by his successor Harry Truman, to use the newly developed atomic bomb on Hiroshima and Nagasaki.

The coming of the Cold War

With the war won, Americans were in no mood to revert back to the isolationism of the 1930s. Amid much hopeful rhetoric, Truman enthusiastically participated in the creation of the **United Nations**, and set up the **Marshall Plan** to speed the recovery of Europe. However, as Winston Churchill announced in Missouri in 1946, an "**Iron Curtain**" had descended upon Europe, and Joseph Stalin was transformed from ally to enemy almost overnight.

1941	**1945**	**1954**
A surprise Japanese attack on Pearl Harbor precipitates US entry into World War II	President Truman's decision to drop atomic bombs on Hiroshima and Nagasaki marks the end of World War II	The Supreme Court declares racial segregation in schools to be unconstitutional

The ensuing **Cold War** lasted for more than four decades, at times fought in ferocious combat (albeit often by proxy) in scattered corners of the globe, and during the intervals diverting colossal resources towards the stockpiling of ever more destructive arsenals. Some of its ugliest moments came in its earliest years; Truman was still in office in 1950 when war broke out in **Korea**. A dispute over the arbitrary division of the Korean peninsula into two separate nations, North and South, soon turned into a standoff between the USA and China (with Russia lurking in the shadows). Two years of bloody stalemate ended with little to show for it, except that Truman had by now been replaced by the genial **Dwight D. Eisenhower**, the latest war hero to become president.

The Eisenhower years are often seen as characterized by bland complacency. Once Senator **Joseph McCarthy**, the "witch-hunting" anti-Communist scourge of the State Department and Hollywood, had finally discredited himself by attacking the army as well, middle-class America seemed to lapse into a wilful suburban stupor. Great social changes were taking shape, however. World War II had introduced vast numbers of women and members of ethnic minorities to the rewards of factory work, and shown many Americans from less prosperous regions the lifestyle attainable elsewhere in their own country. The development of a **national highway system**, and a huge increase in automobile ownership, encouraged people to pursue the American Dream wherever they chose. Combined with increasing mechanization on the cotton plantations of the South, this led to another **mass exodus** of blacks from the rural South to the cities of the North, and to a lesser extent the West. **California** entered a period of rapid growth, with the aeronautical industries of Los Angeles in particular attracting thousands of prospective workers.

Also during the 1950s, **television** reached almost every home in the country. Together with the LP record, it created an entertainment industry that addressed the needs of consumers who had previously been barely identified. **Youth culture** burst into prominence from 1954 onwards, with Elvis Presley's recording of *That's All Right Mama* appearing within a few months of Marlon Brando's moody starring role in *On the Waterfront* and James Dean's in *Rebel Without a Cause*.

The civil rights years

Racial segregation of public facilities, which had remained the norm in the South ever since Reconstruction, was finally declared illegal in 1954 by the Supreme Court ruling on *Brown v. Topeka Board of Education*. Just as a century before, however, the Southern states saw the issue more in terms of states' rights than of human rights, and attempting to implement the law, or even to challenge the failure to implement it, required immense courage. The action of Rosa Parks in refusing to give up her seat on a bus in Montgomery, Alabama, in 1955, triggered a successful mass boycott and pushed the 27-year-old **Rev Dr Martin Luther King, Jr.** to the forefront of the civil rights campaign. While the civil rights cause was fought for most intensely in the segregated South, it also found expression and support in the cities of the North and New England, particularly Boston.

The election of Massachusetts man **John F. Kennedy** to the presidency in 1960, by the narrowest of margins, marked a sea-change in American politics, even if in retrospect his policies do not seem exactly radical. At 43 the youngest man ever to

1962	1963	1968
John Glenn becomes the first US astronaut to go into orbit; President Kennedy faces down the Russians in the Cuban Missile Crisis	Rev Martin Luther King, Jr. delivers "I Have a Dream" speech; President Kennedy is assassinated	With the nation polarized by war in Vietnam, Rev Martin Luther King, Jr, and Robert Kennedy are assassinated

be elected president, and the first Catholic, he was prepared literally to reach for the moon, urging the USA to victory in the Space Race in which it had thus far lagged humiliatingly behind the Soviet Union. The two decades that lay ahead, however, were to be characterized by disillusion, defeat and despair. If the Eisenhower years had been dull, the 1960s in particular were far too interesting for almost everybody's liking.

Kennedy's sheer glamour made him a popular president during his lifetime, while his assassination suffused his administration with the romantic glow of "Camelot". His one undisputed triumph, however, came with the **Cuban missile crisis** of 1962, when the US military fortunately spotted Russian bases in Cuba before any actual missiles were ready for use, and Kennedy faced down premier Khrushchev to insist they be withdrawn. On the other hand, he'd had rather less success the previous year in launching the abortive **Bay of Pigs** invasion of Cuba, and he also managed to embroil America deeper in the ongoing war against Communism in Vietnam by sending more "advisers" to Saigon.

In 1968, the social fabric of the USA reached the brink of collapse. Shortly after President Lyndon B. Johnson was forced by his plummeting popularity to withdraw from the year-end elections, Martin Luther King was gunned down in a Memphis motel. Next, JFK's brother **Robert Kennedy**, now redefined as spokesman for the dispossessed, was fatally shot just as he emerged as Democratic front-runner. It didn't take a conspiracy theorist to see that the spate of deaths reflected a malaise in the soul of America.

Richard Nixon to Jimmy Carter

The misery of 1968 resulted in the election of Republican **Richard Nixon** as president. Nixon's conservative credentials enabled him to bring the USA to a rapport with China, but the war in Vietnam dragged on to claim a total of 57,000 American lives. Attempts to win it included the secret and illegal bombing of Cambodia, which raised opposition at home to a new peak, but ultimately it was simpler to abandon the original goals in the name of "peace with honor". Nixon directed various federal agencies to monitor an emerging vein of radicalism. Increasingly ludicrous covert operations against real and potential opponents culminated in a botched attempt to burgle Democratic National Headquarters in the **Watergate** complex in 1972. It took two years of investigation for Nixon's role in the subsequent cover-up to be proved, but in 1974 he **resigned**, one step ahead of impeachment by the Senate, to be succeeded by **Gerald Ford**, his own appointee as vice president.

With the Republicans momentarily discredited, former Georgia governor **Jimmy Carter** was elected president as a clean-handed outsider in the bicentennial year of 1976. However, Carter's enthusiastic attempts to put his Baptist principles into practice on such issues as global human rights were soon perceived as naive, if not un-American. In 1980 he was replaced by a very different figure, the former movie actor **Ronald Reagan**.

From Reagan to Clinton

Reagan was a new kind of president. Unlike his workaholic predecessor, he made a virtue of his hands-off approach to the job, joking that "they say hard work never killed anybody, but I figured why take the risk?" That laissez-faire attitude was especially

1969	**1987**	**1991**
Neil Armstrong becomes the first man to walk on the moon	Speaking in front of the Berlin Wall, Ronald Reagan challenges: "Mr Gorbachev, tear down this wall!"	Following the Iraqi invasion of Kuwait, the Gulf War begins

apparent in his domestic economic policies, under which the rich were left to get as rich as they could.

In 1988, **George H.W. Bush** became the first vice president in 150 years to be immediately elected to the presidency. Despite his unusually broad experience in foreign policy, Bush did little more than sit back and watch in amazement as the domino theory suddenly went into reverse. One by one, the Communist regimes of eastern Europe collapsed, until finally even the Soviet Union crumbled away. Bush was also president when **Operation Desert Storm** drove the Iraqis out of Kuwait in 1991, an undertaking that lasted one hundred hours and in which virtually no American lives were lost. With the 1992 campaign focusing on domestic affairs rather than what was happening overseas, twelve years of Republican government were ended by the election of Arkansas Governor **Bill Clinton**.

Although Clinton's initial failure to deliver on specific promises – most obviously, the attempt, spearheaded by his wife Hillary, to reform the healthcare system – enabled the Republicans to capture control of Congress in 1994, the "Comeback Kid" was nonetheless elected to a second term. Holding on to office proved more of a challenge in the face of humiliating sexual indiscretions, but the Senate ultimately failed to convict him in **impeachment** proceedings.

The twenty-first century

When Clinton left the presidency, the economy was **booming**. His former vice president, however, **Al Gore**, contrived to throw away the 2000 presidential election, a tussle for the centre ground that ended in a **tie** with his Republican opponent, **George W. Bush**. With the final conclusion depending on a mandatory re-count in Florida, the impasse was decided in Bush's favour by the conservative **Supreme Court**. At the time, the charge that he had "stolen" the election was expected to overshadow his presidency, while the authority of the Supreme Court was also threatened by the perception of its ruling as partisan.

Within a year, however, the atrocity of **September 11, 2001** drove such concerns into the background, inflicting a devastating blow to both the nation's economy and its pride. More than three thousand people were killed in the worst terrorist attack in US history, when hijacked planes were flown into the World Trade Center in New York City and the Pentagon. The attacks were quickly linked to the al-Qaeda network of Osama bin Laden, and within weeks President Bush declared an open-ended "War on Terror".

A US-led invasion of **Afghanistan** in 2001 was followed by a similar incursion into **Iraq** in 2003, ostensibly on the grounds that Iraqi dictator Saddam Hussein was developing "weapons of mass destruction". Although Saddam was deposed, and executed, no such weapons proved to exist, and Iraq degenerated into civil war.

That the Democrats regained control of both Senate and House in 2006 was due largely to the deteriorating situation in Iraq. Similarly, the meteoric rise of Illinois Senator **Barack Obama** owed much to his being almost unique among national politicians in his consistent opposition to the Iraq war. However, while Obama's message of change and optimism, coupled with his oratorical gifts and embrace of new technologies, resonated with young and minority voters, his ultimate triumph over

1998	2000	2001
President Clinton proclaims "I did not have sexual relations with that woman"	The Supreme Court rules George W. Bush to have been elected president	On September 11, more than three thousand people die in the worst terrorist attack in US history

John McCain in that year's presidential election was triggered by a new **recession**. After bankers Lehman Brothers filed for bankruptcy in 2008 – the largest bankruptcy in US history – no element of the economy appeared safe from the consequences of reckless "subprime" mortgage lending.

The exhilaration over Obama's becoming the first black US president soon faded. Despite managing to introduce a universal system of healthcare, which became known as **Obamacare**, he was seen as failing to deliver on many campaign pledges. In particular, he never closed the detention camp at Guantanamo Bay, while his Middle East initiatives had little impact. President Obama's comfortable re-election in 2012 owed much to the role of the Tea Party in drawing the Republican Party ever further to the right. The Republican majority in the House of Representatives, however, continued to impede his agenda, precipitating a two-week **government shutdown** in 2013, and refusing to confirm any nominee to the Supreme Court. During his second term, Obama attempted to govern without Republican support, launching such initiatives as a rapprochement with Cuba, and a deal with Iran over its nuclear programme. Illusions that his rise to the presidency had marked the start of a new "post-racial" era of reconciliation, however, were punctured when the **Black Lives Matter** movement emerged in response to institutionalized indifference to the deaths of young black men.

For the presidential election of 2016, the Republican Party confounded expectations by selecting real-estate tycoon **Donald Trump** as its candidate. Derided by many as a boorish buffoon, Trump had burnished his image as a business mogul by hosting the TV show *The Apprentice*, and came to political prominence advocating the "birther" smear that Obama had supposedly been born outside the US.

Hopes that **President Trump** might put the demagoguery of the campaign trail behind him on assuming power were dashed at his inauguration, when he claimed to see "record crowds" along the visibly depopulated Mall. His term in office saw the US shift towards an isolationist stance, abandoning its commitment to climate-change programmes and withdrawing from the anti-nuclear proliferation agreement with Iran. Although Trump's much-vaunted new Wall along the US-Mexico border was not fully constructed, a ban on immigration from certain Muslim countries was followed by restrictive policies resulting in the forcible separation of migrant families attempting to enter from central America. Constitutional norms were eroded, with minimal dissent from Republicans in Congress; federal agencies placed under the control of anti-government lobbyists; and the courts packed with partisan appointees. Pandering to the hard right, and most at ease addressing rallies of his long-term supporters, Trump survived a first impeachment attempt in 2019 and continued to provoke despair in his opponents as no amount of scandal or blatant "alternative facts" seemed able to bring him down.

However, in early 2020, the worldwide coronavirus (Covid-19) pandemic began to spread across the US. Initially dismissed as a "flu" by Trump that would "miraculously…go away", at the time of writing, the US has suffered the highest Covid-19 death toll in the world, with 898,000 dead and the figure still climbing. Unlike in many countries, stay-at-home orders and social distancing and mask-wearing requirements were made on a state or local level, and orders fluctuated as the country went through and recovered from three successive waves of the virus. By early 2022,

2008	**2016**	**2020**
Barack Obama wins election as the first black president	To worldwide astonishment, Donald Trump is elected 45th president of the United States	The global Covid-19 crisis hits the US hard; Trump is ousted as president by Joe Biden

infection numbers were at record highs, but the 'decoupling' between case numbers and deaths being widely observed in other countries was not holding as true for the United States, owing to the country's high levels of vaccine hesitancy.

The Covid-19 pandemic was ultimately a major catalyst for Trump's downfall. His lack of empathy for its victims, perception he wasn't taking the outbreak seriously enough and frequent flouting of safety protocols (as well as suggesting people might inject bleach to "clean" themselves at a press conference, to the horror of his scientific advisors) – combined with the inevitable economic downturn – conspired to ultimately lose him many swing voters, whose lives had been so hugely impacted by the pandemic.

But this was not the only major crisis in 2020. The Black Lives Matter movement exploded around the country and the world after African-American George Floyd was killed by a police officer kneeling on his neck to restrain him for over eight minutes. It was one of several killings of Black Americans by the police, but the collective anger and taking to the streets of BLM supporters in protest, despite pandemic restrictions, had a profound impact that raised awareness of ongoing racial injustice.

Trump was increasingly out of step with the calls for change and condemnation of police brutality. But after a slow start, the Democrat challenger for the Presidency, Joe Biden, energised the African-American vote with his own support and his selection of Kamala Harris as his running mate, casting his campaign as a "battle for the soul of America". By the time Americans went to the polls in November 2020, the expected result was too close to call. However, Biden prevailed, winning more than 81 million votes, the most ever cast for a candidate in a presidential election, and securing 306 of the electoral college votes to Trump's 232.

President Biden and Vice-President Harris – the first female, African-American and Asian-American to hold the office – had made history. But their win wasn't the last twist in the tale. As Congress gathered to count electoral college votes to formalize Biden's win, ahead of his inauguration, the US Capitol building was stormed and occupied by a pro-Trump mob, seeking to overturn the result. Encouraged to gather by Trump himself, who had failed to concede the election and was alleging vast vote fraud that he claimed had stolen millions of votes, the rioters forced terrified politicians to flee and vandalized and looted the building, while the world watched in real time in horror. For Americans, this attack on the heart of their democratic traditions was traumatizing. Trump failed to call in the National Guard or explicitly denounce his supporters' actions, and in the aftermath, he was impeached for a second time for incitement to insurrection, although he was eventually acquitted.

President Biden was inaugurated on January 20 2021, in a ceremony that looked very different to normal, shorn of crowds due to Covid-19 precautions and with the assembled attendees in face masks. His first year in office witnessed a huge economic relief package to aid pandemic recovery, as well as the successful vaccine roll-out and re-joining of the Paris Climate Accord, although it was marked negatively by the disastrous evacuation of American troops from Afghanistan. Significantly, the conviction of George Floyd's killer, former officer Derek Chauvin, on April 20, has marked a step forward in police accountability. The US remains a country deeply riven by its racial inequalities and entrenched political and cultural perspectives, but with a more centrist President, time will tell if these divides can begin to be bridged.

2021

Pro-Trump militants storm the
US Capitol building; Kamala
Harris makes history as first
female Vice-President

Books

Space not permitting a comprehensive overview of American literature, the following list is simply an idiosyncratic selection of books that may appeal to interested readers. Those tagged with the ★ symbol are particularly recommended.

HISTORY AND SOCIETY

Bill Bryson *Made in America*. A compulsively readable history of the American language, packed with bizarre snippets.

John Demos *The Unredeemed Captive*. This story of the aftermath of a combined French and Native American attack on Deerfield, Massachusetts, in 1704 illuminates frontier life in the eighteenth century.

Brian Fagan *Ancient North America*. Archaeological history of America's native peoples, from the first hunters to cross the Bering Strait up to initial contact with Europeans.

Tim Flannery *The Eternal Frontier*. "Ecological" history of North America that reveals how the continent's physical environment has shaped the destinies of all its inhabitants, from horses to humans.

Shelby Foote *The Civil War: a Narrative*. Epic, three-volume account containing anything you could possibly want to know about the "War Between the States".

John Kenneth Galbraith *The Great Crash 1929*. An elegant and authoritative interpretation of the Wall Street Crash and its implications.

Doris Kearns Goodwin *Team of Rivals*. This detailed story of how Abraham Lincoln marshalled the talents of his unruly cabinet to win the Civil War makes it abundantly clear why he's regarded as the greatest of all US presidents.

David Halberstam *The Best and the Brightest*. Still-relevant, gut-wrenching examination of how America's finest, most brilliant Ivy Leaguers plunged the nation into the first war it ever lost, disastrously.

Aldo Leopold *Sand County Almanac*. A meditation on natural history and landscape by the father of conservation ecology.

Magnus Magnusson and Herman Pálsson (trans)

The Vinland Sagas. If you imagine stories that the Vikings reached America to be no more than myths, here's the day-to-day minutiae to convince you otherwise.

James M. McPherson *Battle Cry of Freedom*. Extremely readable history of the Civil War, which integrates and explains the complex social, economic, political and military factors in one concise volume.

David Reynolds *Waking Giant: America in the Age of Jackson*. Rousing portrait of America in the first half of the nineteenth century, from its clumsy attempt to take Canada in the War of 1812 to its successful Mexican land grab three decades later, with the figure of Andrew Jackson providing the touchstone throughout.

★ **Alan Taylor** *American Colonies*. Perhaps the best book on any single era of American history – a superb account of every aspect of the peopling of the continent, from remote antiquity until the Declaration of Independence.

Henry David Thoreau *Walden*. Few modern writers are more relevant than this nineteenth-century stalwart, whose *Walden* imagined environmentalism one hundred years early, and whose *Civil Disobedience* provided the template for modern activism.

★ **Mark Twain** *Roughing It, Life on the Mississippi* and many others. Mark Twain was by far the funniest and most vivid chronicler of nineteenth-century America. *Roughing It*, which covers his early wanderings across the continent, all the way to Hawaii, is absolutely compelling.

Geoffrey C. Ward, with Ric and Ken Burns *The Civil War*. Illustrated history of the Civil War, designed to accompany the TV series and using hundreds of the same photographs.

TRAVEL WRITING

Edward Abbey *The Journey Home*. Hilarious accounts of whitewater rafting and desert hiking trips alternate with essays by the man who inspired the radical environmentalist movement Earth First! All of Abbey's books, especially *Desert Solitaire*, a journal of time spent as a ranger in Arches National Park, make great travelling companions.

Bill Bryson *The Lost Continent*. Using his boyhood home of Des Moines in Iowa as a benchmark, the author travels the length and breadth of America to find the perfect small town. Hilarious, if at times a bit smug.

Charles Dickens *American Notes*. Amusing satirical commentary about the USA from a jaded British perspective that's still lighter in tone than the author's later, more scabrous *Martin Chuzzlewit*.

Robert Frank *The Americans*. The Swiss photographer's brilliantly evocative portrait of mid-century American life from coast to coast, with striking images contextualized by an introductory essay from Jack Kerouac.

★ **Ian Frazier** *Great Plains*. This immaculately researched 1980s' travelogue holds a wealth of information on the people of the prairielands, from Native Americans to the soldiers who staffed the region's nuclear installations.

William Least Heat-Moon *Blue Highways*. Classic account of a mammoth loop tour of the USA by backroads, interviewing ordinary people in ordinary places. A remarkable overview of rural America, with lots of interesting details on Native Americans.

Jack Kerouac *On the Road*. This definitive account of transcontinental beatnik wanderings now reads as a curiously dated period piece.

James A. MacMahon (ed) *Audubon Society Nature Guides*. Attractively produced, fully illustrated and easy-to-use guides to the flora and fauna of seven different US regional ecosystems, covering the entire country from coast to coast and from grasslands to glaciers.

Virginia and Lee McAlester *A Field Guide to American Houses*. Well-illustrated and engaging guide to America's rich variety of domestic architecture, from pre-colonial to postmodern.

John McPhee *Encounters with the Arch Druid*. In three inter-linked narratives, the late environmental activist and Friends of the Earth founder David Brower confronted developers, miners and dam-builders, while trying to protect three different American wilderness areas – the Atlantic shoreline, the Grand Canyon and the Cascades of the Pacific Northwest.

Bernard A. Weisberger (ed) *The WPA Guide to America*. Prepared during the New Deal as part of a make-work programme for writers, these guides painted a comprehensive portrait of 1930s and earlier America.

FICTION

GENERAL AMERICANA

★ **Raymond Carver** *Will You Please Be Quiet Please?* Stories of the American working class, written in a distinctive, sparse style that perhaps owes something to Hemingway and certainly influenced untold numbers of contemporary American writers. The stories served as the basis for Robert Altman's film *Short Cuts*.

Don DeLillo *White Noise* and *Underworld*. The former is his best, a funny and penetrating pop culture exploration, while the latter is one of those typically flawed attempts to pack the twentieth-century American experience into a great big novel. Worthwhile, though.

★ **Herman Melville** *Moby-Dick*. Compendious and compel-ling account of nineteenth-century whaling, packed with details on American life from New England to the Pacific.

★ **John Dos Passos** *USA*. Hugely ambitious trilogy that grapples with the USA in the early decades of the twentieth century from every possible angle. Gripping human stories with a strong political and historical point of view.

E. Annie Proulx *Accordion Crimes*. Proulx's masterly book comes as close to being the fabled "Great American Novel" as anyone could reasonably ask, tracing a fascinating history of immigrants in all parts of North America through the

fortunes of a battered old Sicilian accordion. The Wyoming-set short stories collected in *Close Range* – which include *Brokeback Mountain* – are also recommended.

George Saunders *Lincoln In The Bardo* The Lincoln in question, suspended in the afterlife, is not Abraham but his son Willie, in this metaphysical examination of the underlying themes of the Civil War.

NEW ENGLAND

Emily Dickinson *The Cambridge Companion*. It took many decades for the innovative work of this pre-eminent poet, which touches on dark emotional themes, to be recognized. This anthology is a good place to start.

Nathaniel Hawthorne *The House of the Seven Gables*. A gloomy gothic tale of Puritan misdeeds coming back to haunt the denizens of a cursed mansion.

John Irving *The Cider House Rules*. One of Irving's more successful sprawling novels, weaving themes of love, suffering and the many facets of the abortion debate against a Maine backdrop.

H.P. Lovecraft *The Best of H.P. Lovecraft*: *Bloodcurdling Tales of Horror and the Macabre*. Creepy New England stories from the author Stephen King called "the twentieth century's greatest practitioner of the classic horror tale".

Film

New England's great beauty has made it much beloved of filmmakers, while the region's long and illustrious literary history has also spawned many adaptations of famous books on the silver screen. Those tagged with the ★ symbol are particularly recommended.

A Connecticut Yankee (1931) Joyful adaptation (with slightly redacted title) of Mark Twain's time-travelling romp.

The House of the Seven Gables (1940) Gothic adaptation of Nathaniel Hawthorne's tale of a man framing his brother for murder, set in Salem.

Adventures of Mark Twain (1944) Frederick March stars as beloved writer Mark Twain in a film which traces his life, including his sojourns in New England.

Plymouth Adventure (1952) Ensemble extravaganza in glorious Technicolor, with Spencer Tracy and Gene Tierney among the Pilgrims on the Mayflower.

Carousel (1956) Boothbay Harbor, Maine is the setting for this adaptation of Rodgers and Hammerstein's classic tale of love and robbery.

★ The Haunting (1963) Classic film adaptation of Shirley Jackson's novel The Haunting of Hill House, set in Massachusetts.

Who's Afraid of Virginia Woolf? (1966). Mike Nichols' directorial debut is a captivating drama starring Elizabeth Taylor as the daughter of a New England college president.

Boston Strangler (1968) Dramatic rendering of the true story of the Boston Strangler, who murdered 13 women in the city – though the case has never quite been solved.

★ Jaws (1975) The fictional town of Amity, Massachusetts is the setting for Steven Spielberg's instant horror classic.

The Dead Zone (1983) Based on Stephen King's novel, this is the story of a Maine schoolteacher who gains supernatural powers after a fairground accident.

Beetlejuice (1988) Tim Burton's ghostly comedy stars Alec Baldwin and Geena Davis as a couple who haunt their former home.

Good Will Hunting (1997) Robin Williams and Matt Damon star in this acclaimed psychological drama set at the Massachusetts Institute of Technology.

★ The Witch (2015) Spooky horror film set in 1630s New England, where strange happenings befall a Puritan family in a woodland settler village.

Small print and index

A ROUGH GUIDE TO ROUGH GUIDES

Published in 1982, the first Rough Guide – to Greece – was a student scheme that became a publishing phenomenon. Mark Ellingham, a recent graduate in English from Bristol University, had been travelling in Greece the previous summer and couldn't find the right guidebook. With a small group of friends he wrote his own guide, combining a contemporary, journalistic style with a thoroughly practical approach to travellers' needs.

The immediate success of the book spawned a series that rapidly covered dozens of destinations. And, in addition to impecunious backpackers, Rough Guides soon acquired a much broader readership that relished the guides' wit and inquisitiveness as much as their enthusiastic, critical approach and value-for-money ethos. These days, Rough Guides include recommendations from budget to luxury and cover more than 120 destinations around the globe, from Amsterdam to Zanzibar, all regularly updated by our team of roaming writers.

Browse all our latest guides, read inspirational features and book your trip at **roughguides.com**.

Rough Guide credits

Editor(s): Kate Drynan
Cartography: Carte
Picture editor: Tom Smyth

Layout: Katie Bennett
Head of DTP and Pre-Press: Katie Bennett
Head of Publishing: Kate Drynan

Publishing information

First edition 2022

Distribution

UK, Ireland and Europe
Apa Publications (UK) Ltd; sales@roughguides.com
United States and Canada
Ingram Publisher Services; ips@ingramcontent.com
Australia and New Zealand
Booktopia; retailer@ booktopia.com.au
Worldwide
Apa Publications (UK) Ltd; sales@roughguides.com

Special Sales, Content Licensing and CoPublishing
Rough Guides can be purchased in bulk quantities
at discounted prices. We can create special editions,
personalised jackets and corporate imprints tailored to
your needs. sales@roughguides.com.
roughguides.com

Printed in Spain

A catalogue record for this book is available from the
British Library

The publishers and authors have done their best to ensure
the accuracy and currency of all the information in **The
Rough Guide to New England**, however, they can accept
no responsibility for any loss, injury, or inconvenience
sustained by any traveller as a result of information or
advice contained in the guide.

Help us update

We've gone to a lot of effort to ensure that this edition of
The Rough Guide to New England is accurate and up-
to-date. However, things change – places get "discovered",
opening hours are notoriously fickle, restaurants and
rooms raise prices or lower standards. If you feel we've got
it wrong or left something out, we'd like to know, and if
you can remember the address, the price, the hours, the
phone number, so much the better.

Please send your comments with the subject line
"Rough Guide New England Update" to mail@
uk.roughguides.com. We'll credit all contributions and
send a copy of the next edition (or any other Rough Guide
if you prefer) for the very best emails.

Photo credits

All images **Shutterstock**

Index

Y

Map symbols

The symbols below are used on maps throughout the book

International boundary	International airport	Spring
State/province boundary	Domestic airport/airfield	National Park
Chapter division boundary	Transport stop	Gate/park entrance
Interstate highway	Parking	State capital
US highway	Post office	Lighthouse
State highway	Information centre	Statue
Pedestrianized road	Hospital/medical centre	Bridge
Path	Cave	Battle site
Railway	Point of interest	Ski
Funicular	Viewpoint/lookout	Mountain range
Coastline	Campground	Mountain peak
Ferry route	Museum	Swamp/marshland
National Parkway	Monument/memorial	Tree
Metro/subway	Fountain/garden	Gorge
Tram/trolleybus	Waterfall	Arch

Boat
Hindu/Jain temple
Church (regional maps)
Church (town maps)
Cemetery
Building
Stadium
Park/forest
Beach
Native American reservation